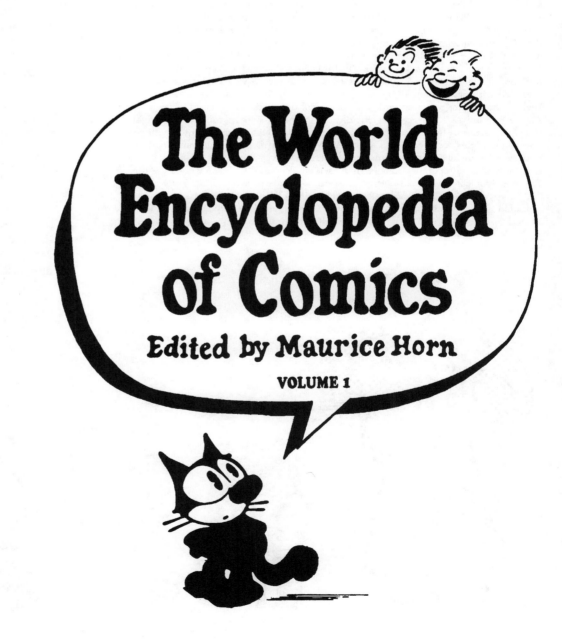

The World Encyclopedia of Comics

Edited by Maurice Horn

VOLUME 1

THE CONTRIBUTORS

Manuel Auad (M.A.), *The Philippines*
Bill Blackbeard (B.B.), *U.S.*
Gianni Bono (G.B.), *Italy*
Joe Brancatelli (J.B.), *U.S.*
MaryBeth Calhoun (M.B.C.), *U.S.*
Javier Coma (J.C.), *Spain*
Bill Crouch (B.C.), *U.S.*
Giulio Cesare Cuccolini (G.C.C.), *Italy*
Mark Evanier (M.E.), *U.S.*
Wolfgang Fuchs (W.F.), *Germany*
Luis Gasca (L.G.), *Spain*
Robert Gerson (R.G.), *U.S.*
Denis Gifford (D.G.), *Great Britain*
Paul Gravett (P.G.), *Great Britain*
Peter Harris (P.H.), *Canada*
Hongying Liu-Lengyel (H.Y.L.L.), *China*
Maurice Horn (M.H.), *France/U.S.*
Pierre L. Horn (P.L.H.), *U.S.*
Slobodan Ivkov (S.I.), *Yugoslavia (Serbia)*
Bill Janocha (B.J.), *U.S.*
Orvy Jundis (O.J.), *The Philippines*
Hisao Kato (H.K.), *Japan*
John A. Lent (J.A.L.), *Asia*
Richard Marschall (R.M.), *U.S.*
Alvaro de Moya (A.M.), *Brazil*
Kalmán Rubovszky (K.R.), *Hungary/Poland*
Ervin Rustemagić (E.R.), *Yugoslavia*
John Ryan (J.R.), *Australia*
Matthew A. Thorn (M.A.T.), *Japan*
Dennis Wepman (D.W.), *U.S.*

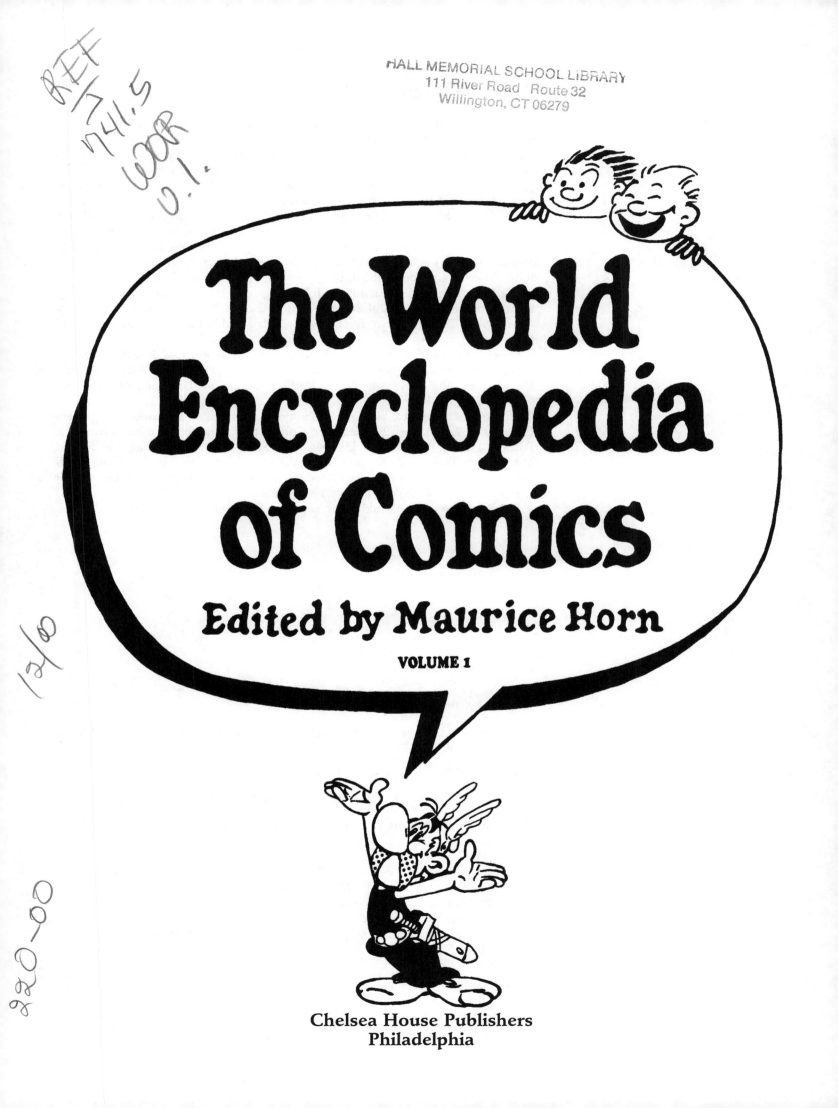

The World Encyclopedia of Comics

Edited by Maurice Horn

VOLUME 1

Chelsea House Publishers
Philadelphia

Acknowledgments

The editors of *The World Encyclopedia of Comics* wish to extend their sincere thanks to the following persons: Bill Anderson, Jerry Bails, Larry Brill, Mary Beth Calhoun, Frank Clark, Bill Crouch, Leonard Darvin, Tony Dispoto, Jacques Glénat-Guttin, Ron Goulart, George Henderson, Pierre Horn, Pierre Huet, S. M. "Jerry" Iger, Jessie Kahles Straut, Rolf Kauka, Heikki Kaukoranta, Roland Kohlsaat, Maria-M. Lamm, Mort Leav, Vane Lindesay, Ernie McGee, Jacques Marcovitch, Victor Margolin, Doug Murray, Pascal Nadon, Harry Neigher, Walter Neugebauer, Syd Nicholls, Tom Peoples, Rainer Schwarz, Silvano Scotto, Luciano Secchi, David Smith, Manfred Soder, Jim Steranko, Ernesto Traverso, Miguel Urrutía, Jim Vadeboncoeur, Jr., Wendell Washer, Peter Wiechmann, Mrs. John Wheeler and Joe Willicombe.

We would also like to thank the following collectors who donated reproductions of art from their collections: Wendy Gaines Bucci, Mike Burkey, Tony Christopher, Russ Cochran, Robert Gerson, Roger Hill, Bill Leach, Eric Sack, and Jim Steranko.

Special thanks also to Michel Mandry, Bernard Trout, José Maria Conget of Instituto Cervantes in New York, Four-Color Images Gallery, Frederik Schodt, David Astor, Alain Beyrand, Manuel Halffter, Dominique Petitfaux, Annie Baron-Carvais, Janice Silverman.

Our appreciation also to the following organizations: Associated Newspapers Ltd., Bastei Verlag, Bulls Pressedienst, Comics Magazine Association of America, Editions Dupuis, ERB Inc., Field Newspaper Syndicate, Globi Verlag, The Herald and Weekly Times Ltd., Kauka Comic Akademie, King Features Syndicate, Marvel Comics Group, San Francisco Academy of Comic Art, Strip Art Features, Walt Disney Archives and Walt Disney Productions.

Finally, we wish to thank Don Manza for his photographic work.

Chelsea House Publishers
1974 Sproul Road, Suite 400
P.O. Box 914
Broomall PA 19008-0914

Typeset by Alexander Graphics, Indianapolis IN

Library of Congress Cataloging-in-Publication Data

The world encyclopedia of comics / edited by Maurice Horn.
   p. cm.
   Includes bibliographical references and index.
   ISBN 0-7910-4854-3 (set). — ISBN 0-7910-4857-8 (v. 1). — ISBN 0-7910-4858-6 (v. 2). — ISBN 0-7910-4859-4 (v. 3). — ISBN 0-7910-4860-8 (v. 4). — ISBN 0-7910-4861-6 (v. 5). — ISBN 0-7910-4862-4 (v. 6). — ISBN 0-7910-4863-2 (v. 7)
   1. Comic books, strips, etc.—Dictionaries. I. Horn, Maurice.
PN6710.W6 1998
741.5'03—dc21   97-50448
                                               CIP

Contents

VOLUME 1:   6 *Preface to the Second Edition*
           7 *Foreword to the First Edition*

           9 *Comics Around the World*
          11 Comics of the World: A Short History
          43 A World Chronology of Comic Art from the 18th Century
             to the Present
          55 The World of Comics: An Analytical Summary

          73 *Alphabetical Entries, A-B*

VOLUME 2: 173 *Alphabetical Entries, C-F*

VOLUME 3: 331 *Alphabetical Entries, G-H*

             Color in the Comics

VOLUME 4: 399 *Alphabetical Entries, I-M*

VOLUME 5: 559 *Alphabetical Entries, N-Son*

VOLUME 6: 717 *Alphabetical Entries, Sor-Z*

          833 *More About the Comics*
          835 A History of Newspaper Syndication
              by Richard Marschall
          843 The Comic Paper in America
              by William Henry Shelton
          847 The Humor of the Colored Supplement
              by Ralph Bergengren
          851 Glossary of Comic Strip Terms

VOLUME 7: 859 *U.S. Senate Hearings*

          915 *Still More About the Comics*
          917 Selected Bibliography
          920 Notes on the Contributors

          927 *Appendices*
          929 A: Code of the Comics Magazine Association of America
          930 B: Reuben Award Winners
          931 C: Directory of Newspaper Syndicates
          932 D: Directory of Comic Book Publishers

          933 *Indices*
          935 A: Proper Name Index
          955 B: Title Index
          983 C: Media Index
          991 D: Contributors Index
         1001 E: Geographical Index
         1011 F: Illustration Index
         1021 G: Subject Index

Preface to the Second Edition

This is an updated, enlarged edition of what has become, since its publication more than 20 years ago, the standard reference work in the field of comics: *The World Encyclopedia of Comics*. Building upon that foundation, we have conserved all the entries as originally written, only updating those (some 600 of them) that needed updating. Additionally, over 200 entries on features, artists, and writers that have come to the forefront of the field in the past 20 years have been added to this edition, bringing the total number of entries to more than 1,400. Written by experts from around the world, some of them former contributors, some new to the *Encyclopedia*, these additional entries widen the panorama of world comic art as it has evolved over the last two decades. We are particularly proud to have made this edition even more encyclopedic and even more universal with the inclusion of entries on artists and comics from countries—mostly from Asia, Africa, and eastern Europe—that, for political or practical reasons, were absent from the first edition.

The front and back matter (history, chronology, bibliography, and essays) have also been updated to reflect the changes that have occurred since the first publication of the *Encyclopedia*. These updates will provide the reader with a global perspective and a current time line to a living art form that doesn't cease to reinvent itself. More than 120 new black-and-white illustrations and additions to the color section will further enhance the usefulness and pleasure provided by this *Encyclopedia*.

This edition of *The World Encyclopedia of Comics* is intended for use not only as a scholarly reference tool, being the most comprehensive survey of the medium ever realized, but also as an endless source of enjoyment for the reader. The information contained in this *Encyclopedia* covers the developments in the comic art field through December 1997. It is the intention of the publisher to further update and revise the work at periodic intervals.

Foreword to the First Edition

The World Encyclopedia of Comics is the first book to cover the entire field of comic art in all of its aspects—artistic, cultural, sociological, and commercial—on a global scale. To this purpose we have assembled an international team of 15 contributors from 11 different countries, each a recognized authority in his field. (Short biographies of these contributors may be found on pages 920-926 of this work.) The exhaustive data compiled for this book has, for the most part, been obtained firsthand by direct examination and reading of the sources, and through interviews with the artists, authors, editors and publishers involved. The text, therefore, is lively and fascinating reading, aside from its value as a straight reference work.

The more than 1200 cross-referenced entries constitute the main body of this encyclopedia. These entries have been organized alphabetically for easy reference, and fit in two classifications: biographical and bibliographical. The biographical entries deal with comic artists, writers and editors, and provide a succinct summary of the subjects, with emphasis on their work in the comics, their stylistic and thematic contributions, their influence on other artists or writers and their achievements in general. The bibliographical entries, which relate to the comic features themselves, contain a brief history, including the names of the artists and writers who created and worked on them, a summary of themes, plots and leading characters, a discussion of the place held by each particular feature in the history and art of the comics and their adaptations into other media. Many relevant anecdotes, parallels and asides are also included in the entries (which are valuative as well as informative).

To supplement the individual entries and give the reader a "bird's eye view" of the comic art form, the volume contains a number of informative articles, including a world history of the comics (providing a global overview of the more than 80 years of comic art), a chronology of important events in comics development, a history of newspaper syndication, an analytical summary dealing with the language, themes and structures of the comics and an extensive glossary of comic terms.

This book constitutes not only a definitive study of a very important and influential art form, it also illuminates many facets and peculiarities of 20th-century culture, and of Western civilization as a whole. It is, therefore, an invaluable tool for historians, sociologists, art instructors, folklorists and critics.

There are also a bibliography and a number of appendices included. Of particular usefulness are the indices which provide easy access to additional information on thousands of authors and titles apart from the individual entries in their names. Illustrated with over 700 black-and-white pictures and 100 color reproductions, the encyclopedia is the most extensive and representative anthology of comic works ever assembled.

The World Encyclopedia of Comics has been designed not only as a reference work on the subject, but also as a source of endless hours of enjoyment for scholars and laymen alike. The data contained herein covers the developments in the comic art field through December 1975. It is the intention of the publisher to update, revise and enlarge *The World Encyclopedia of Comics* accordingly, at a later date.

The Editors

Comics Around the World

A Short History
A World Chronology
An Analytical Summary

Comics of the World:
A Short History

The following essay represents the first attempt at a history of world comic art. The only other international history of the comics, *A History of the Comic Strip,* not only fails to deal with comic books, but is largely confined to the productions of the United States and Western Europe. This account presents a more balanced world picture, and while the American and European productions receive the largest share of attention, reflecting their preeminent position in the world of comics, they are placed in a wider context that includes the very important contributions made by Japanese comics, as well as those from countries of Asia, Latin America, and the Pacific, in a truly global overview of the 100 or more years of comic art.

In this historical narrative I have tried to chronicle the evolution of the world's comics, pinpoint their heights and valleys, describe their trends and cycles, and analyze their accomplishments and failings, in the context of 20th-century culture. I have also attempted to capture the spirit, feel, and flavor of comic history by concerning myself with the thrust of events and happenings, rather than with historical details. For more detailed information the reader should refer to the chronology and to the bio-bibliographical entries for the authors and features mentioned in the text.

William Hogarth, "Gin Lane."

Genesis

As cannot be sufficiently reiterated, the comic strip is emphatically *not* a medium of graphic narration. The narrative in the strip is not conveyed visually, but is expressed in both pictures and words. While emphasis may be given to one of the dual aspects of the strip over the other, the interest most often shifts back and forth, according to the demands of the action or the needs of characterization and atmosphere. It is therefore futile, as some uninformed critics still do, to relate the comics to early modes of visual narration: there is as much generic distance between the comics and the Trajan Column or Queen Mathilde's tapestry as exists between the cinema and shadow theater. They simply do not aim at the same effect. To pretend otherwise is to make a regrettable confusion of categories.

It is probably in Leonardo da Vinci's notebooks that one finds the first deliberate strivings toward a new language that would retain the cognitive and normative elements of the written word and flesh them out with visual expletives. Leonardo devised his scheme in answer not to an aesthetic problem, but to a philosophical dilemma. It was becoming apparent to the artists and thinkers of the Renaissance that the preeminence of the printed word was leading man to isolation from his fellow men. Leonardo thought that only the image, which bears an immediately recognizable relationship with external reality, could help liberate language from the alienating power (to use a modern phrase) of the printed word.

In spite of limited experiments, text and illustration followed different paths. It fell upon the genius of the English illustrator William Hogarth to reassemble the two heterogenous elements of text and image into a single whole. In his picture series, like *The Rake's Progress* or *Marriage à la Mode*, he reestablished the sequential nature of visual narrative, while at the same time depicting the action as if it were a stage play, thus giving it dramatic impact. His creations were so clearly different from the traditional illustrations of his time that a new name had to be coined for them, "cartoons." The dramatic setting of these cartoons clearly called for the systematic use of the balloon (a form that has been in use sporadically over a long period), and thus the definitive characteristics of the cartoon were established. Refined later by Thomas Rowlandson and introduced to the Continent by the fame of James Gillray, these techniques led in a roundabout way to the creation of the comic strip.

The 19th century witnessed a flourishing of illustrated narratives, spurred on by such technical innovations as zincography and, later, photoengraving. But these narratives ("Images d'Epinal" in France, "Bilderbogen" in Germany) still kept text and pictures separate from each other. Artistically these picture-stories

Wilhelm Busch, "Max und Moritz."

reached their highest point with the Swiss Rodolphe Töpffer, whose work, abundantly praised by Goethe, signaled not the beginning of a new art form, as some have contended, but the brilliant end of an already outdated artistic concept.

More important in the history of the comic strip was the German Wilhelm Busch, whose creation, *Max und Moritz*, contributed mightily (if accidentally) to the birth of the American comic strip. As H. Arthur Klein, Busch's talented translator, ably put it, "We may call Busch the stepfather, if not the father, of an important group of comics in the United States." Another early pioneer of the budding art of the comics, the Frenchman Georges Colomb (who used the pen name "Christophe"), introduced stylistic innovations such as actions depicted from odd angles and accelerated narratives, which foreshadow some of the techniques of the strip. His work was years ahead of such artistically disreputable frolics as W. F. Thomas's *Ally Sloper*.

At the end of the 19th century the stage was set for the grand entrance of a new mode of expression. It was to come from an altogether unexpected direction.

Birth of the comic form

From the vantage of hindsight, the birth and subsequent rise of the comic strip in the United States seem as inevitable as they are spectacular. At the end of the 19th century, however, nothing pointed to an American breakthrough in a field

Rudolph Dirks, "The Katzenjammer Kids."

that had been pioneered and explored almost exclusively by Europeans. American artists were lagging far behind their European counterparts in the art of pictorial storytelling. In fact, the original impetus came not from the artists themselves, but from the publishers, who, in the Sunday supplement, created the medium best suited for the expression of their artist's ideas.

Around 1880 a number of American daily newspapers started publishing on Sundays (despite a campaign for the continued observance of the Sabbath), but it was Joseph Pulitzer who first seized upon the Sunday supplement as a showcase for his newspaper, the *World*. To attract readers to his newspaper, Pulitzer made increasing use of color and illustrations, including cartoons. The conjunction of these innovations directly led to Richard Outcault's historic *Yellow Kid* on February 16, 1896 (actually, color had already been applied to Outcault's panel as early as July 1895, but the results had not been considered entirely satisfactory). *The Yellow Kid* was not yet a comic strip as we define it today, but its creation was pivotal, signaling as it did the birth of the comics as a distinct medium.

In the pages of the *World*, therefore, were gathered all the essential elements of the form—the sequential narrative, continuing characters, dialogue enclosed within the picture—but their synthesis was brought about not by Pulitzer, but by his redoubtable young competitor, William Randolph Hearst, who had just bought out the *Morning Journal* from Joseph's brother, Albert. Not only did Hearst share Pulitzer's conviction that the Sunday supplement had a remarkable future, but further, he saw that the cartoons constituted its main pillar of strength. As it turned out, he was right on both counts. Hearst's weapon against Pulitzer was to launch a new color supplement, *The American Humorist* (self-described as "eight pages of polychromatic effulgence that make the rainbow look like a lead pipe") in 1897. In these pages appeared the work of artists who, under the vigilant gaze of Hearst, unconsciously forged a new language that, together with the movies, brought a new way of looking at external reality. In these developments Hearst's role should not be slighted. Granted that his methods and ethics left something to be desired—at one point he bought out the entire staff of the *World*—his judgment and discrimination in selecting his artists were uncanny. He can rightly be regarded as the godfather of the new form (only much later to be called the "comics").

In the stable of artists assembled by Hearst for his *American Humorist* three stand out: Richard Outcault, James Swinnerton, and Rudolph Dirks, respectively the authors of *The Yellow Kid* (bought out along with its creator from the *World*), *The Journal Tigers*, and *The Katzenjammer Kids* (this last feature was probably the single most important creation in the entire history of the comic strip).

Every period of great innovation must be followed by a period of consolidation. The early cartoonists were developing new themes and creating new conventions at such a furious pace that they were in danger of outrunning themselves. Clearly, a new man was needed who would bring some order into the chaotic cartoon world, who would channel all the heady, bold, and often contradictory experiments going on at the same time into a distinct pattern and along a central direction. Such a man was Frederick Burr Opper. His Happy Hooligan prefigured Charlie Chaplin's tramp just as his Gloomy Gus already wore Buster Keaton's mask. His peculiar brand of dark humor and slapstick found further development in the comedies of Mack Sennett. Even his narrative techniques point in some of the directions that the movies later took.

Such were the four men most responsible for the art of the comic strip as we know it today. Their work might seem coarse and vulgar, but they were also vital and vibrant. They were pioneers, innovators. Delicacy of line, shade of meaning, subtlety of design were subordinated to the sheer joy of being able to express themselves in an entirely new idiom. Their creations were imbued with an overwhelming sense of discovery, a reckless abandon to the seemingly endless possibilities of the medium. They left to a new generation of cartoonists (and to their older selves) the task of refining and disciplining their artistic impulses. Improvisation and spontaneity, not skill and purpose, were their main concerns.

If their collective contributions can be summarized at all, it might be said that they stand in the history of comic art in the same position that the artists of the Quattrocento occupy in the history of Western art in general.

F. B. Opper, "Happy Hooligan, © King Features Syndicate.

The new order and the old

By the early years of the 20th century the rough outlines of the new medium were already apparent. The vital conventions and vocabulary of the comics—speech balloons, onomatopoeia, motion lines, frame-enclosed pictures—were already in use as the accepted norm and were finding their way into the public consciousness. Venturing forth, as they were, into unknown territory, the first practitioners of the medium sought to preserve a lifeline with the older and established form, the humor cartoon. This helps to explain the more than casual resemblance they bear to one another. In style, if not in intent and treatment, they remained close to their immediate sources—the linearity and simplicity of the cartoon. The next period (circa 1905) saw the first break between the comic strip and the cartoon, and the first conscious strivings for the creation of an altogether autonomous and original art form.

Winsor McCay was the artist who, above all others, proved to be the guiding genius of this aesthetic revolution. His single-minded and masterly research into new semantic structures and thematic variations, starting with *Little Sammy Sneeze* and deepening into *The Dreams of the Rarebit Fiend,* found its most accomplished and dazzling expression in *Little Nemo in Slumberland.*

In *Little Nemo* McCay achieved a unity between plot and theme that is rarely found among the comics (or in other art forms, for that matter).

The only artist of the period who could be compared to Winsor McCay was the German-American painter Lyonel Feininger. His two short-lived creations for the comic medium, *Wee Willie Winkie's World* and *The Kin-der-Kids,* endowed as they are with the artist's whimsical vision, seem in retrospect to have captured

Lyonel Feininger, ''The Kin-der-Kids''

the *Zeitgeist* of the comic strip form, caught between its cartoony beginnings and its painterly aspirations. If in style Feininger owes little to the tradition of the American cartoon (and much to the school of German caricature), in spirit he is closer to Dirks (as the name ''the Kin-der-Kids'' indicates) than McCay was ever to be.

No man, however, has contributed to the basic ''look'' of the comic strip as much as George McManus, a young cartoonist who came into his own around the same time. McManus had begun unobtrusively in 1900, but as early as five years later he was already displaying his almost awesome mastery of line, his uncanny feel for situations, and his unerring ear for dialogue in such creations as *Panhandle Pete* and *The Newlyweds,* harbingers of things to come.

In a position somewhat apart from the others stands Charles William Kahles. At a time when all cartoonists were eager to stake out their own particular provinces, Kahles pursued his craft with self-indulgence. He seems to have been in love with the medium itself and was so intoxicated by its multivariegated possibilities that he could not tie himself to any one of the paths open to him.

Winsor McCay, "Little Nemo."

Louis Forton, "Les Pieds-Nickelés." © SPE.

Each of the four men discussed here brought his own unique contribution to the developing medium; each enlarged and greatly enriched the scope of the comic strip, refined its artistry, and invented many of the narrative and visual devices that are now part of the language of the comics. Their contributions may seem unequal, yet it was in the interaction of their diverging styles that they achieved a sense of unity. They bore more resemblance to one another than to any of the preceding generation of cartoonists. If their inspirations were disparate, their aims were similar, and together they lifted the comics to what was already recognizable as an exacting and original art form.

While all this was happening in the United States, Europe was lagging far behind. Even the more successful among European comic strips, such as *Weary Willie and Tired Tim* and *Airy Alf* in England, *Les Pieds-Nickelés* and *Bécassine* in France, and *Bilbolbul* in Italy, still did not make use of the balloon, but put captions of sometimes substantial size under the pictures, thereby divorcing the image from the text. It was some time before Europe (and the rest of the world) caught up with the United States in this field.

In Japan, on the other hand, Rakuten Kitazawa, founder of the famous *Tokyo Puck* (modeled on the American *Puck*) in 1905, wholeheartedly adopted the techniques and innovations brought about by the American cartoonists in his comic strip creations, such as *Doncia* and *Tonda Haneko*.

The advent of the daily strip

At about the same time that McCay and Feininger were bringing the comics to formal perfection, Bud Fisher firmly established the daily strip as one of the most important features in the newspaper. *Mutt and Jeff* (created in 1907 as *Mr. A. Mutt*) was not the first comic to appear across the page of a daily newspaper, but it was the first to do so with lasting success. After 1910, when it was evident that the daily strip was there to stay, many newspapers followed suit, timidly at first; then, as the new form met with growing readership, the practice of running daily comic strips inside the newspaper became general throughout the United States.

Bud Fisher, "Mutt and Jeff." © H. C. Fisher.

G. A. Van Raemdonck, "Bulletje en Bonestaak." Bulletje and Bonestaak "pay a visit" to Jopie Slim and Dickie Bigmans of the London Evening News. © Het Volk.

It was lucky for Fisher's reputation (as well as for his finances) that his "discovery" was so universally recognized, for his artistic standing was not on a par with that of his illustrious contemporaries. *Mutt and Jeff*'s style was clearly derivative of the conventions of the early cartoon. Even the characters (the mismatched duo) and the theme (the enjoyment of idleness) owed much to Opper. Fisher's contribution was more basic: by creating the black-and-white daily comic strip (by which name the whole medium soon became known), he opened up new aesthetic possibilities (not to mention almost endless commercial opportunities) that later cartoonists were able to explore and enlarge.

Still, the new format did not take hold immediately: the traditions of the Sunday color supplement and the comic page were strong. Only when a satisfactory way of tying daily and Sunday readership was found did the comic strip become the social phenomenon that it is today.

Parenthetically, it is interesting to note that *Mr. A. Mutt* and its most widely heralded predecessor, Clare Briggs's *A. Piker Clerk*, both started as horse-race tip sheets: they were conceived as part and parcel of the daily newspaper, and not as an extension of the weekly color comics to the black-and-white eight-column page.

At any rate, the progress of the newfangled feature was slow. The daily strip met with the opposition, if not downright hostility, of newspaper editors (a tradition still alive today). A few newspapers tried daily strips, but only Hearst (who had bought out Fisher and his strip in 1908) wholeheartedly embraced the new format (again showing both artistic judgment and business acumen). At first he used the black-and-white strips for experimental purposes (they were cheaper to produce than full-color Sundays). *Bringing Up Father* and *Krazy Kat*, for instance, originated in the daily newspaper pages, but, later, daily strips became established in their own right.

Captain Joseph Patterson, publisher of the Sunday-less *New York News* (at least until 1924), was instrumental in the growth of the daily strip. Not only did he help produce such standards as *The Gumps* and *Little Orphan Annie*, but, when the *News* finally added a Sunday section, he introduced the concept of the synchronized daily/Sunday comic feature. This was devised as a commercial ploy, but it definitively established the comics as an integral part of American newspapers.

The spread of the daily strip format to other parts of the world was slow and patternless. Outside the United States and Canada there existed no strong tradition of the Sunday supplement, and the daily strip provided the comics with their first foothold in the adult newspaper (they had been confined up to then mainly to children's publications). At first these were reprints of American imports (*Mutt and Jeff* appeared as early as 1910 in Argentina and Japan), but slowly a national production began to emerge in many countries. This progress is interesting to follow: England got its first original newspaper strip in 1915 (Charles Folkard's *Teddy Tail*, published in the *Daily Mail*), followed by Argentina (Arturo Lanteri's *El Negro Raul*, 1916) and Australia (*The Potts*, 1919).

With the general acceptance of the daily strip in American newspapers in the 1920s, the form grew rapidly abroad: in Sweden (*Adamson*, known as *Silent Sam* in the United States, 1920), the Netherlands (*Bulletje en Bonestaak*, 1921), Mexico (*Don Catarino*, 1921), and Japan (Yutako Asō's *Nonkina Tousan*, 1924). A national newspaper strip production also began around that time in Canada, Denmark, and Finland.

There were important holdouts, however; the first French newspaper strip, *Le Professeur Nimbus*, appeared only in 1934, while the Italians had to wait until 1968 to see their first national strip (Bonvi's *Sturmtruppen*). As a form, however, the daily strip is now an accepted part of most newspapers throughout the world.

A time of consolidation

Every period of intense creation and daring innovation—such as characterized the first decade of the American comic strip—has to be followed by a breathing space, a time of recapitulation and consolidation. After 1910 the cartoonists, looking back on past achievements, went into a reflective or analytical pause, according to their particular temperament. Their mood was best exemplified by the work of the greatest artists of the period, George Herriman and George McManus, whose accomplishments, while seemingly divergent in purpose and outlook, were actually strikingly similar in form and substance. Both consciously sought to express themselves in the language of the comics and solely on its terms—and their inspiration (however literary it seemed at the outset) owed more to the art of the comic strip than to any exterior source.

So much ink has been spilled in praise of these two artists (especially Herriman, who in recent years has attained the status of a quasi-literary saint) that we forget how funny they were—and how their funniness directly derived from the bumptiousness of the early cartoons. In line, Herriman owed as much to Opper as McManus did to Swinnerton, while the brick tossed by Ignatz at Krazy Kat and the rolling pin thrown at Jiggs by Maggie were the logical extensions of the

George McManus, *"Bringing Up Father."* © King Features Syndicate.

George Herriman, *"Krazy Kat."* © King Features Syndicate.

HOW TO GET UNCLE MANFRED OFF CHAIR AFTER THANKSGIVING DINNER

SOCIETY (A) DISPLAYS DIAMONDS AT OPENING OF METROPOLITAN OPERA — JITTERY BOOKMAKER (B) THINKS IT IS ATOMIC FLASH AND DIVES UNDER BUREAU (C) —

HE UPSETS FIFTEEN-CENT GLASS OF BEER (D) WHICH FALLS ON JIMMY DURANTE'S NOSE (E) — MORTIFIED AT SUCH WASTE, JIMMY BREAKS UP PIANO (F) —

FALLING KEYS CAUSE GAVEL (G) TO CALL MEETING OF GENERAL ASSEMBLY IN PARIS AND VISHINSKY (H) HOLDS UP PHONY DOVE OF PEACE (I) —

STRING (J) ATTACHED TO EIFFEL TOWER (K) PULLS UNCLE MANFRED (L) OUT OF CHAIR AND DEPOSITS HIM ON COUCH WHERE HE STAYS TILL CHRISTMAS DINNER.

One of Rube Goldberg's famed "inventions." © Reuben L. Goldberg.

traditions of slapstick and destruction ushered in by *The Katzenjammer Kids*. A fresh look at *Bringing Up Father* and *Krazy Kat* seems, therefore, in order.

In the world of comic art *Krazy Kat* and *Bringing Up Father* represent two aesthetic opposites. The questionings of the former are contrasted with the certainties of the latter. The same correspondence obtains in the dialogues, graphic styles, backgrounds, themes, situations, and attitudes. Herriman is lyrical and McManus is earthy, Herriman is complex and McManus is direct, Herriman is a dreamer and McManus is a pragmatist, and so on all the way down the line. They represent, almost ideally, the dual direction in which subsequent comic artists would travel. One may be called entertainment and the other may be called art, but they are indissolubly tied together by the very nature of the form. Intellectual snobbishness recognizes *Krazy Kat* as art, while popular success marks *Bringing Up Father* as entertainment, but the truth, as usual, lies somewhere in between. Herriman is as much an entertainer as he is an artist, and McManus teases the mind as much as he pleases the eye. Both reached a summit in comic strip expression, and their divergent styles were responses to the demands of the medium, as they perceived them.

This early chapter of the comics' turbulent history can best be summed up, however, by the feature that, in many ways, started it all—*The Katzenjammer Kids*. Due to some artistic cloning and legal acrobatics, the terrible twins had in the meantime duplicated themselves. One set (under the title *Hans and Fritz*, then *The Captain and the Kids*) remained under the direction of Rudolph Dirks; the other passed into the hands of Harold Hering Knerr, who also kept the original title—and the race was on! In trying to outdo each other, Knerr and Dirks, each in his own inimitable style, set the tone, pace, and flavor of the whole period, outrageously swiping characters, ideas, and entire situations from each other, exuberantly escalating the antics of their heroes, letting the action run wild, pulling out all stops—both of them encapsulating at once the vibrant spirit of the comics in the sublime effrontery of it all.

The comics bloomed in all directions in the second decade of the 20th century, testifying to the vigor of the form and the growing self-sufficiency of its practitioners. If Ray Ewer's *Slim Jim* prolonged the stylistic experiments of Feininger and McCay, the work of Milt Gross and Rube Goldberg amplified Opper's thematic concerns. The cartoonists' choice of themes—the escaped lunatic facing an even more insane outside world (*Count Screwloose of Tooloose*), the innocent set upon by a savage society (*Boob McNutt*), the little man trampled down by cruel fate (*Nize Baby*)—had a peculiarly disturbing, even neurotic, ring, showing that the comics, even at that time, were not as insulated from the intellec-

Two of Milt Gross's zany creations: "Looy Dot Dope" and "That's My Pop." © Milt Gross.

tual mainstream as their detractors pretended them to be. The underlying current of paranoia could be detected in even as innocuous a strip as *Abie the Agent*, which Arthur Brisbane once called (in a typical display of ignorance) "the first of the adult comics in America."

The end of the devil-may-care days of the medium occurred some time between 1920 and 1925. All of a sudden the comics grew into maturity. At the same time that they became an art form, they also became a business, big business, and the responsibility was to be taken from the artists, an unreliable and impractical lot, as everybody knows. Because of the enthusiastic efforts of the early cartoonists, the comics had evolved the most important elements of their vocabulary and their own syntax. To be sure, much *terra incognita* still remained to explore, but the shape and outline of the medium were now entirely known.

The family strip

By the 1920s the comics had become so vast a field that specialization was inevitable. The freewheeling days of the early decades, when each man could embark on wild flights of fancy taking him in all directions, were over. The powers-that-be decreed that each artist was to stick to his own theme (or, more often than not, to a given formula). If this resulted in an unhappy narrowing of focus for the strips concerned, it did not affect the medium as a whole. Strips like *The Katzenjammer Kids* or *Krazy Kat* remained as free and delightfully unpredictable as ever. What had changed was not the content but the spirit of the comics.

What brought about these changes was the generalization of the syndicate distribution system and the limitations that system entailed (a discussion of the syndicate system can be found in another part of this encyclopedia). The American newspaper had become a family institution, and to that institution the comics held the comforting illusion of a rose-colored looking glass. No one was more responsible for this trend than Captain Joseph Medill Patterson, publisher of the *New York Daily News*, who is said to have had an uncanny flair for identifying himself with the middle-class aspirations of the very audience he sought. Home from a (supposedly) bad day's work at factory or office, a father could chuckle at the doings and sayings of characters bearing enough resemblances to himself that they could elicit delighted glimmers of recognition; yet, they remained so unlike him in their stylized attire and stereotyped responses that he could laugh at them without laughing at himself. In turn, a mother could look appreciatively

Children of the Comics

From the outset, kids in the comics have been an unruly lot. They are lazy, conniving, sloppy, occasionally cruel, always rebellious. Fortunately, the advent of the family strip did not appreciably change the remarkably candid and realistic appraisal of children as cheerful barbarians. In a world beset with conformity and hypocrisy, there is a welcome absence of sham in the actions of the comics' children. In strips like Skippy, Reg'lar Fellers, *and the Sunday version of* Winnie Winkle, *the trend is glaringly exposed. Perry and his gang,* Skippy, Puddin'head, *and the others may not possess the diabolical imagination of the Katzies, but their revolt against the adult world is no less real for its being more concealed.*

The children of the comics retain enough innocence to believe in dreams, in the brotherhood of clubhouse pals, the vastness of nights under the stars, the magic of an afternoon at the circus; and they have acquired enough wisdom to know that the adult world is the enemy of dreams. Therefore they lie, cheat, and dissemble—the typical response of the bright and weak to the stupid and strong. But even in their deceit, delinquency, and self-aggrandizement, and in the hollowness of their victories, they are never made to look inane or ridiculous. We never laugh at the children as we do at their adult victims; we laugh with them.

This is not accidental, of course. The cartoonists are tipping the scales in favor of the kids. It is as if, in an act of like rebellion, they too are crying out against the stupidities and iniquities of middle-class life, which they are supposed to uphold and enshrine.

M.H.

at "funnies" which were not coarse or vulgar, but in which the wife, more often than not, was one up on her husband.

The archetype of this new wave of family strips was *The Gumps*, directly conceived and named by Captain Patterson. There is no doubt that the fearless captain intended the strip to be a shining example of his stewardship over the newly created Tribune-News Syndicate, as well as the prototype for the new comic strip age to come.

Sidney Smith, "The Gumps." © Chicago Tribune-New York News Syndicate.

It is well to remember that the family genre is not deplorable in itself and has produced a few masters who have managed to transcend both the limitations of the setting and the literalness of the situation by breathing into their creations the intents and characteristics of established and respected forms. Under the daily ludicrous happenings in *Blondie*, there is a lively comedy of manners that gives substance and meaning to the strip; the sense of the implacable flow of time overwhelms the gentle pieties of *Gasoline Alley*, while *Moon Mullins* turns the very facts of family life into the frightening structure of a black comedy.

Little Orphan Annie is the most extreme case of all. First designed as a story about an orphan (in the vein of the screen tearjerkers of the time), it was transformed by its creator into a dark parable of Good and Evil, a brooding metaphor of life, in which all characters took on the translucence of symbols, and all situations became permeated with a haunting sense of betrayal and doom—a far cry from the idyll of domestic romance!

The family-type comics were created to attract a female readership, and nowhere was this as apparent as in the so-called girl strips. Aimed particularly at the growing number of working girls, they presented a flattering self-picture of independence, attractiveness (even glamour), and poise, the image of self-reliance mixed with charm. Despite the implications of their titles (*Tillie the Toiler, Winnie Winkle, the Breadwinner*), there was little depiction of their actual work in these strips, for they were more devoted to play and romance. A combination gossip column, fashion illustration, and advice for the lovelorn, most deserve only the sleep of oblivion.

A couple of girl strips have managed, however, to rise above the norm. Cliff Sterrett's *Polly and Her Pals* is notable for its very intricate design and composition and for its goofy and somewhat surreal atmosphere. The same pixieish charm can be found in *Winnie Winkle*, whose author, Martin Branner, was able to display a fine sense of comedy and irony.

The domestic strips met with growing (even astonishing) popularity in the United States, but failed to set the world of comics on fire. In the 1920s, when the family strip was at its zenith in North America, the rest of the world, by and large, failed to take notice. There were *The Potts* (originally *You and Me*) in Australia, *Don Pancho Talero* (*Bringing Up Father* with a Latin accent) in Argentina, *Dot and Carrie*, a misguided attempt to bring the American-type girl strip to the English masses, and that was about all. Even the genuine article, the American-grown domestic feature, often got short shrift abroad: in France, for instance, *The Gumps* was edged out after a few years by Alain Saint-Ogan's upstart *Zig et Puce*,

The "Gasoline Alley" cast of characters as seen by Dick Moores. © Chicago Tribune-New York News Syndicate.

Jim Russell, "The Potts." © The Herald and Weekly Times Ltd.

while only the Sunday page of *Winnie Winkle* (featuring the pranks of brother Perry and his pals) got published in France and the Netherlands.

One reason for this international failure was the fact that the comics, outside of the North American continent, were still aimed mainly at children, and the kids, with remarkable discernment, simply loathed the genre. Also, the figure of the *pater familias* was still very much respected in most parts of the world (especially in Japan). One can see how a Jiggs or an Andy Gump would have failed to fit the bill. (It took the American occupation of Japan to bring about the first Japanese family strip—*Sazae-san*—in 1946.) However, over the years a few non-American domestic strips made their appearances: *Vater und Sohn* (Germany), *La Familia Burrón* (Mexico), *Patatras* (as a replacement for *Gasoline Alley*, France), *La Familia Ulises* (Spain). But, as a genre, the family strip never really succeeded outside of the United States.

End of an era: 1929

By the end of the 1920s the comics had reached a high plateau of public adulation. They certainly rivaled the movies (which had just begun to talk—or stammer) in popularity, especially in the United States. Comic creation, while giving some signs of fatigue and repetition, continued at a fast pace. The years 1918-1928 were exceedingly fecund. Some of the comics produced in this period have been noted elsewhere; three American features deserve special mention at this point.

Billy DeBeck's *Barney Google* was an earthy example of the traditional comic strip. It exhibited a good-natured humor, as well as a graphic style that represented the epitome of the well-crafted cartoon strip. With *Little Orphan Annie* Harold Gray introduced a not entirely welcome innovation into the field of comic features: the advocacy of a political ideology (in this case, that of the Right) within the confines of his strip. Elzie Segar's *Thimble Theater* derived from the zaniness of Milt Gross and Rube Goldberg's comic creations and from the lyrical humor of *Krazy Kat*. Segar was a master of creating inimitable characters and bewildering situations.

The scene was not limited to the United States, however. The comic strip had by then assumed the proportions of a worldwide social and artistic phenomenon. In England, H. S. Foxwell with *Tiger Tim* (created by J. S. Baker), A. B. Payne with *Pip, Squeak and Wilfred,* and Mary Tourtel with *Rupert* brought the animal strip to new heights of popularity, while J. Millar Watt's *Pop* acquired international fame. At the other end of the globe, Japan produced many cartoonists of talent in this period, the most prolific being the aforementioned Yutako Asō.

In France, where children rather than animals were favorite subjects, Louis Forton (creator of the earlier *Les Pieds-Nickelés*) produced *Bibi Fricotin,* and Alain Saint-Ogan came out with *Zig et Puce,* the first French comic feature to make use of the balloon exclusively. Italian comics, on the other hand, remained faithful

Willy DeBeck, "Barney Google." © King Features Syndicate.

to the illustrated story with captions, in such creations as Sergio Tofano's *Signor Bonaventura*, Antonio Rubino's *Quadratino*, and Carlo Bisi's *Sor Pampurio*.

Comic strip production did not remain confined to its traditional bastions in the U.S.A., England, France, Italy, and Japan. National comic strips sprouted everywhere—in Spain (where K-Hito created the very funny *Macaco*), in Scandinavia (*Pekka Puupää* in Finland, *Adamson* in Sweden, and others), in Latin America (*Chupamirto* in Mexico, Arturo Lanteri's creations in Argentina), in Australia (*Ginger Meggs, Fatty Finn),* even in China, where an original comic strip production began as early as 1920 in Shanghai.

Thus, at the beginning of 1929 the world's comics presented an image of success and stability that was to be shattered that same year by the introduction of narrative techniques and stylistic devices of an altogether different type.

Mary Tourtel, "Rupert." © Beaverbrook Newspapers Ltd.

The adventure strip

Adventure and the unknown have always exercised a fascinating appeal upon the imagination and the human spirit. Ever responsive to popular aspirations, the comic strip was prompt to seize upon these dreams. If Charles Kahles was the first to mine this rich lode in his strips, he did not long remain the only prospector. The first decades of the century were a time of explorers and discoverers, and the travel accounts of these hardy spirits soon found their way into the comic pages. Poetically transposed or devastatingly parodied, they gave extra color to the erratic wanderings of Felix the Cat, the mock heroics of Boob McNutt, the round-the-world odyssey of the Gumps, and the cataclysmic cruise of the Katzenjammers.

The early strips, however, used adventure merely as an added fillip, a ploy aimed at setting off the familiar pyrotechnics of slapstick and buffoonery. Roy Crane was the first to break away from the confining conventions of caricature and broad humor by introducing to his strip *Wash Tubbs* the dashing figure of Captain Easy, soldier of fortune. A little later Harold Foster's *Tarzan* and Nowlan and Calkins's *Buck Rogers* completed this transformation. From that moment on, the adventure strip was going to play it straight (January 1929).

Some interesting aesthetic consequences arose from this deliberate choice of interpretation. Artistically, the new strip form abandoned the caricatural style and free-flowing line of the early cartoon and moved closer to magazine illustration (in its graphic design) and figurative art (in its composition), while aiming at duplicating the sequential flow of the cinema in its effect. This judicious blending of forms gave the new strips the illusion of movement, of reality, of life. At the same time the traditional forms of storytelling adopted by the older strips—the comic fable, the morality play, the familiar anecdote, the fairy tale— were discarded in favor of the narrative continuum of the novel and the heroic tone of the epic. Even as the movies were beginning to talk, the comics started to move. They had gone all the way from static entertainment to dynamic spectacle.

In one respect the continuity strip has a definite advantage over the movie. The uninterrupted flow of happenings unfolding day after day, week after week, gives the strip a quality of timelessness and a diversity of approaches within a single framework that the movie cannot possibly hope to equal. There is an excitement and expectation in the words "to be continued" that should not be dismissed. The adventures go on for all eternity, the end of each episode being but the starting point of the next one, and part of their fascination comes from watching this unceasing parade, this sea of characters, places, and incidents endlessly rolling on.

It has been said that the adventure strip confronts its readers with only a few basic situations. This is true, as it is true with all forms of narrative literature, but the variations exercised upon the primary themes were and are the measure of any artist. In this respect the cartoonists displayed an astonishing range and an unequaled evocative power. They took over and assimilated into their strips preexisting narrative forms; they drew upon the historical novel and the movie serial, the mythological legends and the pulp magazines, the wisdom of folklore and the sensationalism of dime novels, giving them unity and continuity within the unique structural framework of the comic strip.

Harold Foster, "Tarzan." © ERB, Inc.

Chester Gould, "Dick Tracy." © Chicago Tribune-New York News Syndicate.

While *Tarzan* and *Buck Rogers* both owed their inspiration to existing novels, in 1931 Chester Gould created the first successful, originally conceived adventure strip, *Dick Tracy*, a tale of mystery and detection. *Dick Tracy's* importance lay in its plotting and its locale. It did not take place in some future century or some distant jungle, but in the here and now.

In quick succession, scores of adventure strips saw the light between 1929 and 1934. In addition to *Dick Tracy*, other strips of note were Frank Godwin's *Connie* (originally begun as a girl strip), Hal Forrest's *Tailspin Tommy* and Lyman Young's *Tim Tyler* (both started in 1928, but taking their definitive character only some time later), and *Brick Bradford*, a space strip drawn by Clarence Gray. The greatest artist of the time, however, proved to be Alex Raymond, who produced three strips of worldwide renown: *Secret Agent X-9, Jungle Jim*, and *Flash Gordon*, the latter being especially beloved.

Then came the flood. Lee Falk brought out two adventure strips of great originality: *Mandrake the Magician* (with Phil Davis) and *The Phantom* (with Ray Moore). Milton Caniff created the much-admired *Terry and the Pirates*; Foster went on to produce *Prince Valiant* while the talented Burne Hogarth took over *Tarzan*. This was also the time of *Radio Patrol, King of the Royal Mounted, Don Winslow, Charlie Chan, Red Ryder*, and Noel Sickles's *Scorchy Smith*, ably continued by Frank Robbins.

The spirit of adventure pervaded the whole comic field in the 1930s: even the humor strip turned to all-out derring-do. The classic example was provided by Segar, who developed the heroic (albeit comical) figure of Popeye the Sailor. Adventure was also present in the daily escapades of Mickey Mouse (who joined the comic pages in 1930) and of his predecessor from the cartoon film, Felix the Cat. Al Capp's *Li'l Abner* also started its satirical career on a fairly adventurous note and, of course, such features as *Alley Oop* and *Oaky Doaks* were conceived as strips of humorous adventure from the start.

The rapid development and extravagant popularity of the American adventure strip overwhelmed the fledgling competition from other comic-producing countries. By 1940 the American syndicates were inundating Europe and the rest of the world with their enormous output. The English strip was marking time, the South American production faltering, the Japanese set back; the French made a timid effort at renewing the outdated outlook of their comic features with René Pellos's imaginative science-fiction strip, *Futuropolis*, but this effort remained isolated. The Italians did better, following the ban of American comics by Musso-

Hergé (George Rémi), "Tintin." © Editions Casterman.

lini in 1938 with such excellent creations as *Kit Carson, Gino e Gianni, Virus,* and *Dottor Faust.* The best and most imaginative comic strip to come out of Europe in this period, however, was indisputably Hergé's *Tintin,* which was to become a worldwide success, rivaling even the best-known American features.

Spurred on by the success of American adventure comics, many publishers hastily decided to develop their own homegrown varieties, with mixed results. Thus, the decade witnessed the birth of action-oriented features all over the world: in England (*Buck Ryan*), Japan (*Hatanosuke Hinomaru*), Spain *(Cuto),* Yugo-slavia (*Stari Mačak*), Australia (*Larry Steele*), and Argentina (*Hernan el Corsario*). What checked the seemingly inexorable American expansion was not the desultory competition, but the outbreak of World War II. The American comic industry was cut off from its most lucrative markets in Europe and had its sales

Phil Nowlan and Dick Calkins, "Buck Rogers." © National Newspaper Syndicate.

Cast of characters of "Ninja Bugeichō." © *Sanpei Shirato.*

further limited in those countries still open, because of paper rationing and embargoes on nonessential imports.

The rise of the comic book

Contrary to what many people believe, the comic book is not an American innovation of the 1930s. It may be argued that Rodolphe Töpffer's *Histoires en Estampes* was the first genuine attempt at collecting comic stories in book form. In Germany, in the second half of the 19th century, all of Wilhelm Busch's stories appeared within book covers, as did Christophe's creations a few years later.

In the United States comic strip reprinting started with *The Yellow Kid* as early as 1897. In the early 1900s F. A. Stokes published color reprints of *Buster Brown, The Katzenjammer Kids, Foxy Grandpa,* et al., in book form. Other books from different companies reproduced the *Mutt and Jeff* strips, Tad's comic creations, and others, all in black and white. These were succeeded by the Cupples and Leon books of the 1920s and 1930s, which reprinted such standards as *Bringing Up Father, Little Orphan Annie,* and *Dick Tracy.*

It was the Japanese, however, who published the first cheap, mass-produced, regularly scheduled comic books in the 1920s. Printed (sometimes in color) on pulp paper and distributed on a monthly basis, they actually predated the American comic book by a good 10 years. Eventually original material began to appear in these books, some of artistic merit—Suimei Imoto's *Nagagutsu no Sanjūshi* appeared there in 1930, for instance. The comic book format was soon so successful with Japanese children that it gave rise to lending libraries specializing exclusively in comic books, the "kashibonya manga." These special libraries then began to produce their own comic books for rent, and this practice was successful enough to last well into the 1960s. Many young cartoonists started their career in rental comic books: Gōseki Kojima, Sanpei Shirato, Hiroshi Hirata, Shinji Mizushima, among others. Several successful features also got their start in these limited-circulation comic books before graduating to regularly published, newstand-sold publications (*Hakaba no Kitarō* and *Ninja Bugeichō* being the two most notable).

The first modern American comic book, *Funnies on Parade,* appeared in 1933 as a promotional giveaway for Procter and Gamble. In May 1934 the Eastern Color Printing Company issued the first commercial comic book, *Famous Funnies,* a monthly collection of newspaper strip reprints. The next year saw the birth of the first comic book containing exclusively original material, all of it humorous, called *New Fun.* Adventure features were not far behind, and they ensured the success of the new format. In January 1937 *Detective Comics* was first with a comic book devoted to a single protagonist. By the end of the 1930s the comic book was clearly a medium in search of a hero; he finally appeared in the first issue (June 1938) of *Action Comics.* His name was Superman and he made comic history.

Superman was conceived as far back as 1933 by the writer/artist team of Jerry Siegel and Joe Shuster, who had unsuccessfully submitted it to every imaginable newspaper syndicate. When the lone survivor of the planet Krypton arrived in the pages of *Action Comics,* he became an immediate hit. Eventually *Superman* made countless millions for a number of people (but not for its creators, who had sold all their rights).

The phenomenal success of *Superman* spawned a host of imitations; by the time of America's entrance into World War II, the legion of superheroes had virtually taken over the comic book medium. Most of the creations were worthless, but a few managed to survive and even to flourish: Bob Kane's *Batman,* Carl Burgos's *The Human Torch,* Bill Everett's *Sub-Mariner,* and Jack Cole's *Plastic Man* have become classics of sorts. None of them, however, could compete in wit and imagination with C. C. Beck's 1940 creation, *Captain Marvel.*

The unholy proliferation of comic books was feverishly abetted by scores of entrepreneurs eager to cash in on the superhero craze. Two such men deserve special notice: Harry Donnenfeld, who single-handedly created the D.C. empire (now National Periodicals, part of Warner Communications), and S.M. "Jerry" Iger, an indefatigable discoverer of new comic book talent.

Among Iger's discoveries were Lou Fine, Jack Kirby, and Will Eisner, Iger's special protégé. In 1940 Eisner created *The Spirit,* not for sale on newsstands, but as

ALIGHTING ON THE EDGE OF THE HUGE VAT, **SUPERMAN** SUCCEEDS IN CATCHING LOIS....

GOT YOU!

Jerry Siegel and Joe Shuster, "Superman." © *National Periodical Publications.*

part of a comic book supplement to be carried by Sunday newspapers. Both the feature and the format proved successful—so much so that comic book supplements were soon offered by King Features and the News-Tribune Syndicate (*Brenda Starr* first appeared there). This step was the newspaper syndicates' ultimate recognition that the comic book was there to stay.

World War II and the comics

Unlike World War I, which affected the American comic strip only superficially, World War II caused a profound and permanent upheaval in the comics. Most comic strip heroes rushed into the armed services and helped America's psychological war preparation. Joe Palooka, Jungle Jim, Captain Easy, and countless others found themselves enthusiastically battling against the Axis forces or fighting spies and saboteurs on the home front. Most typical was Caniff's *Terry and the Pirates*, whose episode dated October 17, 1943, was the first comic strip ever to be reprinted in the *Congressional Record*.

War comics, as distinct from the already existing adventure strips–turned–service features for the duration, became a staple of the times, the two most noteworthy being Roy Crane's *Buz Sawyer* and Frank Robbins's *Johnny Hazard*. In contrast, Crockett Johnson's poetic *Barnaby* was also born in this period.

The comic books, led by Joe Simon and Jack Kirby's *Captain America*, proved even more bellicose than the newspaper features. The titles of some of the books published in this period suffice to give a clue as to their character: *Spy Smasher, Commando Yank, Major Victory, Captain Flag, The Fighting Yank, The Unknown Soldier. . . .* But the war also gave rise to another phenomenon—comic strips especially created for servicemen. The most notable of these were George Baker's *The Sad Sack*, Milton Caniff's *Male Call*, and Dave Breger's *GI Joe*, whose title became a synonym for the average "buck private."

The American heroes of the comics were not alone in battling the Axis. The British comic characters had been at it since 1939, going to war in a spirit at first cheerful (one early war comic was called *Musso the Wop*) and, after the fall of France, with grim determination as well as humor. If *Derickson Dene* was a good example of the former, *Jane* (whose scantily clad heroine joined the British

Joe Simon and Jack Kirby, "Captain America." ® Marvel Comics Group.

equivalent of the WACs, to the enjoyment of soldiers of all ranks) provided much of the latter. Australia and Canada also helped with such contributions to the war effort as *Bluey and Curley* and *Rex Baxter*.

The Axis countries, however, were going tit for tat. Germany had no war comics, for Hitler loathed the form, but the Italians fielded *Romano il Legionario*, *Fulmine* (formerly *Dick Fulmine*), and *Il Mozzo del Sommergibile* ("The Submarine Cabin-Boy"), while the Japanese had *Norakuro* and a number of other war comics created for the occasion. The war also echoed in comic strips produced in neutral countries from Spain to Argentina, and Sweden to Switzerland.

Long after V-E and V-J days, the war continued to be fought in the comics, in some cases well into the 1950s, both in America and in liberated Europe. World War II thus proved the single most important real-life experience ever to be reflected in the comics.

A period of uncertainty: 1945-1950

Paradoxically, the end of World War II fostered among American cartoonists a feeling of malaise and a spirit of self-doubt that contrasted sharply with the self-assurance, even cockiness, of the war years. This disarray was perceptible everywhere, in comic books and in newspaper features, in gag strips as well as in adventure stories. As was noted in *A History of the Comic Strip*: "It is understandable that after a conflict that had cost 30 million human lives, humorists found it a bit difficult to be funny. The adventure strip authors, for their part, had a still more complex problem: compared with the silent heroism displayed by millions of combatants, famous or anonymous, the exploits of their characters suddenly seemed contemptible, futile, and almost unseemly."

The desire for change, for a new departure, was most sharply reflected among the adventure strip artists, who, unlike their colleagues working in the humorous vein, did not have a long tradition to fall back on. It is no surprise, therefore, that three of the most prestigious artists of the comics, Alex Raymond, Milton Caniff, and Burne Hogarth, decided at about the same time (1945-1947) to break with their own pasts and forge ahead with entirely new creations. In varying degrees, and for divergent reasons, all three features failed in their intent: Hogarth's *Drago* petered out after one year, Raymond's *Rip Kirby* was cut short by the untimely death of its creator (while ably continued by John Prentice, the feature lost most of its electricity and mystique), and Caniff's *Steve Canyon* sank into the morass of the Cold War. The American adventure strip proved unable to rejuvenate itself, and this portent (while it went unnoticed at the time) signaled the irremediable decline and ultimate death of the genre.

BUT BOOM-BOOM IS IMPATIENT AND FALLS FOR AN OLD TRICK... HIS SLUG DOES RIP'S HAT NO GOOD....

Alex Raymond, "Rip Kirby." © King Features Syndicate.

The funny strip and the comic book reacted differently to the changes wrought by the coming of peace. While only one worthwhile feature appeared in the humor field—Walt Kelly's *Pogo*, which more properly belonged to the next decade, the comic book publishers engaged in frenzied activity, dropping old titles, starting new categories, forever tampering with formats and concepts, but generally getting nowhere in the changed atmosphere of the postwar years.

The same confusion reigned in Europe, in Latin America, and in Japan. The desire to go back to things as they were before was strong; there was much repetitiveness, sterility, and imitation in the comics born in the immediate postwar era, but there were also the first stirrings of a youthful and exuberant creative spirit about to burst onto the claustrophobic scene. In France Raymond Poïvet and Roger Lécureux started the seemingly played-out science-fiction strip on a fresh path with *Les Pionniers de l'Espérance*; Hans Kresse started *Eric de Noorman* in Holland; in England Wally Fawkes (Trog) created the delightful *Rufus* (later retitled *Flook*), while Aurelio Galleppini in Italy perpetuated the Western myth with *Tex Willer*. But the newly found mood of creativity expressed itself strongest in tiny Belgium, where a whole new batch of exciting and enduring features saw the light of print between 1945 and 1950: Morris's classic of Western parodies, *Lucky Luke*, Jacques Martin's tale of the Roman empire, *Alix l'Intrépide*, Willy Vandersteen's endearing *Suske en Wiske*, and, best of all, E. P. Jacobs's scintillating science-fiction series, *Blake et Mortimer*.

After an initial period of prostration, the Japanese cartoonists also rebounded with their legendary resiliency. The American occupation had the beneficial effect of cutting the Japanese strip loose from some of its more desiccated storytelling traditions, and Japanese comics acquired a more occidental outlook, with forays into science fiction (*Fushigina Kuni no Putchā*), jungle adventure (*Shōnen Oja*), and even domestic humor (*Sazaesan*).

The late 1940s also witnessed a strong surge of interest in the cultural and social potentialities of the comic form (the first comprehensive survey of the medium, Coulton Waugh's *The Comics*, appeared in 1947). There was also widespread (if sometimes grudging) recognition of the contributions made by the comics to the folklore and mythology of our times; Superman, Krazy Kat, Popeye, Dagwood, and Li'l Abner were now perceived in a new light, not just as slapstick or cardboard characters, but as emblematic figures representative of deep nostalgia and longing. For the comics, the age of innocence was over.

Milton Caniff, "Steve Canyon." © Field Newspaper Syndicate.

E. P. Jacobs, "Blake at Mortimer." © Editions du Lombard.

The eventful decade of the 1950s

The 1950s were marked by the slow but irreversible decline of the American comic industry in terms of creativity, leadership, prestige, and viability. The causes for this erosion were many, but a few can be singled out.

The very popularity of the newspaper comics was, paradoxically, one cause of their decline. In order to capitalize on the comics' pull on their readers, many newspapers started cramming four, five, or even as many as eight features onto a standard page, resulting in an unseemly overcrowding of the comic page; like food piled up on a cafeteria tray, the mess eventually turned off all but the less discriminating customers. The daily strip fared no better, being further and further reduced in size to suit editors' whims. By the end of the 1950s the newspaper strips were a shambles. Older readers were slow to notice, but younger people gradually stopped reading them.

The action strip, which suffered most grievously from these strictures (the humor strip could adapt more easily to the reduction in format), was dealt a further blow by the retirement or death of some of its most outstanding practitioners (Burne Hogarth quit the field in 1950, Alex Raymond was killed in a car accident in 1956, Clarence Gray died in 1957, and Frank Godwin died in 1959). The American adventure strip never recovered from this quadruple loss.

The comic book, meanwhile, had its own problems. After the boom of the war years, readership fell off drastically. Many publishers went out of business, and those remaining had to fight fiercely to keep their share of the shrinking market. The novelty of the medium had by now worn thin, and its most popular feature, the superhero, was no longer able to pull in the customers—even Superman fared badly. In order to bolster sales, some publishers turned to unbridled violence, in the form of crime stories, or to horror. The most extreme case was that of William Gaines's E.C. Comics.

Some of the titles that E.C. put out in the early 1950s speak for themselves: *Crypt of Terror, The Vault of Horror, The Haunt of Fear.* Latter-day apologists of the E.C. horror comics speak in hushed tones of the high quality of art and writing that went into these books. There is some truth to their arguments, as far as they go. Most of the art and writing was only good in comparison to those in other comic books; furthermore, E.C. artists and editors, while arguably setting some

---

Comic Strip Mythology: Sadie Hawkins Day

Sadie Hawkins Day takes place annually in the Dogpatch of Al Capp's Li'l Abner *strip every November, no particular date in November being "official." Essentially, it is a traditional mountain-culture ceremony, invented by Capp for his rural hill characters, in which all the eligible bachelors of the Dogpatch community are pursued, after being given a "fair" running start, by all the eligible females, age or physical condition notwithstanding. Males "drug" over the finish line in the heart of the town by midnight have to marry the girls who capture them; in the meantime, the men can hide anywhere, so long as they remain within the city limits of Dogpatch (which covers a good bit of open hill country). The girls may use any means they like to capture the man of their choice, from a club to tear gas—and almost every conceivable device has been used in the course of the* Li'l Abner *strip.*

Introduced in a Li'l Abner *narrative beginning on November 13, 1937, Sadie Hawkins Day was named for the daughter of "one of the earliest settlers of Dogpatch, Hekzebiah Hawkins," to quote Capp's text. Homely, Sadie had gone without suitors until she was 35, and her father was grimly furious. Taking a gun, he rounded up by cajolery and/or force all of the eligible young men in the town, laid down the rules (in Capp's initial version, the girl only had to catch the boy to be able to marry him; for drama's sake, Capp added the fin-*

ish line a bit later), and fired his gun to start the boys running, then fired it again to set the girls on their trail a brief time later. The Dogpatch spinsters, Capp wrote, "reckoned it were such a good idea that Sadie Hawkins Day was made an annual affair." As presented in Li'l Abner, *Abner was usually the fearful figure followed by the reader during the yearly event in the strip, until his actual marriage to Daisy Mae forced Capp to feature other characters in subsequent years' events.*

For several decades, Capp reprinted the original two 1937 daily episodes, explaining the origin and rules of Sadie Hawkins Day every successive November. He deliberately left the date of the day in November unfixed, however, to permit himself continuity leeway from year to year. The dates announced in the narrative have varied from November 7 (1942) to November 25 (1967) and are obviously valid only for the year concerned. The Sadie Hawkins Day idea was seized upon almost from its inception by college, community, and office groups eager to dress up in hillbilly regalia and "switch" the roles of the sexes for a day. It has been estimated that 500 to 1,000 such parties or actual chases take place annually in the United States. Marriage, however, does not seem to be the pursuit of these get-togethers.

B.B.

A horror comic book. © E.C. Publications.

new trends in graphic storytelling, also displayed (in a succession of gruesome stories and gory covers) a callous disregard for civilized sensitivities. This trait, while acceptable, perhaps even desirable, in formats designed for mature readers (such as the later underground comics), was certainly objectionable in a popular medium overwhelmingly aimed at children. It seemed like a sure way to bring censure to the comic book.

The comics had always had their share of detractors (some were legitimately concerned educators, others were plain cranks), but these had proved no more than mere nuisances. Toward mid-century, however, the clouds above the comics grew increasingly more dark and threatening, and the horror comics bore the largest share of the blame. The controversy reached its crescendo in 1954 with the Estes Kefauver senatorial hearings and the publication of Dr. Frederic Wertham's *Seduction of the Innocent*. That same year, to fend off impending censorship, the publishers established the Comics Code Authority, a self-regulating body (the standards set forth by the code, as later revised, can be found in Appendix C). If it saved the industry from probable ruin (a fact conveniently overlooked by its more rabid critics), the establishment of the code also resulted in the total emasculation of the medium. As a creative force, the comic book simply ceased to exist for the remainder of the decade.

The newspaper strips fared somewhat better. There was a discernible loss of creativity, not only in the adventure field (the only noteworthy entry was *The Cisco Kid* and, symptomatically, it was drawn by a foreign artist, the Argentinian José-Luis Salinas), but in the traditional humor strip as well. *Beetle Bailey*, by Mort Walker, and *Dennis the Menace*, by Hank Ketcham, both appeared at the beginning of the decade and were the only strips whose popularity rivaled that of the established funny strips.

The 1950s also witnessed the rise of the soap-opera comics. Started as a genre in the 1930s (with *Mary Worth* as its standard-bearer), the soaps prospered and multiplied in this, America's most problem-ridden decade. There were *Judge Parker*, written by Dr. Nicholas Dallis (significantly, a psychiatrist and the author of the earlier *Rex Morgan, M.D.*), Stan Drake's *The Heart of Juliet Jones*, Leonard Starr's *On Stage*, and a host of others.

Comic Publishing in the Philippines in the 1970s: A Case Study

For several decades Ace Publications has been the dominant comic book company in the Philippines. It is controlled by Ramon Roces, the owner of Roces Publications and the most successful publisher in the field.

On June 14, 1947, the first issue of Pilipino Komiks appeared in the Philippines, a country that has the most avid comic book readers in the world. Many of the comic publications were geared toward the masses; they catered to the tastes and demands of the adult population, as well as those of the younger generation.

Pilipino Komiks *became such a tremendous hit that other comics were brought out in the 1950s.* Hiwaga, Espesyal Komiks, Tagalog Klasiks, Kenkoy Komiks, *and* Educational Klasiks *were added to the roster.*

The guiding force behind the success of Ace Publications was Tony Velasquez, the most popular cartoonist in the Islands. He wrote and illustrated Kenkoy, *the most famous cartoon character in the history of Philippine comics. Velasquez also had worked for* Halakhak, *the first comic book to be published in the country.*

Also working for Roces Publications were comic book pioneers Francisco Reyes (the illustrator of Kulafu, *the Filipino jungle hero), Carlos Francisco (the foremost muralist in the country), and Francisco V. Coching (the most imitated and admired writer-artist in the medium). Other early participants were Jesse Santos (of* DI 13 *fame), Larry Alcala (creator of* Kalabog en Bosyo, *the funniest duo to appear in komix), Noly Panaligan (one of the finest komik technicians), Fred Carillo, Teny Henson, Ruben Yandoc, and Elpidio Torres.*

The writers who joined the fold were Clodualdo del Mundo, Mars Ravelo, Gregorio Coching, Pablo Gomez, Virgilio Redondo, and Damy Velasquez. And some of the more well-known cartoonists were Deo Gonzales, Sabala Santos, Malang Santos, and Menny Martin. Among the list of top artists who became internationally known are Nestor Redondo, Alfredo Alcala, Tony Zuñiga, and Alex Niño.

Many of the classics of the Philippine graphic-novel appeared in the pages of the comics that carried the Ace insignia. Among them are Kabibe, Satur, Lapu-Lapu, El Indio, Barbaro, Dumagit, Maldita, Pulot-Gata, Waldas, Gigolo, Buhawi, Darna, Diwani, Ukala, Ifugao, Infanta Judith, Yamato, Warspite, Mikasa, Guerrero, Kurdapya, Monica, Pandora, Hokus-Pokus, Buntot-Page, Payaso, Brix Virgo, *and a host of others.*

Numerous other artists and writers have contributed their talents through the years to Ace. Among them are Federico Javinal, Alcantara, Jess Jodloman, P. Z. Marcelo, Rico Rival, Nestor Leonidez, Tuning Ocampo, Jim Fernandez, Tony Caravana, Rene Rosales, Manuel Carillo, Cirio H. Santiago, Rico Bello Omagap, and Jaime Vidal.

O.J.

Charles Schulz, "Peanuts." © United Feature Syndicate.

Walt Kelly, "Pogo." © Walt Kelly.

Then the nation's fears, doubts, and hopes found their expression in a remarkable group of intellectual and sharply questioning new strips: *Peanuts, Feiffer, B.C.* (to which should be added the earlier *Pogo*). Their authors, Charles Schulz, Jules Feiffer, Johnny Hart, and Walt Kelly, often pioneered in their innovative use of the medium, as well as in their sharp and unblinking commentary on contemporary social, political, and psychological ills. That they did indeed strike a responsive chord is best exemplified by the extraordinary success of *Peanuts*.

The rest of the world was no longer taking its cue from the American comics, however. National comic strip productions were again springing up everywhere. This was hastened by the proliferation of comic weeklies, which turned more and more to local talent to replace an American production grown increasingly stale. Art, like nature, abhors a vacuum, and as the American production went down, both quantitatively and qualitatively, non-American features correspondingly came to the fore.

This phenomenon was nowhere as apparent as with the action strips. While American syndicates were dropping adventure titles right and left, the rest of the world was busy turning out new ones. In the science-fiction field there were Frank Hampson's *Dan Dare*, Sidney Jordan's *Jeff Hawke*, Osamu Tezuka's *Tetsuwan-Atom*; the Western gave birth to Arturo Del Castillo's *Randall* and Joseph Gillain's *Jerry Spring*; the police strip had *Ric Hochet* and *Gil Jourdan*. Other types of adventure stories also found their representation in such strips as *Akadō*

Osamu Tezuka, "Tetsuwan-Atom." © Shōnen.

Arturo Del Castillo, "Randall." © Frontera.

Suzunosuke, *Air Hawk, El Capitan Trueno, Michel Tanguy,* and *Ninja Bugeicho,* to mention only the best or the most popular.

In the humor field the American strip also met with stiff competition from France (where *Astérix,* born in 1959, soon became a worldwide success), Belgium (*Gaston Lagaffe, Max*), Japan (*Kappa*), Germany (*Nick Knatterton*), Spain (*Mortadelo y Filemón*), Italy (*Cocco Bill*), and especially England, with Reg Smythe's *Andy Capp,* which has since conquered the American public.

Where America still held an advantage was in the realm of the sophisticated strip. No other country could boast of a feature as philosophical as *Pogo* or as penetrating as *Peanuts.* But, even there, the situation soon changed.

A shift in direction

After its brilliant, but essentially limited, renaissance in the 1950s, the American newspaper strip began to suffer from the worst artistic and economic slump in its history. In the 1960s and early 1970s few new strips achieved acclaim or notice, and only three reached the top of the lists: Johnny Hart and Brant Parker's *The Wizard of Id,* Garry Trudeau's *Doonesbury,* and Dik Browne's *Hägar the Horrible.* Economic disaster went hand in hand with artistic failure; the 1975 edition of *Editor & Publisher*'s syndicate directory listed less than 200 current strips being nationally syndicated, an all-time low. (Some syndicates also offered reprints of defunct comic features, such as Harold Gray's *Little Orphan Annie,* a most damning admission of creative failure.)

Granted that the economic factors that led to the syndicates' predicament (such as the declining readership of American newspapers) were not of their making (though it can be argued that, since the comic strip has historically been the most popular feature in newspapers, more people would have read the papers if they could find better comics in their pages), the unmitigated artistic disaster resulting was entirely the syndicates' own doing. Despite an undisputably large pool of new cartooning talent being turned out each year by the art schools (to mention only one source), the syndicate editors were unwilling or unable to tap these resources. Only a handful of nationally syndicated strip cartoonists were under 35 years of age, and only one, Garry Trudeau, was in his twenties (significantly, he was discovered by a small-time organization, which grew big, thanks to their judgment).

In point of fact a majority of cartoonists were in their sixties and seventies, and while old age is not necessarily synonymous with senility, it can hardly be looked upon as a fount of creative ideas. (Lest the reader gets the false impression that old-timers are paragons of productivity in their later years, one must hasten to add that most older cartoonists—and quite a few younger ones as well—resort to the infamous practice of "ghosting": they hire anonymous hacks to do their work while they play golf or watch their health.) It is no wonder, therefore, that the syndicate system literally crumbled under such appalling dead weight.

Garry Trudeau, "Doonesbury." © G.B. Trudeau.

Stan Lee and John Romita, "Spider-Man." © *Marvel Comics Group.*

In the 1960s the comic book broke with the pattern of repetitiveness and uniformity that had become associated with the medium in the preceding decade. Editor/writer Stan Lee, particularly, started experimenting with new designs and concepts, with the help of a talented stable of artists that included Jack Kirby, Steve Ditko, and Jim Steranko. This was the famous age of Marvel's "superheroes with problems," characters such as the Fantastic Four, Thor, and, especially, Spider-Man, who became a symbol for a whole generation of college students. National also tried to revamp its comic book lineup to suit the new age of relevance, but with markedly less success.

In the 1970s the comic books came down from the high peak of their popularity. The publishers tried to diversify, with new titles coming out practically every month (some lasting only one or two issues), but only the adaptation in comic form of Robert Howard's *Conan the Barbarian* took hold with the readers. In 1975 the drawn-out legal battle between National and *Superman*'s creators was finally settled out of court, with National's parent company, Warner Communications, agreeing to pay Jerry Siegel and Joe Shuster a lifelong annuity—a welcome plus for an industry that has been plagued with much adverse publicity.

The foremost comic book innovations came, however, from the so-called underground comics (or "comix" as they are commonly called), which allied

"Hef's Pad." © Robert Crumb, Jay Lynch, Skip Williamson.

James Holdaway and Peter O'Donnell, "Modesty Blaise." © Beaverbrook Newspapers Ltd.

great freedom of subject matter (including pornography and scatology) with a return to the original sources. Begun in such publications as *The East Village Other* and *Zap Comix*, the undergrounds enjoyed a tremendous boom throughout the decade, despite harassment, censorship, and lawsuits. Eventually the underground cartoonists gained recognition, and some, like Robert Crumb (whose most popular creations are *Fritz the Cat* and *Mr. Natural*) and Gilbert Shelton (author of *The Fabulous Furry Freak Brothers*), became famous.

Some enthusiastic critics (this writer included) predicted a long and glorious future for the new breed. Unhappily, the undergrounders' staying power did not match their talent; most of them lacked the self-discipline indispensable to any artist, and soon many dropped out of the comix scene for the same reasons they had dropped out of straight society—out of adolescent self-indulgence. While the underground movement cannot be entirely written off, it is certainly no longer the model that it was in its heyday.

The 1960s and the first half of the 1970s witnessed the exuberant growth of the comic form in the rest of the world. The English cartoonists enjoyed a surge of creativity; British humor asserted itself in Frank Dickens's hilarious account of office life, *Bristow*, and reached new heights of outrageousness with such iconoclastic confections as Bill Tidy's *The Fosdyke Saga* and Nicholas Garland's *Barry McKenzie*. In a more serious vein were Peter O'Donnell and James Holdaway's fast-moving *Modesty Blaise,* Pat Tourret and Jenny Butterworth's lighthearted soap opera, *Tiffany Jones,* and the superlative creations of Frank Bellamy, England's most gifted draftsman (*Frazer of Africa* and *Heros the Spartan*).

Across the Channel the French comic strip flourished. Two excellent comic features, *Achille Talon* by Greg (Michel Régnier) and *Gai Luron* by Marcel Gotlib, saw the light of print in this period; adventure was well represented by such outstanding creations as *Lieutenant Blueberry*, Jean Giraud's brooding Western; *Philémon*, a delightful work of fantasy by Fred (Othon Aristides); and Jean-Claude Forest's sex-cum-science-fiction strip, *Barbarella*.

The other major French-speaking country, Belgium, contributed the adventure strip, *Bernard Prince,* and the Western, *Comanche,* both drawn by Hermann (Huppen) and written by Greg, as well as François Craenhals's period strip, *Chevalier Ardent,* and the whimsical *Les Schtroumpfs* by Peyo (Pierre Culliford).

Jean-Claude Forest, "Barbarella." © *J.C. Forest.*

In Italy the 1960s saw the establishment of the "black hero" type of strip: *Diabolik* by Angela and Luciana Giussani opened the way, followed by *Kriminal* and others. The sick humor strip found its representation in Franco Bonvicini's *Sturmtruppen*. Two of the most remarkable artists of the comics came into their own in this period—Hugo Pratt, who injected new life into the adventure strip with *Una Ballata del Mare Salato* and *Corto Maltese*, and Guido Crepax, who revolutionized the content and style of the modern comic strip in such creations as *La Casa Matta*, *Bianca*, and, above all, the hauntingly beautiful *Valentina*.

Quality of design and draftsmanship was the hallmark of the Spanish cartoonists of this period: Carlos Giménez (*Delta 99*, *Dani Futuro*), Victor de la Fuente (*Haxtur*), and Esteban Maroto (*Cinco por Infinito*, *Wolff*) were the most outstanding. For his part, Enric Sío carried out interesting experiments with layout and color in his strips, *Nus* and *Sorang*.

European comic production was, in the 1970s, more vigorous and diversified than at any time in its history. Every European country seemed to be participat-

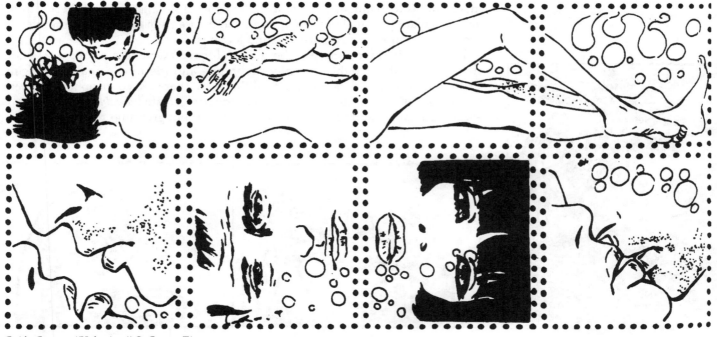

Guido Crepax, "Valentina." © *Crepax/Figure.*

ing in the comic sweepstakes, from Denmark (*Rasmus Klump*) to Germany (*Roy Tiger*, Rolf Kauka's comic creations), from the Netherlands (*Dzjengis Khan*) to Yugoslavia (*Herlock Sholmes*). Even in the Soviet Union the comics enjoyed a modest boom. So excellent did the European features become that, while they did not reach the United States in any sizable number (the success of *Andy Capp* notwithstanding), they successfully competed with American comics in such traditional American markets as Canada and South America.

Japan was the only non-Western country with a major comics production. Japanese creations were both numerous and notable in the 1960s and the first half of the 1970s. Osamu Tezuka added to his string of successes with the allegorical *Hi no Tori*, but he received artistic and commercial competition from Sanpei Shirato (*Sasuke, Kamui Den*), Gōseki Kojima (*Kozure Okami*), Tetsuya Chiba (*Harisu no Kaze, Ashita no Joe*), and Takao Saitō (*Golgo 13*). Two remarkable draftsmen reached their stride in this period: Hiroshi Hirata, who excelled in the depiction of violent, pulsating action scenes, and Koo Kojima, a master of subtle eroticism. Modern brands of black comedy and nonsense found able exponents in Shunji Sonoyama (*Gyatoruzu*), Fujio Akatsuka (*Osomatsu-kun*), and Tatsuhiko Yamagami (*Gaki Deka*); while Shinji Nagashima created what may be the first autobiographical novel in comic form with his trilogy, *Kiiroi Namida*.

The comics are a world phenomenon. To cite every comic-producing country would be tantamount to a roll call at the United Nations. One must mention, however, the Philippines (*Voltar*), Mexico (*Alma Grande*), Argentina (*Mafalda*, a Latin version of *Peanuts*), and China, whose flourishing comic book productions are slowly finding their way into the West.

The comics today: a new perspective

One of the most significant developments in the recent history of comic art, and perhaps the one most likely to affect its course in the future, has come not from within the profession, but from without: the formation in the 1960s of groups devoted to the study and preservation of the comics. In the past there had been individuals who had written cogently on the subject, but their efforts remained isolated and they went largely unnoticed. Not so with those militant organizations whose voices became increasingly audible. Soon there were international comic conferences (the first one, held at Bordighera, Italy, in 1965, was followed by the yearly congresses in Lucca); major art exhibitions were organized (the 1967 "Bande Dessinée et Figuration Narrative" at the Louvre and the 1971 "75 Years of the Comics" at the New York Cultural Center were two milestones); comic art museums were established (the first one, the City Museum of Cartoon Art, opened in Omiya, Japan, in 1966); and specialized, professional magazines (succeeding the amateurish "fanzines") sprang up everywhere. Strong and articulate personalities emerged in the field and manifested themselves in scores of histories, essays, articles, and lectures.

This activity in turn brought about a heightened awareness among a substantial segment of the public (usually the young and the intellectuals), changing them into ardent readers and critics of the form (there are comicophiles as there are cinephiles). Put in simple terms, there has been created *a public*, whose enthusiasm and appreciation make up for their small (but growing) numbers.

A page from a Chinese comic book.

Shunji Sonoyama, "Gyatoruzu." © Sonoyama.

Like their counterparts in other disciplines, the comic critics fulfill two main functions. One is the rediscovery, reevaluation, and preservation of the past (the works and artistic reputations of Winsor McCay, Alex Raymond, and Burne Hogarth, among others, have all been saved from oblivion by this continuing process of reappraisal). Their second—and perhaps more important—function is to express an educated judgment on the current production. Here, too, the critics have been successful in pointing the way; certainly artists as diverse as J. C. Forest, Guido Crepax, Shinji Nagashima, and Robert Crumb owe a large part of the recognition they have received to perceptive critics and an enlightened public.

Twenty years of American comics

Starting in the late 1970s, however, there has been a strong resurgence of fresh, innovative humor strips. In 1977 the Pulitzer Prize-winning editorial cartoonist Jeff McNelly created *Shoe*, a hilarious newsroom satire in which the assorted characters are birds of a different plumage; and the following year Jim Davis's *Garfield*, the quintessential cat strip, made its appearance. The trend culminated with the publication of Berke Breathed's *Bloom County* (1980), starring, among other outlandish characters, a sententious penguin, a liquor- and drug-crazed cat, and a 10-year-old scientific genius and convicted hacker named Oliver Wendell Jones.

Other newspaper strips followed along the same path, including *Zippy the Pinhead*, an iconoclastic feature concocted by Bill Griffith for underground comic books in the 1970s and transplanted to the newspaper pages a decade later; Scott Adams's minimally drawn but brilliantly written office comedy *Dilbert*; and two by yet more Pulitzer Prize winners, Mike Peters's *Mother Goose and Grimm* and Doug Marlette's *Kudzu*. The most original, innovative, and delightful comic strip to come out in the last decade—perhaps in the last quarter-century—was *Calvin and Hobbes*, about a hyperactive six-year-old and his pet tiger, created by Bill Watterson in 1985 and ended much too soon 10 years later.

Doug Marlette, "Kudzu." © Jefferson Communications.

Women and minorities were finally given their due in the past 20 years. Following such pioneering strips of the 1960s and 1970s as Morrie Turner's *Wee Pals* and Ted Shearer's *Quincy*, the last decade witnessed an ample flowering of newspaper comics on black themes: mention should be made of Ray Billingsley's *Curtis*, Stephen Bentley's *Herb & Jamaal*, and Robb Armstrong's *Jump Start*. Similarly, two distinctive and award-winning features written and drawn by women, Cathy Guisewite's *Cathy* (1976) and Lynn Johnston's *For Better or For Worse* (1978) gained strong readership among both genders.

The story strips, however, have continued on a downward spiral. The last 20 years tolled the end for such long-lasting features as *Brick Bradford, Captain Easy, Secret Agent Corrigan*, and *Joe Palooka*. Bucking the trend, Tribune Media Services in 1995 revived *Terry and the Pirates* in a new, jazzed-up version. The year 1996 marked the 100th birthday of comics, with numerous celebrations taking place across the United States, including the issuance by the U.S. Postal Service of a 20-stamp set of "Newspaper Strip Classics," and this in turn may signal the resurgence of a form that some had already written off as dead a few short years ago.

With newsstand sales plummeting and many companies folding, the comic-book medium was only saved at the end of the 1970s by a revolutionary method of distribution: the so-called direct market, consisting of a network of specialized comic stores (totaling almost 5,000 by the mid-1990s) that bought comic-book titles on a nonreturnable basis. Thus bolstered by guaranteed sales of their product, comic-book publishers quickly rebounded.

Marvel preserved its dominant position in the comics industry with its incredibly successful line of *X-Men* comics; started as early as 1963, they only gained a large public following in the late 1970s. By the 1980s the series had spawned an entire line of spin-offs, most starting with the letter "X" (*X-Factor, X-Force*, etc.). Other Marvel titles of note have been *Alpha Flight, The New Mutants*, and the Frank Miller-scripted *Daredevil*; but overall the Marvel production suffered a sharp decline in both quality and popularity in the 1990s, a trend hastened by the flight of some of their top talents, who went on to form Image Comics. The spate of bad news culminated in December 1996, when Marvel filed for bankruptcy.

Meanwhile, DC Comics maintained a steady course, bolstered by their traditional titles, which were strongly helped by the box-office success of the *Superman* and *Batman* movies. This allowed them to experiment with new and interesting titles, such as *The New Teen Titans, Camelot 3000, Starman*, and especially *Watchmen* (1985) by the British team of Alan Moore and Dave Gibbons.

The direct market also allowed a host of small comic-book publishers, the so-called independents, to survive and occasionally flourish. Many of the most innovative creations emanated from the independents, including Howard Chaykin's *American Flagg!*, Harvey Pekar's *American Splendor*, and Dave Sim's *Cerebus*, not to mention the incredibly successful *Teenage Mutant Ninja Turtles*.

The period also saw the generalization of the graphic novel, an extended narrative told in comic-book style. The form allowed for some of the most powerful statements ever made on significant and/or controversial themes. *Maus*, done by Art Spiegelman over the span of 10 years, is an allegory of the Holocaust, in which the Jews are depicted as mice and the Nazis as cats. In 1995, Howard Cruse told a poignant coming-of-age (and coming-out-of-the-closet) tale with *Stuck Rubber Baby*; the following year Joe Kubert produced *Fax from Sarajevo*, a gripping story of the civil war in Bosnia; while Will Eisner has created several autobiographical novels (*A Contract with God, The Dreamer, Dropsie Avenue*). Comic books have finally grown up.

The last 17 years have witnessed what can only be called the "Hollywoodization of the comics," from the release of *Flash Gordon* in 1980 to the 1997 movie *Batman and Robin*. In the intervening years, these comic characters have made it onto the big screen: *Popeye, The Mask, Superman* and its sequels, *Dick Tracy, Barb Wire, The Phantom, Teenage Mutant Ninja Turtles, The Crow, Dennis the Menace*, even the British *Judge Dredd*, among others, with many more to come.

The globalization of the comics

The past two decades have been a period of great creativity in all parts of the planet, led, but no longer dominated by, the traditional comics-producing countries of western Europe, the United States, and Japan. In Britain the trend has been toward the creation of superpowered characters based on the American model, such as Judge Dredd and Marvelman. Across the Channel, French cartoonists continued to be active in all genres: social satire (*Les Bidochon*, about a lowbrow French family, is a good example), erotic humor (Georges Pichard's

Art Spiegelman, "Maus." © Art Spiegelman.

many creations), romantic adventure (François Boucq's *The Magician's Wife* and others), and science fiction (a genre in which Yugoslav-born Enki Bilal excels). Italy hasn't lagged far behind, with such creations as Vittorio Giardino's political thrillers (*Hungarian Rhapsody*, *Orient Gateway*), Stefano Tamburini and Tanino Liberatore's punk epic *Ranxerox*, the cartoon spoofs of Massimo Mattioli, and the many graphic novels of erotic fantasy by Milo Manara.

Following the death of the dictator General Francisco Franco, a remarkable flowering of the art took place in Spain. Mention should be made of Fernando Fernández, author of an impressive adaptation of *Dracula* (1984); of Daniel Torres, creator of the tongue-in-cheek futuristic adventures of Rocco Vargas; of the transplanted Argentinians Carlos Sampayo and José Muñoz, who uncannily re-created the mood of 1940s *film noir* in their thriller, *Alack Sinner*; and of Jordi Bernet, whose dynamic style has given distinction to the gangster tales of *Torpedo*. Other creations of note have come out of Germany (with the remarkable *Bell's Theorem* by Matthias Schultheiss), the Netherlands (where Jost Swarte holds sway with his surreal vignettes of daily life), Denmark (*Valhalla*, a tongue-in-cheek chronicle of the gods).

In the 1990s the western European production suffered a marked loss of creativity (and a consequent loss of readership), which was only partially offset by the emergence of new talent coming out of eastern Europe (Gzregorz Rosinski and Jerzy Wroblewski in Poland, Karel Saudek in the Czech Republic, and others). Even Russia, where comics had been frowned upon by the Soviet regime, enjoys a small but growing output of comic publications.

In the Americas, the Canadian Dave Sim is the author of the aforementioned *Cerebus the Aardvark*; Mauricio de Souza of Brazil spearheads a flourishing production of children's comics, of which *Monica* is the best known internationally; and Mexico continues to pour out an average but steady flow of comic *novelas*. While the Argentine output was temporarily put into artistic eclipse by the advent of the military regime in the late 1970s, the return of democracy has brought a renewal of the medium to the country. This is particularly true of Robin Wood, whose many creations have captured an international public, and of Alberto Breccia (1919-1993), who topped his long career with *Perramus*, a wrenching meditation on the meaning of life and memory.

Japan has now the distinction of being the largest producer of comic books in the world, in terms of number of copies sold. The Japanese comic books range from romance comics (Riyoko Ikeda's *The Rose of Versailles*) to thrillers (*Golgo 13* by Takao Sato) to whimsical comedy (Rumiko Takahashi's *Ranma 1/2)* to the very Japanese genre of "salary men" comics, depicting the tribulations of office workers. Of special note have been Shotaro Ishinimori's *Japan Inc.*, a fictional (or perhaps not so fictional) account of the workings of the Japanese economy, and *Gen of Hiroshima*, a very long narrative started in 1973 by Keiji Nakazawa and now totaling over 2,000 pages, about the horrors of nuclear war. Japanese comics (or *manga*) are sold in all parts of the world, including North America and western Europe.

For a long time Japan had inundated the rest of Asia with its production, but in recent years a vigorous comics industry has sprung up in every country of the region. It would be fastidious to name them all, but mention should be made of the Indonesian *Djon Domino* by Johnny Hidajat, of Rafiqun Nabi's *Tokai* in Bangladesh, of Lat's *Kampung Boy* in Malaysia. India has had a thriving comics industry, which is somewhat hampered by the number of regional dialects in the country. The cartoonist Pran has somehow surmounted this handicap with his many children's comics, which have earned him the title "Walt Disney of India." China's comics tradition goes back to the 1920s, but after the Communist takeover most of the comics industry was devoted to propaganda and nationalistic themes. A steady flow of comic strips (or rather "comic boxes," since Chinese comics usually come in a square rather than a horizontal format) has been produced since the 1950s, a production slowed (but not ended) by the Cultural Revolution. Of late, cartoonists such as Ye Quianyu and Zhang Leping have dealt with contemporary and even satirical themes in their comic strips.

Australia and New Zealand have maintained their long tradition of homespun newspaper strips. The former spawned Allan Salisbury's punning *Snake Tales*, while the latter harbors Murray Ball's barnyard-flavored *Footrot Flats*. The comics have now become a universally accepted form of expression, and examples can be found from South Africa (where the most popular newspaper strip, *Madam and Eve*, stars a white matron and her black maid) to Algeria, whose eminent cartoonist, Sid Ali Melouah, has won many awards in Europe for his comic strips. Most importantly, cartoonists and their creations are now transcending national borders, with European artists coming to the United States, American cartoonists working in Europe and Japan, and many national publications open to talent from the entire world. This trend can only continue well into the next century.

With festivals, exhibitions, and conventions (not to mention comic art museums) springing up all over the world, there now seems to be a universal acceptance of the comics as a legitimate form of popular culture, despite resistance in some academic circles, to validate the important contributions the comics have made to the consciousness and culture of people worldwide.

One of the more hopeful (as well as one of the more exciting) developments in recent years has been the introduction of comics on the Internet. There are now forums for discussion on the comics during which fans can voice their opinions and exchange views on the latest comics offerings, thereby providing word-of-mouth support to an art form too often neglected by mainstream media; just as importantly, comics old and new are being broadcast over the Net. Some of the syndicates offer daily installments of their most popular strips, and creators also use the Web to promote their strips, independently of their syndicates. As Lee Salem of Universal Press Syndicate recently noted, "Whatever cyberspace becomes may well afford cartoonists other creative outlets, and it's easy to envision thousands—even millions—of people subscribing to a cartoonist's work for a penny a day." The number of comic strips thus beamed out increases every day, and there has been a promising growth in the number of international, independent, and underground comics that have joined the ranks of more established features. It is possible that to a great extent the future of comics in the 21st century lies in that direction.

Maurice Horn

A World Chronology of Comic Art
From the 18th Century to the Present

1734:

William Hogarth's *A Harlot's Progress* published.

1735:

W. Hogarth's *A Rake's Progress* published.

1745:

W. Hogarth's *Marriage à la Mode* appears.

1790-1815:

James Gillray publishes his series of patriotic cartoons, extolling British virtues and excoriating the vices of Republican (and later Napoleonic) France.

1809:

Thomas Rowlandson produces his most famous cartoon series, *The Tour of Doctor Syntax*, with verses by William Combe.

1814:

First volume of *Hokusai Manga* ("The Hokusai Cartoons") published in Japan.

1815:

T. Rowlandson publishes his satirical cartoon series, *English Dance of Death*.

1841:

Punch magazine started in London.

1846-47:

Rodolphe Töpffer's picture-stories collected in book form as *Histoires en Estampes*.

1885:

Wilhelm Busch's *Max und Moritz* published in Germany.

First real newspaper syndicate, A. N. Kellogg News Company, established in the United States.

1867:

First adventure of *Ally Sloper* published in England by Charles Henry Ross.

1877:

English-language version of the comic weekly *Puck* published in the United States.

1881:

Judge magazine starts publication as *The Judge*.

1883:

Life magazine established.

James Gillray, "Tales of Wonder."

Richard Outcault, "The Yellow Kid."

1889:

Christophe's *La Famille Fenouillard à l'Exposition* published in France.

1890:

Comic Cuts and *Chips* started in England.

1893:

New York Recorder publishes its first color page, one week ahead of the *New York World*. James Swinnerton's *Little Bears* starts as a spot filler in the *San Francisco Examiner*.

1895:

R. F. Outcault's character, the Yellow Kid, makes his first appearance in the *World*.

1896:

The *Yellow Kid* definitively established as a weekly feature.

In England *Weary Willie and Tired Tim* created by Tom Browne.

1897:

Outcault leaves the *World* for the *Journal*. "The American Humorist," the *Journal*'s color Sunday supplement established (first issue features *The Yellow Kid* and Rudolph Dirks's *The Katzenjammer Kids*).

1900:

Carl "Bunny" Schultze creates *Foxy Grandpa* for the *New York Herald*. F. B. Opper's *Happy Hooligan* appears.

1902:

R. F. Outcault starts *Buster Brown* in the *New York Herald*.

J. S. Baker's *Casey Court* started in England.

First publication in France of *Le Jeudi de la Jeunesse* magazine.

First Swedish comic strip, *Mannen som gör vad som faller honom in* ("The Man who Does Whatever Comes to His Mind") by Oskar Andersson (O.A.), appears.

1903:

Gustave Verbeck's reversible strip, *The Upside Downs*, starts publication in the *Herald*. Clare Briggs's weekday strip, *A. Piker Clerk*, starts in the *Chicago American*.

1904:

George McManus creates *The Newlyweds*. *The Dream of the Rarebit Fiend* by Silas (Winsor McCay) starts in the *Evening Telegram*. James Swinnerton originates *Little Jimmy*.

J. S. Baker's *Tiger Tim* started in England.

Comic weekly *L'Illustre* (later changed to *Le Petit Illustré*) established in Paris.

First French-Canadian newspaper strip, *Le Père Ladébauche*, started in *La Presse* by J. Charlebois.

C. W. Kahles, "Hairbreadth Harry."

1905:

Winsor McCay creates *Little Nemo in Slumberland* for the *Herald*. G. Verbeck starts *The Terrors of the Tiny Tads*.

Bécassine by Pinchon and Caumery published in France.

First publication of the comic magazine *O Tico Tico* in Brazil.

Tokyo Puck founded in Japan.

1908:

C. W. Kahles originates *Hairbreadth Harry*. From Germany, Lyonel Feininger creates *The Kin-der-Kids* and *Wee Willie Winkie's World* for the *Chicago Tribune*.

1907:

First successful daily strip, H. C. "Bud" Fisher's *Mr. A. Mutt* (later changed to *Mutt and Jeff*), appears in the *San Francisco Chronicle*.

1908:

The comic weekly *L'Epatant* established in Paris; in issue number 9 Louis Forton creates *La Bande des Pieds-Nickelés*.

In England *Billy Bunter* started by Frank Richards.

Il Corriere dei Piccoli established in Italy with Attilio Mussino's *Bilbolbul* featured in first issue.

1909:

L'Espiègle Lili created by Jo Valle and André Vallet (France).

1910:

Desperate Desmond created by Harry Hershfield. First appearance of George Herriman's *The Dingbat Family*.

Antonio Rubino's *Quadratino* published in Italy.

1911:

Sidney Smith creates *Old Doc Yak*.

1912:

International Feature Service founded by William Randolph Hearst. Rudolph Dirks leaves the *Journal*; Hearst starts lawsuit against Dirks to prevent him from drawing *The Katzenjammer Kids* for the *World*. Cliff Sterrett's *Polly and Her Pals* started as *Positive Polly*.

1913:

George McManus originates his most famous creation, *Bringing Up Father*. First appearance of George Herriman's *Krazy Kat* as a regular strip.

1914:

Hearst v. Dirks lawsuit settled in appeal; *The Katzenjammer Kids* remains in the *Journal* (illustrated by H. H. Knerr), while Dirks retains right to draw his characters for the *World*, under the title *Hans and Fritz* (changed to *The Captain and the Kids* during World War I). Harry Hershfield starts *Abie the Agent*.

1915:

Fontaine Fox definitively establishes *Toonerville Folks*. Rube Goldberg creates *Boob McNutt*. Merrill Blosser's *Freckles and His Friends* appears. King Features Syndicate founded by Moses Koenigsberg as a consolidation of International Feature Service and other Hearst newspaper interests.

First British daily strip, *Teddy Tail* by Charles Folkard, appears in the *Daily Mail*.

1916:

Arturo Lanteri's *El Negro Raul* started in Argentina.

1917:

Sidney Smith starts *The Gumps*.

In Italy *Il Signor Bonaventura* created by Sto (Sergio Tofano).

1918:

Frank King originates *Gasoline Alley*.

First professional association of cartoonists, the "Manga Kourakukai," founded by Rakuten Kitazawa in Japan.

1919:

Billy DeBeck creates *Barney Google*. *Thimble Theater* started by E. C. Segar. *Harold Teen* originated by Carl Ed.

Pip, Squeak and Wilfred created by Bertram Lamb and A. B. Payne in England.

The Potts (originally *You and Me*) started by Stanley Cross in Australia.

Sto (Sergio Tofano), "Il Signor Bonaventura." © Corriere dei Piccoli.

James Bancks, ''Ginger Meggs.'' © *Australian Consolidated Press Ltd.*

1920:

Martin Branner creates *Winnie Winkle*.

Rupert created by Mary Tourtel in England.

Oscar Jacobsson's *Adamson* started in Sweden.

1921:

Ed Wheelan creates *Minute Movies*. Russ Westover originates *Tillie the Toiler*. *Out Our Way* started by J. R. Williams.

Birdseye Center started (as *Life's Little Comedies*) by James Frise in Canada.

John Millar Watt creates *Pop* in the *London Daily Sketch*.

First successful Dutch daily strip, *Bulletje en Bonestaak*, by G. A. Van Raemdonck, appears in *Het Volk* (preceded by a few months by the short-lived *Yoebje en Achmed*).

Ginger Meggs (originally *Us Fellers*) created by James Bancks in Australia.

Don Catarino daily strip started by Salvador Pruneda in Mexico.

1922:

Smitty created by Walter Berndt.

In Argentina Arturo Lanteri creates *Don Pancho Talero*.

Fatty Finn created by Syd Nicholls in Australia.

1923:

Pat Sullivan's *Felix the Cat* syndicated as a newspaper strip. *The Nebbs* started by Sol Hess, with drawings by W. A. Carlson. *Moon Mullins* created by Frank Willard. Ad Carter produces *Just Kids*.

Nonkina Tousan created by Yutaka Asō in Japan.

1924:

Harold Gray creates *Little Orphan Annie*. Roy Crane's *Wash Tubbs* started. *Boots and Her Buddies* created by Edgar Martin.

In France Louis Forton creates *Bibi Fricotin*.

Nonkina Tousan becomes Japan's first original daily strip.

1925:

Ella Cinders started by Charles Plumb and Bill Conselman. Alain Saint-Ogan creates *Zig et Puce* in France.

In Finland Ola Fogelberg starts *Pekka Puupää*.

Longest-running Australian strip, Mary Gibbs's *Bib and Bub*, appears.

1926:

In Mexico Jesús Acosta Cabrera creates *Chupamirto*.

1927:

Frank Godwin creates *Connie*.

1928:

Tim Tyler's Luck created by Lyman Young. Hal Forrest and Glen Chaffin introduce *Tailspin Tommy*. Ham Fisher starts *Joe Palooka*. Percy Crosby's *Skippy* syndicated by King Features.

Macaco created by K-Hito (Ricardo García López) in Spain.

1929:

The adventure strip definitively established in the comic pages with P. Nowlan and R. Calkins's *Buck Rogers* and Harold Foster's *Tarzan*. Popeye makes his appearance in Segar's *Thimble Theater*. Clifford McBride's *Napoleon* established.

In Belgium Hergé (Georges Rémi) creates *Tintin*.

Sor Pampurio created by Carlo Bisi in Italy.

Tony Velasquez's *Kenkoy* appears in the Philippines.

1930:

Walt Disney's *Mickey Mouse*, drawn by Ub Iwerks, starts syndication as a daily strip. Chic Young creates *Blondie*.

Speed Tarō created by Sako Shushido in *Japan*.

1931:

Chester Gould creates *Dick Tracy*.

Patoruzú started as an independent strip by Dante Quinterno in Argentina.

In Japan *Norakuro* created by Suihou Tagawa.

1932:

Martha Orr creates *Apple Mary* (later changed to *Mary Worth*). C. D. Russell's *Pete the Tramp* starts national syndication.

Norman Pett starts *Jane's Journal* (later *Jane*) for the *London Daily Mirror*.

Fiki-Miki created by Makusynski and Walentinowicz in Poland.

Globi, by J. K. Schiele and Robert Lips, appears in Switzerland.

In Sweden *91 Karlsson* started by Rudolf Petersson.

1933:

Funnies On Parade issued for Procter and Gamble. Zack Mosley starts *Smilin' Jack* (originally *On the Wing*). William Ritt and Clarence Gray create *Brick Bradford*. Milton Caniff starts *Dickie Dare*. *Alley Oop* created by V. T. Hamlin.

1934:

A bumper year for the American comic strip: *Flash Gordon* and *Jungle Jim* (both by Alex Raymond), *Secret Agent X-9* (by A. Raymond and Dashiell Hammett), *Mandrake the Magician* by Lee Falk and Phil Davis, *Li'l Abner* by Al Capp, *Terry and the Pirates* by Milton Caniff, *Red Barry* by Will Gould, *Don Winslow* by F. Martinek and L. Beroth. Noel Sickles takes over *Scorchy Smith* (created 1930). Otto Soglow's *Little King* starts syndication.

First French daily strip, *Le Professeur Nimbus*, created by A. Daix.

In Germany *Vater und Sohn* started by Erich Ohser (E. O. Plauen).

First Japanese superhero strip, *Tanku Tankurō*, created by Gajō.

1935:

Zane Grey's *King of the Royal Mounted* started by Allen Dean. Ralph Fuller creates *Oaky Doaks*. Publication of *New Fun* comic book. Bob Moore and Carl Pfeufer create *Don Dixon*. *Smokey Stover* started by Bill Holman.

In Spain Jesús Blasco originates *Cuto*.

Luis Palacio creates *Don Fulgencio* in Argentina.

1936:

Lee Falk and Ray Moore create *The Phantom*.

Martha Orr, "Apple Mary." © Publishers Syndicate.

K-Hito (Ricardo García López), "Macaco." © K-Hito.

Will Eisner, "The Spirit." © Will Eisner.

Ted McCall and C. R. Snelgrove originate *Robin Hood and Company* for the *Toronto Telegram*.

Riyūichi Yokoyama's *Edokko Ken-chan* (later changed to *Fuku-chan*) started in Japan.

1937:

Harold Foster creates *Prince Valiant*. Burne Hogarth takes over the *Tarzan* Sunday page. *Detective Comics* established.

Jack Monk starts *Buck Ryan* in England.

In France *Futuropolis* created by René Pellos.

In Italy Rino Albertarelli originates *Kit Carson*. Cesare Zavattini and Giovanni Scolari create *Saturno contro la Terra*.

Andrija Maurović's *Stari Mačak* published in Yugoslavia.

H. Dahl Mikkelsen's *Ferd'nand* appears in Denmark.

Creation of Gabriel Vargas's *La Familia Burron* in Mexico.

Larry Steele created by Reg Hicks in Australia.

1938:

Fred Harman creates *Red Ryder*. Fran Striker's *The Lone Ranger* adapted to the comics by Ed Kressy. Al Andriola begins *Charlie Chan*. *Superman*, by Jerry Siegel and Joe Shuster, appears in *Action Comics*. *The Shadow* started as a newspaper strip by Vernon Greene.

The comic weekly *Spirou* established in Belgium.

Mussolini enacts a law barring all American comics (except *Mickey Mouse*) from Italy. *Virus* created by Federico Pedrochhi and Walter Molino. *Dick Fulmine* originated by Carlo Cossio.

Just Jake started by Bernard Graddon in England.

Djordje Lobacev's *Princeza Ru* appears in Yugoslavia.

1939:

Batman, by Bob Kane and Bill Finger, created in *Detective Comics*. Carl Burgos creates *The Human Torch*. Bill Everett originates *Sub-Mariner* in *Marvel Mystery*.

Barlog creates *Die Fünf Schreickensteiner* for the *Berliner Illustrirte*.

1940:

Dale Messick creates *Brenda Starr*. Will Eisner produces *The Spirit*. Lou Fine's *The Black Condor* appears in *Crack Comics*. *Captain Marvel* created by Bill Parker and C. C. Beck. Gardner Fox and Harry Lampert start *The Flash*.

In Australia *Bluey and Curley* created by Alex Gurney. Stan Cross starts *Wally and the Major*.

1941:

Gus Arriola creates *Gordo*. *Vic Jordan* by Payne and Wexler starts. *Captain America* created by Joe Simon and Jack Kirby. *Wonder Woman*, by William Marston and H. G. Peter, appears in *All-Star Comics*. Jack Cole creates *Plastic Man* in *Police Comics*. Bob Montana starts *Archie*. *Green Arrow* created by Mort Weisinger and George Papp.

Fred Harman, "Red Ryder." © NEA Service.

In Spain Jesús Blasco creates *Anita Diminuta*.

1942:

George Baker creates *The Sad Sack*. Crockett Johnson starts *Barnaby*. Dave Breger introduces *G. I. Joe* (formerly *Private Breger*) in *Yank*. Charles Biro and Bob Wood start *Crimebuster*. Carl Barks begins his comic book association with *Donald Duck*.

1943:

Milton Caniff creates *Male Call* for Camp Newspapers. Roy Crane creates *Buz Sawyer*. *Captain Easy* taken over by Crane's assistant, Leslie Turner. Al Andriola starts *Kerry Drake*. Walt Kelly's *Pogo* appears in *Animal Comics*.

Garth started by Steve Dowling in England.

1944:

Frank Robbins creates *Johnny Hazard*.

Marijac's underground strip, *Les Trois Mousquetaires du Maquis*, appears in France.

1945:

Burne Hogarth creates *Drago*. Ray Bailey begins *Bruce Gentry*.

Les Pionniers de l'Espérance created by Raymond Poïvet and Roger Lécureux in France.

Willy Vandersteen starts *Rikki en Wiske* (later changed to *Suske en Wiske*) in Belgium.

1946:

Alex Raymond creates *Rip Kirby*. The National Cartoonists Society established, with Rube Goldberg as its first president.

In France Claude Arnal starts *Placide et Muzo* and Pierre Liquois originates *Guerre à la Terre*.

In Belgium Morris creates *Lucky Luke*. *Tintin* magazine started (in first issue E. P. Jacobs's *Blake et Mortimer* and Paul Cuvelier's *Corentin* appear).

El Coyote, by José Mallorqui and Francisco Batet, begins in Spain.

1947:

Milton Caniff creates *Steve Canyon*, leaving *Terry* to George Wunder. Coulton Waugh publishes the first book-length study of the American comic strip, *The Comics*.

In Belgium creation of *Buck Danny* by V. Hubinon and J. M. Charlier.

In Japan *Fushigira Kuni* started by Fukijiro Yokoi.

1948:

Walt Kelly's *Pogo* appears as a daily strip in the *New York Star*. *Rusty Riley* created by Frank Godwin. *Rex Morgan, M.D.* appears.

Jacques Martin creates *Alix l'Intrépide* (Belgium).

Shōnen Oja created by Soji Yamakawa in Japan.

Raymond Poïvet, "Les Pionniers de l'Espérance." © Editions Vaillant.

José-Luis Salinas and Rod Reed, "The Cisco Kid." © King Features Syndicate.

1949:

In England Trog (Wally Fawkes) creates *Rufus* (later retitled *Flook*).

1950:

Charles Schulz's *Peanuts* appears. Mort Walker creates *Beetle Bailey*. E. C. Comics launches its "new trend" of horror comics.

Eagle comic weekly started in England (*Dan Dare*, by Frank Hampson, appears in first issue).

1951:

Rod Reed and José-Luis Salinas start *The Cisco Kid*. In an interval of a few days, Hank Ketcham in the United States and David Law in England each create a different kid strip by the same name—*Dennis the Menace* (March 12 and 17).

In Japan *Tetsuwan-Atom* created by Osamu Tezuka.

1952:

Judge Parker started by N. Dallis and Dan Heilman. *Mad* magazine starts publication.

Eiichi Fukui creates *Igaguri-kun* in Japan.

1953:

In Belgium Raymond Macherot creates *Chlorophylle*.

Jimmy das Gummipferd started by Roland Kohlsaat in Germany.

1954:

Mort Walker and Dik Browne create *Hi and Lois*. Dr. Frederic Wertham publishes his anti-comic book essay, *Seduction of the Innocent*, in April; in October the Comics Code Authority is established as a reaction.

Jeff Hawke originated by Sydney Jordan in England.

In Japan *Akadō Suzunosuke* created by Eiichi Fukui.

1955:

Gus Edson and Irwin Hasen create *Dondi*.

Max l'Explorateur, by Bara, starts in the Paris daily *France-Soir*.

1957:

Leonard Starr creates *On Stage*. Mel Lazarus starts *Miss Peach*.

Reg Smythe creates *Andy Capp* in England.

Gaston Lagaffe created by André Franquin in England.

In Italy Benito Jacovitti originates *Cocco Bill*.

1958:

Johnny Hart creates *B.C.* John Dirks takes over *The Captain and the Kids* from his father, Rudolph Dirks. *Feiffer* begins national syndication. *Rick O'Shay* created by Stan Lynde. *Short Ribs* created by Frank O'Neal. Irving Phillips starts *The Strange World of Mr. Mum*.

China's longest-running strip, Shen Pei's *Little Tiger*, debuts.

1959:

Stephen Becker's *Comic Art in America* published by Simon and Schuster.

The French comic weekly *Pilote* started (in the first issue *Astérix*, by René Goscinny and Albert Uderzo, and *Michel Tanguy*, by J. M. Charlier and Uderzo, appear).

Ninja Bugeichō created by Sanpei Shirato in Japan.

John Dixon's *Air Hawk and the Flying Doctors* started in Australia.

Johnny Hart, "B.C." © Field Newspaper Syndicate.

1960:

Peyo's *Les Schtroumpfs* established in Spirou.

1961:

Stan Lee and Jack Kirby create *The Fantastic Four*. *Apartment 3-G* started by N. Dallis and Alex Kotzky.

Alma Grande produced by Pedro Zapiain and José Suárez Lozano in Mexico.

1962:

Harvey Kurtzman and Will Elder's *Little Annie Fanny* starts publication in *Playboy*. Stan Lee creates *Spider-Man*, with Steve Ditko, and *Thor*, with Jack Kirby.

Bristow started by Frank Dickens in England.

Creation of the Club des Bandes Dessinées in France. Marcel Gotlib starts *Gai Luron* (first called *Nanar et Jujube*). J. C. Forest creates *Barbarella*.

In Italy *Diabolik* created by Angela and Luciana Giussani.

1963:

In England creation of *Modesty Blaise* by Peter O'Donnell and James Holdaway. Alex Graham starts *Fred Basset*.

Achille Talon, by Greg, and *Fort Navajo* (later *Lieutenant Blueberry*), by Charlier and Gir (Jean Giraud), created in France.

Alfredo Alcala starts *Voltar* in the Philippines.

1964:

Johnny Hart and Brant Parker create *The Wizard of Id*.

Tiffany Jones started by Pat Tourret and Jean Butterworth in England.

SOCERLID established in France (among its founders were Pierre Couperie and Maurice Horn).

Maxmagnus and Bunker create *Kriminal* in Italy.

In Argentina Quino (Joaquin Lavado) creates *Mafalda*.

1965:

Wee Pals created by Morrie Turner. *Nick Fury, Agent of SHIELD* created by Jack Kirby in *Strange Tales*. First appearance in print of Robert Crumb's *Fritz the Cat*.

First International Comics Convention held in Bordighera, Italy. The comic monthly *Linus* starts publication in Milan. In its pages appears Guido Crepax's *Neutron* (later to become *Valentina*).

1966:

In Belgium creation of *Chevalier Ardent*, by François Craenhals, and *Bernard Prince*, by Greg and Hermann.

The City Museum of Cartoon Art opened in Omiya, Japan.

First version of China's most famous comic book, *The Red Detachment of Women*, published in Peking.

1967:

Redeye started by Gordon Bess. *Zap Comics* appears. Gilbert Shelton creates *The Fabulous Furry Freak Brothers*. Robert Crumb originates *Mr. Natural*. The Academy of Comic Art established by Bill Blackbeard in San Francisco.

The Musée des Arts Décoratifs (Palais du Louvre) shows a comprehensive exhibition of comic art, "Bande Dessinée et Figuration Narrative," organized by SOCERLID. Philippe Druillet's *Lone Sloane* appears in book form. *Philémon*, by Fred, established.

Comic monthly *Eureka* started in Italy.

In Japan *Hi no Tori* created by Osamu Tezuka.

1968:

The English version of *Bande Dessinée et Figuration Narrative, A History of the Comic Strip*, by Pierre Couperie and Maurice Horn, published. John Saunders and Al McWilliams start *Dateline: Danger! The Dropouts* created by Howard Post.

Bonvi's *Sturmtruppen*, Italy's first successful daily strip, appears.

Exhibition "La Historieta Mundial" organized in Buenos Aires, Argentina.

1969:

The Collected Works of Buck Rogers in the 25th Century published by Chelsea House Publishers, New York.

Golgo 13 created by Takao Saitō in Japan.

In Italy *Alan Ford* originated by Magnus and Bunker (Luciano Secchi and Roberto Raviola).

In India Pran creates his best-known strip, *Chacha Chaudary*.

Jack Kirby, "Thor." © Marvel Comics Group.

Takao Saitō, "Golgo 13." © Big Comic.

1970:

Broom Hilda created by Russell Myers. Garry Trudeau's *Doonesbury* starts national syndication. Jim Lawrence and Jorge Longaron produce *Friday Foster*. Marvel Comics starts comic book adaptation of *Conan*.

Corto Maltese created by Hugo Pratt for the French weekly *Pif*.

Djon Domino starts publication in Indonesia.

1971:

Maurice Horn organizes the exhibition "75 Years of the Comics" at the New York Cultural Center, the first comic exhibition ever held in a major American museum.

Stop Me! The British Newspaper Strip published by Denis Gifford in England.

1972:

Comics: Anatomy of a Mass Medium, by Reinhold Reitberger and Wolfgang Fuchs, appears in English translation.

Zack comic weekly starts publication in Germany.

1973:

Dik Browne creates *Hägar the Horrible*.

1974:

Joe Brancatelli starts *Inside Comics*, the first professional magazine on comic art in America. The Museum of Cartoon Arts opens in Greenwich, Connecticut.

Tatsuhiko Yamagami creates *Gaki Deka* in Japan.

1975:

The Cartoon Museum opens in Orlando, Florida.

First International Festival of Comics held at the University of Montreal, Canada.

Guido Crepax's *Histoire d'O* published simultaneously in Italy and France.

Mètal Hurlant magazine starts appearing on French newsstands: Jen Giraud, using the name "Moebius," will publish his most ground-breaking comics there.

Alack Sinner created by José Muñoz and Carlos Sampayo in Italy.

Dik Browne, "Hägar the Horrible." © King Features Syndicate.

1976:
Harvey Pekar begins his *American Splendor* comic-book series.
First edition of *The World Encyclopedia of Comics* published.
1977:
Jeff McNelly's *Shoe* starts syndication.
Dave Sim's *Cerebus* appears.
Publication of *The Smithsonian Collection of Newspaper Comics*.
1978:
First appearance of *Garfield*.
Wendy and Richard Pini begin publication of *Elfquest*.
1979:
For Better or For Worse first appears. *Little Orphan Annie* resurrected as *Annie*, following the success of the eponymous musical comedy.
1980:
Berke Breathed creates *Bloom County*.
The World Encyclopedia of Cartoons published.
1982:
Torpedo 1936 begins its long international run in Spain.
Martin Mystère produced in Italy.
In Japan creation of *Akira*.
1984:
Teenage Mutant Ninja Turtles launched.
In Argentina Alberto Breccia creates *Perramus*.
Duan Jifu's *Lao Ma* produced in China.
First issue of *Comic Art* magazine released in Rome.
1985:
Bill Watterson's spirit-renewing *Calvin and Hobbes* starts syndication.
Strip, Poreklo i Znacaj ("Comics, Their Origins and Importance") published in Yugoslavia.

Jim Davis, "Garfield." © United Feature Syndicate.

A Chinese "comic box": "Lao Ma's Adventures" by Duan Jifu. © Duan Jifu.

1986:

Alan Moore and Dave Gibbons produce *Watchmen*.

Monumental *Historia de los Comics* completed in Spain.

1989:

Scott Adams creates the extraordinarily successful *Dilbert*.

1991:

Jim Lee, Rob Liefeld, Todd McFarlane, and others found Image Comics (official announcement is made in January 1992).

First auction of comics and comic art held at Sotheby's Auction House in New York.

Javier Coma's *Diccionario de los Comics* published in Spain.

1994:

First three volumes of John A. Lent's four-volume *International Bibliography of Comic Art* released. (Fourth volume follows in 1996.)

1995:

Terry and the Pirates revived by Tribune Media Services.

In anticipation of the 100th anniversary of the comics, the U.S. Postal Service issues a 20-stamp set of "American Classic Comic Strips."

1996:

In this anniversary year of the birth of the comics the International Museum of Cartoon Art opens in Boca Raton, Florida; *100 Years of American Newspaper Comics* is published. The occasion is also marked by exhibitions in the United States and around the world, notably in Brussels, Barcelona, Buenos Aires, Tokyo, Belgrade, and Rome.

In December Marvel Comics files for reorganization under Chapter 11 of the U.S. bankruptcy laws.

1997:

For the first time in Spanish history, the National Library in Madrid organized a conference on the comics in January.

As of December 1997, the Marvel Comics legal proceedings were still not resolved.

The World of Comics:
An Analytical Summary

The following essay constitutes not a general theory of comic art (this will have to wait until such time as a new set of aesthetic principles specifically applying to 20th-century art forms, as well as to the traditional arts, has been formulated), but an inquiry into the nature and workings of the art form itself. My thoughts on the subject were first expressed in "What is Comic Art?", which I wrote as the introduction to the 1971 New York Cultural Center exhibition, "75 Years of the Comics." In turn, that introduction served as the basis of my lecture series, "Language and Structure of the Comics," which I have been giving at universities in North America and Europe since 1973.

The New York Cultural Center catalogue has been out of print for a number of years now (and the New York Cultural Center itself out of existence since 1975), but since then a number of writers have appropriated my positions (sometimes my very words) as their own, in publications from Montreal, Québec, to Buenos Aires, Argentina, and from Richmond, Virginia, to Rome, Italy. Imitation, as everyone knows, is the sincerest form of flattery, and I am flattered to see my ideas given such wide currency. However, I also feel that any personal body of ideas is best expressed in the words of its originator, so as to allow a reader to form an educated opinion and to evaluate the validity of such ideas in full knowledge of their exact formulation.

In the 20 years that have elapsed since the first publication of the *Encyclopedia*, there have been a few efforts to arrive at a definition of this medium, most of them by practicing cartoonists from the limited perspective of their craft. (Picasso once observed to fellow painter and budding art critic André Lhote that he could choose between being a good painter or becoming a good critic but couldn't be both. Lhote took the hint, abandoned painting, and turned himself into the leading modern art theoretician of the first half of the 20th century.) In this context I have decided to leave this essay in the form in which it originally appeared in the first edition of *The World Encyclopedia of Comics*.

The comics: a working definition

What is comic art? To this question it is already possible to give a tentative answer. It was Coulton Waugh who, in his pioneering book *The Comics* (1947),

Text and pictures reinforce each other: "Krazy Kat." © King Features Syndicate.

Panel: Paul Robinson, "Etta Kett." © King Features Syndicate.

first propounded an analytical definition that came to be widely accepted as the groundwork on which to build any serious study of the comics. Summarily put, the comics are a form necessarily including the following elements: a narrative told by way of a sequence of pictures, a continuing cast of characters from one sequence to the next, and the inclusion of dialogue and/or text within the picture.

Unfortunately, Waugh and his subsequent followers did not fully comprehend the significance of their discovery. Instead of realizing that they had just described the broad features of a new art form calling for an accordingly new set of standards, they kept trying to fit this newcomer into the alien mold of older and accepted forms. It is therefore not surprising that this conceptual aberration led its author into further and further aesthetic confusion. Thus Waugh, in the conclusion of his massive study, asked the question, "Is artistic and literary development [in the comics] possible?"—hardly an earthshaking pronouncement at the end of a 360-page volume.

Aside from the naiveness of believing content could somehow develop independently of form and structure (and elaborate structure at that), Waugh and his followers correlatively failed to recognize that the descriptive definition they themselves had given precluded any development outwards and that all subsequent improvements had to be organic to a preexistent and self-contained form. Within the external structure of the comics, there had to be an internal cohesiveness that could not be gained from surface observation.

Strip: Noel Sickles, "Scorchy Smith." © AP Newsfeatures.

The above definition, then, does not give us insight into the essence of the comics any more than the formula for *pi* gives us knowledge of the nature of the circle. It is as a methodological tool that it can be of invaluable use. By clearing away much of the semantic confusion surrounding the comics, it narrows the scope of research and puts the subject into a more accurate and more sharply defined focus.

The language of the comics

It would not occur to the serious scholar or critic to pronounce judgment on a novel on the evidence of a few paragraphs or to review a play on the basis of one or two scenes. Yet this practice is widely accepted in the criticism of the comics. Most art critics have not accepted the very simple and legitimate notion that a comic feature should be judged within its proper context, and on its own terms. In other words, a working knowledge of the language of the comics is necessary for any intelligent discussion of the subject, and because it is specialized knowledge, many a critic who sets out to expose the comics only succeeds in exposing his own ignorance.

Balloon: René Goscinny and Albert Uderzo, "Astérix." © Editions Dargaud.

Even when honestly trying to judge the comics, the unwitting critic is likely to evaluate the text and the pictures independently, whereas the most original feature of the comics is the blend of these two elements into one organic whole. Expression in the comics is the result of this interaction between word and picture, the product and not the sum of its component parts. The art and the writing reinforce (or pull down) each other in a variety of ways. When the writing (plot, situations, dialogue) is good, it can carry passable or even poor art along; conversely, good art can sometimes make up for any weakness in the writing. When both art and writing are exceptional, the result is a masterpiece (George Herriman's *Krazy Kat* is one good example); when art and writing are both terrible, the result validates all the criticism leveled at the comics (unfortunately, as in all arts, the bad is much more common than the good).

The basic element in the language of the comics is the panel, a simple drawing most often enclosed in a rectangular or square frame, that stands both in isolation from, and in intimate relation to, the others, like a word in a sentence. It is the simplest form of the comics, in the strict sense of gestalt, the contents of which are perceived as one unit. It is therefore futile to try to judge the artistry of a comic by the drawing of one panel (or a number of panels, each examined in isolation). To separate image content from narrative content is to do violence to the whole concept of the comics.

The panels themselves are grouped, again like words in a sentence, into strips (superficially a horizontal succession of panels) or pages whose format widely varies but whose chief characteristic, as opposed to a strip, is to present a vertical as well as a horizontal combination of frames. In turn these strips and pages articulate themselves, in a more or less complex manner, into sequences and episodes.

For their vocabulary the comics borrow both from common language and the language of (representational) art. Over the years they have developed a peculiar set of conventions, of which the balloon is the most widely known and used, and invented an array of new signs and symbols, mainly in the form of word-pictures and visual puns. Thus a lamp comes to represent a bright idea, a black cloud over the head of a character a feeling of grief or despair. The examples are endless.

Visual pun: H. H. Knerr, "The Katzenjammer Kids." © King Features Syndicate.

Today the language of the comics, with its innovations, its symbols, its colorful onomatopoeia (pow, vroom, ka-boom!) is as familiar and commonly accepted as the language of the movies. Together they have forced upon Western man a new way of looking at external reality.

The comics as communication

Even before the advent of Marshall McLuhan, the comics were usually viewed in terms of communication, without much attention being paid to them as art, whether actual or potential. There is some validity in seeing the comics in this light exclusively, and this prejudice has been reinforced in no small measure by those organizations engaged in selling the comics as a product (the same atti-

Comics used in advertising: Chester Gould, Autolite.

tude was also prevalent among the movie studios as regarded the motion pictures, and it contributed largely to the decline and fall of Hollywood).

The two main supports of the comics have historically been the book and the newspaper, and this resulted in the development of two different publics, with some overlap between them. As the heir to the picture book, the book of comics (and later the comic book narrowly defined) addressed itself mainly to younger readers, while the comic strip, being part and parcel of the daily newspaper, was generally conceived as a more adult form of expression. The gap, however, has been narrowing over the years, with the growth in the United States of comic books mainly destined for adults, and in Europe of illustrated weeklies encompassing a greater range of features. One of these papers styles itself, fittingly enough, "the newspaper of young people from 7 to 77."

There is no doubt that the public reads the comics primarily for their entertainment value, but even so one must make a distinction between routine readership (the reader who turns to the comics page from force of habit upon opening his newspaper) and active readership, which consists in looking at the comics for some form of specific satisfaction (it might be artistic, or nostalgic, or even campy). We find that those adults most interested in the comics are located at both ends of the educational spectrum. It would seem that the less educated enjoy the comics for their uncomplicated immediacy, and the sophisticates have increasingly adopted the medium (in Europe first, and now in the United States) for its anticultural qualities. If the medium is the message, then the message of the comics, with their flouting of the rules of traditional art and of civilized language, can only be subversion. (This point in one form or the other has always been the leading argument of the enemies of the comics. Now it is being utilized *a contario* by the exponents of the counterculture.)

A word must be said about the comics as specialized communication, however. The comics have been used in advertising ever since the Yellow Kid, and their utilization as propaganda has also been widespread, from the crude patriotizing of English and French comics in World War I to Steve Canyon and Buz Sawyer fighting the good fight in Vietnam, and American "imperialist" soldiers being lambasted in Chinese comics (at least before Nixon's visit to Peking).

Among its more sedate pursuits, the medium has been used in the dissemination of information ("Dennis-the-Menace and dirt" for the Soil Conservation Society of America and "Cliff Merritt sets the record straight" for the Brotherhood of Railroad Trainmen) and as a valuable teaching tool—two recent textbooks prepared by the University of Illinois for the teaching of the new math rely heavily on the comic form.

Compared to other forms of mass media, the comics are not a highly effective instrument of either suasion or enlightenment. They are not as overwhelming as the movies, as authoritative as the written word, or as pervasive as television. That they function best as a form of expression may be a commercial drawback, but that very fact also testifies to the integrity of their form.

The intellectual confusion about the comics

As has happened with the cinema, the popular success of the comics as a mass medium has obscured their preexistence as a form. Surveying the forest but ignoring the individual trees, the critics have seized upon the comics as a sociological object to be clinically studied, thereby denying *a priori* that aesthetic qualities could be attributed to them. This, of course, helped conceal the social critic's ignorance of the dynamics of creation in the comics.

Actually, the comics are a much more personal mode of expression than the movies, television, or even most modern manifestations of art and music. Whether there are several authors or only one, each feature is done in a craftsman's manner; this applies not only, as should be expected, to the writing and drawing, but to the lettering and tracing of the balloons also. Quite often this applies to the delineating of the frames surrounding each panel as well. While there exist some chemically pretreated materials, the cartoonist's instruments remain primarily ink, pen, brush, and paper. This, of course, does not give a comic strip a personal look unless the artist has some personal ideas to express, but it serves to prove that the comics are far from being the mechanized process that some pretend them to be. It is true that the comics are often a team effort,

Page: Harold Foster, "Prince Valiant." © King Features Syndicate.

Charles Schulz, "Peanuts." © United Feature Syndicate.

with assistants working on the backgrounds, the lettering, even the inking, and there is no denying that more often than not it is a case of too many cooks spoiling the broth. Predictably enough, the best authors are those who retain the strongest direction (Charles Schulz, for instance, does everything on *Peanuts*, including the lettering) and therefore give their features the most accomplished sense of unity.

Since artistic creation is present (or at least potential) in every feature of the comics, the temptation is great to apply to this new form the canons of traditional aesthetics, but again there is the danger of intellectual confusion. Because the comics present so many facets, each mirroring the rules of different art forms, they present some thorny epistemological problems that need to be cleared away if one desires to achieve any understanding of the form.

Guido Crepax, "La Casa Matta." © E.D.I.P.

The comics as graphic art

Since a comic, any comic, is first perceived visually, the tradition has always been to classify the comics as graphic art and to link them ("lump them" would probably be a more accurate choice of words) with illustration and caricature. And indeed, as one can see, there is a direct affiliation between the cartoon and the comic strip, just as there is a strong bond between the story strip and illustration. The differences, however, are obvious: the cartoon and the illustration highlight only one point, be it a punch line or the dramatic climax in a narrative, while the comics must keep the continuity of a whole sequence flowing.

This is not meant to play down the artistic skills required to draw a comic feature. Karl Fortess's assertions that "the comic strip artist is not concerned with art problems, problems of form, spatial relationships, and the expressive movement of line" and that "the comic strip has failed to produce a Daumier or a Hogarth" are utter nonsense. The best of the comic artists are very much concerned with artistic problems, although from a different vantage point than that of the traditional draftsman. On this score I simply let the illustrations in the color selections of this work speak for themselves. As for excellence of drawing, the comics can boast of a long line of outstanding artists from Winsor McCay to Burne Hogarth, from Frank Bellamy to Guido Crepax. All artistic currents have found expression in the comics, and a collection of the best works in this field presents an astonishing retrospective of the history of graphic art.

It would thus be perfectly possible to judge the comics entirely on their artistic merits, just as it would be feasible to judge a motion picture on its photography alone. Of course, that would mean that one is willing to place undue restrictions on other ways of appreciating the comics. But the image in the comics is not fixed in some point in time; rather, it inserts itself within the time flow of the narrative. It is a *diffuse* image whose projection in space, overlapping from one frame to another, mirrors a projection in time, forwards and backwards. Because of that fact the artistic concerns of the comic artist are not wholly coincidental with the concerns of the traditional artist, so it is only axiomatic to conclude that traditional aesthetics cannot be wholly coincidental with the aesthetics of the comics.

Mythology in comics: the legend of Theseus told in a Hungarian comic strip by Istvan Endrody.

The comics as narrative literature

Functionally, the comics would seem to belong to some literary discipline, as they are chiefly meant to be *read*, and the persistent public indifference to silent or pantomine strips bears this out. Some critics, therefore, have tried to link the comics with folk literature. There again similarities can be found; certainly the argument of many a comic sequence closely parallels such folk forms as the tale, the fable, or the parable. Harold Gray in *Little Orphan Annie*, Al Capp in *Li'l Abner*, and Walt Kelly in *Pogo* are especially fond of these forms. As one can see, however, the comics are the expression of individual artists and run counter to the collective processes that have contributed to the vast body of folk literature. What the comic artists have done is simply to weave these inchoate or unformed mythologies into their own scheme of things, in ways not dissimilar to those of artists and writers everywhere.

Winsor McCay, "Little Nemo."

Narration, however defined, remains the essence of the comics: their purpose is to tell a story. Because they aim at a large public, the comics have come to compete with, and eventually displace, older forms of popular literature like the dime novels, the pulps, and the magazine serials. Their superiority to these earlier forms comes not, as is widely assumed, from the fact that they can tell the story in graphic terms, but from the fact that, because of their graphic elucidation of detail and background, they can tell the story in more economical terms. As some wit put it, "They give you more bangs in less time."

Building on these premises, some authors have tried to fashion their comics into a monumental novel, with all that it implies in terms of a self-contained universe governed by its own laws, dynamics, and motivations. It would do them injustice to compare them exclusively with the picaresque novels. Some have deliberately aimed higher. Gray's *Little Orphan Annie* offers perhaps the closest example of a novel in comic form. Not only are there undertones of Dickens and Hugo, but the obsessing and rhythmic repetition of motif and echo is very close to the preoccupations of modern novelists. In *Gasoline Alley* Frank King sets out to describe the lives and times of a small midwestern community with a tenderness and serenity worthy of Goethe's *Wilhelm Meister*. Other examples could be cited with equal justification.

If I have insisted on the literary qualities present in the comics, it is because they are not so readily apparent as their graphic values. There again I must be careful not to beg the question and judge the comics in terms of literary standards alone. The comics is indeed a literary form, but one that should not be reduced to its literary elements lest its very raison d'être be subverted.

The comics as a dramatic form

A case can be made (and indeed has been made) for the comics being a latter-day outgrowth of the dramatic arts. It may be said without irony that the comics, more than any other 20th-century literary form, follow Aristotle's rule of a beginning, a middle, and an end. In the 80 years of their existence they have accomplished much the same progression as Western drama since the Middle Ages; starting with the farce or pantomime (*Yellow Kid, Katzenjammer Kids, Happy Hooligan*), they have assimilated the elements of the comedy of observation and manners (*Bringing Up Father, Moon Mullins*) before proceeding to the themes of the social comedy and the melodrama (*Mary Worth, Steve Canyon*) and the drama of ideas (*Little Orphan Annie*). The great dramatic currents of the 20th-century world have also found their spokesmen in the comics with the likes of George Herriman, Walt Kelly, Jules Feiffer, and Georges Wolinski.

The foregoing argument should not be slighted. Because of the ubiquitous use of the balloon, the dialogue constitutes the strongest and most prominent literary feature of the comics. While most cartoonists use dialogue chiefly as a means to convey essential information and to carry the plot forward, many others have become aware of its dramatic powers and played skillfully upon them. They have called upon dialogue to establish character and motivation (George McManus, Milton Caniff, Hergé), to create suspense and anticipation (Harold

Dream balloons: Mort Walker, "Beetle Bailey." © King Features Syndicate.

Theatrical strip: "Feiffer." © Jules Feiffer.

Gray, E. P. Jacobs, Milton Caniff), to reveal the central themes and ideas of their work (George Herriman, Walt Kelly, Charles Schulz), to establish tone and rhythm, and to give purpose to the action. The examples are endless, but dramatic conventions and stage devices are the special domain of two artists— George McManus and Walt Kelly, whose work has always been more dramatic than narrative.

In the context of action the balloon plays an ambivalent role: by function it is a dramatic device, by nature a graphic form, thus creating possibilities that great cartoonists have been prompt to explore. By using the graphic elements of the balloon (its shape, the lettering and the symbols within it) in a literal way, they are able to translate the nonverbal aspects of language: tone, pitch, rhythm, and accent. More importantly, the balloon can transcend speech, addressing itself to the naked thought (thought balloon), and even free itself of all the restraints of organized expression. Thus, one sees the balloon changing its form, slowly dissolving, or suddenly exploding. It is used as a ploy, a mask, a shield, an attack weapon. One also sees an analogy with the symbolic use of props in the modern theater.

Comics and cinema

For many reasons, some of which we have already mentioned, the comics come closer to the movies than to any other art form. Not only were they both born around the same time and from the same artistic and commercial preoccupations, but both tended to the same end: the creation of dialectical movement, either through optical illusion (cinema) or through kinetic suggestion (comics). It is well to point out at this juncture that many techniques which came to be called "cinematic" originated in the comics. Montage was the rule in the comics well before Eisenstein came along, and the techniques of cutting, framing, and panning were used by such early practitioners as Opper, McCay, and Feininger. As for the "audio," the comics had ample time to develop the voice-off, the

Cinematic Montage: Jim Steranko, "Nick Fury." © Marvel Comics.

Cinematic Montage: Jim Steranko, "Nick Fury." © Marvel Comics.

voice-over, and overlapping dialogue during the 30 years when the movies had at their disposal only the barbarous subtitle. Even the grammar of the comics and the movies was almost identical; the concepts of "shot" (as opposed to the static "scene") and "sequence," the variations of angle and perspective, and the possibility of tracking forward and backward are present in both forms.

The influence of the movies on the comics has been great; not only have they given the comics better techniques for the suggestion of movement in the transposition to paper of the equivalents of cinematic lighting, depth of field, silhouetted backgrounds, etc., but they also proved a major source of inspiration. The movie serials were as much the forerunners of the adventure strip as the dime novel or the pulps, and their distinctive syncopated rhythm became the hallmark of most of the action series of the 1930s.

Comic strips and animated cartoons

The constant cross-fertilization between the comics and the cinema soon produced its first legitimate offspring: the animated cartoon, a peculiarly modern union of art and technology. In their book *The Cinema as Art*, Ralph Stevenson and J. R. Debrix declare that "the accepted definition of an animated film is, not that it is drawn by hand, but that it is created frame-by-frame," which, of course, is how the comics are also created. This fact goes a long way toward proving that the animated cartoon owes more to the comics than to the cinema.

Another important point should also be made in this connection. Animation of still drawings predates the invention of the movie camera by quite a number of years. Using colored cartoons drawn on strips of paper (comic strips, literally!), such early inventors as the Belgian Plateau with his phenakistoscope, and the Englishman W. G. Horner with his zoetrope, were able to animate sequences of drawings as early as the 1830s.

The most important early pioneer in the field of animation was the Frenchman Emile Reynaud, who invented the praxinoscope and was the first to project animated cartoons onto a screen (his Théâtre Optique opened in 1892). In his study *Animation in the Cinema*, Ralph Stevenson unequivocally states, "He [Reynaud] not only invented a technique, he originated a genre and was the first to develop the animated film . . . into a spectacle." It was only years later, through the efforts of the American J. Stuart Blackton, that animation became irrevocably tied (for better and worse) to the cinema.

Many comic strip artists were also pioneers of the animated film; Winsor McCay is the most notable example, but Bud Fisher and George McManus also

Interdependent relationship between comics and animated cartoons: "Mutt and Jeff." © H. C. Fisher.

Interdependent relationship between comics and animated cartoons: "Popeye." © *King Features Syndicate.*

dabbled in animation, and Pat Sullivan worked on comic strips in Australia, England, and the United States before going into film cartooning.

The early cartoon films drew most of their inspiration and techniques from the comics, as well as many of their most popular characters: *Mutt and Jeff, The Katzenjammer Kids, Krazy Kat, Bringing Up Father, Happy Hooligan* (an early Blackton effort), *Les Pieds-Nickelés*, among others, were turned into successful cartoon series. In the 1920s, however, the animated cartoon started giving some of its own characters back to the comic strips with *Felix the Cat*. But even in the 1930s, when *Mickey Mouse, Donald Duck*, and other Disney creations massively invaded the comic pages, the comics were still contributing to screen animation in a notable way (with O. Soglow's *Little King* and especially E. C. Segar's *Popeye*).

In recent times animators have turned more and more toward experimentation and abstraction and away from the aesthetics of the traditional cartoon. Deprived of an important source of fresh ideas, commercial studios everywhere have again turned to the comics: in the United States (*Peanuts, Archie, Spider-Man*), France (*Astérix*), Belgium (*Tintin, Lucky Luke, Les Schtroumpfs*), Japan (*Tetsuwan-Atom*, alias "Astroboy"), and many other places. The romance between the comic strip and the animated cartoon is not over.

A search for new standards

By now it is apparent that the comics cannot be reduced to fit into any preconceived formula. By their very existence they seem to baffle any attempt at epistemological elucidation and offer an obdurate resistance to traditional aesthetics. One can very well sympathize with the resentment and frustration of the critic who finds all his neat little formulas of little or no use in any sane explication of the medium. The comics simply refuse to be pigeonholed. One solution (and it is the most frequent, if the least enlightening) is to put the comics beyond the pale, to write them off as non-art, non-literature, and non-significant. This approach is applied to the movie also, but to the astonishment of only the ignorant, both comics and movies have been able to survive the excommunication of the would-be defenders of Art, Truth, Beauty, and the preservation of the cultural status quo.

It is a peculiar form of intellectual perversity that consists in doggedly trying to berate the comics in the name of art or literature, in the face of overwhelming evidence that the comics do not answer to either. In the presence of an altogether new and original form, intrinsic values must be objectively assessed. This is no easy task, hardly easier than it has been with the movies. A thorough knowledge of the field must be obtained, with the same assiduity as is required of any other discipline; the *a priori* judgment that this is an inferior form only deserving of inferior scholarship is an especially galling piece of tortuous reasoning. It is only by serious study that one can arrive at an understanding of the underlying structures of the comics and formulate any critical conclusion.

Space and time in the comics

The problems of spatial representation have bedeviled the comic artist ever since the inception of the medium. Because the cartoonist deals not with one, but with an organic sequence of pictures, these problems cannot be solved by perspective alone. Simple perspective would give the same uniform depth value to all of the panels and thus tend to flatten them out, giving them the same

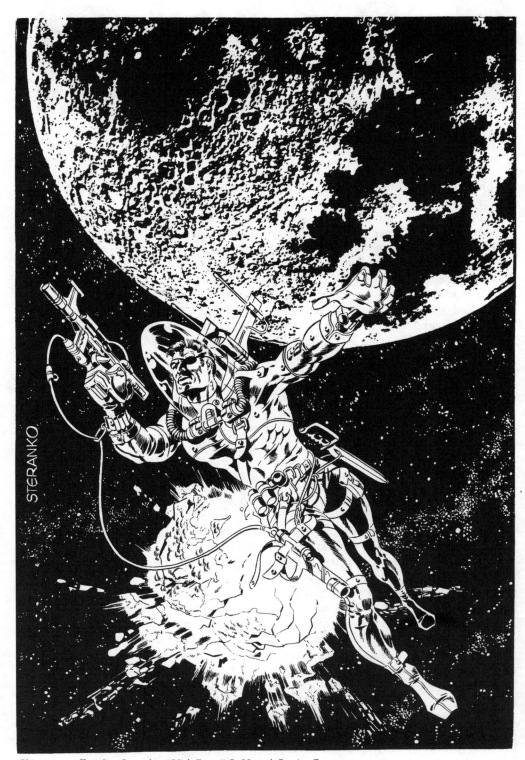

Chiaroscuro effect: Jim Steranko, ''Nick Fury.'' © Marvel Comics Group.

appearance as the friezes on the walls of Egyptian mastabas. Some artists, notably Chester Gould, put this principle to good aesthetic use, but in the hands of less gifted craftsmen, this only produces a succession of still drawings.

In order to create depth, other artists have resorted to the effects of chiaroscuro, or to a manipulation of scale that subtly distorts traditional perspective and forces a perception of volume from the reader, much as a composed photograph does. In the Sunday pages (as well as in the comic books) foremost artists such as Winsor McCay, Burne Hogarth, and Hiroshi Hirata have created spatiality out of the multilinearity (horizontal, vertical, or diagonal) of the layout by means of expanding or projecting figures along carefully worked-out vectors. The drawings seem literally ready to burst out of their frames.

In the comics time is a function of space (this is their most important difference from the movies); the frames of a strip or page are divisions of time. Thus narrative flow, which is how the author conceives of the passing of time in a particular sequence, and time flow, which is how it is perceived by the reader, are seldom coincidental. Furthermore, they both must be weighed against actual (or reading) time, which may be very long (as in the case of many newspaper strips) or quite short (as with a comic book). The resulting confusion further adds to the sense of unreality that comics produce. Even a feature like *Gasoline Alley*, which purports to keep apace with real time and whose characters age along with the reader, does not escape the rule.

Time in the comics seems to have no organic function; all that happens happens not by necessity but by accident or chance. Time is limitless and open-ended; it can also be reversible: often the characters will go back 10, 20, or more years in time and start the cycle again in a different direction. The comics are ahistorical not because they refuse to deal with their times (they often do), but because real time is irrelevant to their purpose. There is an almost complete absence of teleology in the comics: the events that took place last year have not the slightest influence on the events taking place now, at least not in the strictly causative sense. The same can be argued of popular literature, but words have not the same suggestive power as pictures. By confronting us with a direct representation of reality, the image involves us much more closely in the process. As the Bogart cult demonstrates, only the movies might have been more effective than the comics in this respect, if actors were not made of mortal flesh. Thus the comics are uniquely qualified to take us into a paradoxical universe where time is neither consumed nor abolished: the universe of the eternal present tense.

Themes of the comics

Aesthetic preoccupations and commercial considerations have always conspired to limit the thematic range of the comics. Commercially, the comics are a mass medium, and their authors must give the public something immediately and easily recognizable. Yet at the same time the action must have a certain exemplarity if it is to rise above the level of the simple anecdote. The problem of creating a milieu at once ordinary and different is the lot of all mass media that also aspire to becoming art forms. To answer the challenge, the comics may resort to the wholesale creation of a mythical ontogeny, as in the case of Superman and most other superheroes, or of a dream kingdom (*Little Nemo* is the best example), but few are the comics that have not made some use of the device.

The protagonists of the comics, whether by design or by necessity, go back to the fount of our collective memories and aspirations. They represent some emblematic figure, some archetype linking us to the primeval drives and forces across the night of history. It is as if the comics had taken it upon themselves to embody all our collective longings and try to give them some channel for fulfillment. And yet at the same time it is asked that they toe the social line, and this dichotomy has often led to ambivalence and frustration.

However ridiculous the family may appear in *Bringing Up Father*, for instance, the notion of family itself is never under attack. As one press release once stated: "Jiggs never struck Maggie and will never divorce her." The same ambivalence can be noted in relation to society itself. The first comics were genuinely anarchistic and nihilistic (*The Katzenjammer Kids* is, of course, the classic example), but soon they learned to compromise and eventually to accept the rules of social

Mythical ontogeny: "Superman" and his cohorts.
© *National Periodical Publications.*

Well-balanced page: Burne Hogarth, "Tarzan." © ERB, Inc.

order, however ludicrous. The free spirit of the comics could not be kept down, however, and emerged among the so-called underground comics and in such creations as *Gaki Deka, Sturmtruppen,* or *Barry McKenzie.*

In one of the most revealing pages of *Pogo*, Walt Kelly says of the comics that they are "like a dream . . . a tissue of paper reveries . . . it glows and glimmers its way thru unreality, fancy an' fantasy." Even to an intellectual (by any standard) artist like Kelly, the intellectual limitations of the comics are apparent. But these limitations are also their strength. By their very inability to sustain for long any lofty and more relevant theme, they retain the virtue of timelessness, thus refusing to become another dreary exercise in ephemeral literature.

Stylistics

In order to shape the two heterogeneous elements of the comics into one artistic whole, each cartoonist has to evolve his own distinctive signature (at least those cartoonists who take some pride in their craft do). Two different approaches soon emerge: in the first one the picture takes precedence over the text and the story is told in purely narrative and graphic terms (this method was traditionally the trademark of the great draftsmen from McCay and Feininger to Foster and Hogarth; it can still be found in the work of cartoonists like Hirata and Maroto); the second solution to this stylistic problem gives primacy to the text, as happens in such features as *Little Orphan Annie, Li'l Abner,* and *Pogo.* On the other hand, a more fluid type of narrative emerged in the 1930s, with the use of dramatic dialogue and cinematic techniques combining to preserve a skillful if delicate balance between the literary and the graphic elements of the comics. Milton Caniff was its foremost exponent, and Hugo Pratt later became its most skilled practitioner.

To maintain the integrity of a sequential narrative within the framework of contiguous, but separate, pictures presents another set of problems. Of course the cartoonist can construct an exact visual correlative to the written narrative, but the redundancy and wastefulness of such a method are obvious. It would seem preferable by far to have text and picture carry the action alternately rather than simultaneously. Will Eisner and Milton Caniff are recognized masters of such techniques: in their features they use verbal understatement as a counterpoint to violent visual action or, conversely, they set off visual metaphors to relieve long stretches of dialogue or monologue.

The breaking down of the story into panels and sequences is also mainly a problem of style. The comic artist may prefer to carefully prepare and build up the action, as Harold Gray or Chester Gould do, or to collide head-on with the happenings, an aggressive approach more associated with the comic book and the underground comics. To endow his images with atmosphere, the cartoonist may choose the use of solid black masses or the ambiguous delineation of background; or, to the contrary, he may resort to visual objects violently etched into the foreground—the range is infinite. In this respect color can play an important role by calling attention to important points in the narrative; it can also help link dialectically different frames in a sequence by carrying the same tonal value from one picture to another.

The comics have also at their disposal the syntax of the other literary and artistic forms: iteration, distortion, amplification, stylization, etc. It is up to the artist to make a discreet use of these devices and to avoid the sins of overdramatization and redundancy. In the comics, as in all art, less is more.

A few words in conclusion

It is the fate of all new art forms to be greeted with derision. Attic tragedy was decried as sacrilegious, Italian opera put down as unseemly cacophony, and the cinema termed (not so long ago) "an art for drunken ilotes." Against the comics the laughter has been longest and loudest. For the major part of their 100-year existence the comics have everywhere been held up to public scorn, censure, and ridicule.

This is no longer so; scholarship and analysis have replaced prejudice and ignorance. Yet the comics' growing cultural acceptance has brought with it the added burden of responsibility. Now that they are no longer dismissed as grubby purveyors of mindless entertainment, the cartoonists and their employers must

Narrative redundancy: Harry Hall and Ted McCall, "Men of the Mounted." © Toronto Telegram.

expect to be called into account on aesthetic and ethical grounds (just as novelists, book publishers, playwrights, and filmmakers are). Some may resent this fact and yearn for the good old days when cartoonists could labor in reassuring obscurity and syndicates and publishers could peddle their wares in lucrative self-complacency; there is no turning back.

Maurice Horn

Alphabetical Entries

AASNES, HÅKON (1943-   ) Håkon Aasnes, Norwegian comic artist, born February 13, 1943, in Oslo, grew up in the nearby village of Aurskog, and started drawing at the age of two—with a carpenter's pencil on wrapping paper. *The Phantom* fascinated him from his earliest years and made him want, at the age of five, to become a comic artist. He even drew his own *Phantom* stories, and at ten, he had created about 50 heroes of his own, abandoning them after two or three strips. At 17 he created a first version of *Tobram*. It was not until August 6, 1972, however, that an updated version, *Seidel og Tobram,* ("Seidel and Tobram") was first published in the Norwegian press. Before that came to pass, Aasnes tried his hand at a number of jobs, running the gamut from door-to-door salesman to industrial worker to foreign worker in Germany and South Africa. Here, he gained the experience on which to base his comic strip, in order to create an atmosphere of credibility and to flesh out the characters of his heroes.

Seidei og Tobram originally started out as two country bumpkins, but eventually developed into two members of the fictitious village of Ulvedal and are usually haunted by misfortune. *Seidel og Tobram* is a popular, robust comedy played out against the background of contemporary Norwegian provincial life. The strip is drawn in a simple, uncluttered style with speech balloons neatly integrated with the artwork. Håkon Aasnes's style is strongly influenced by Sy Barry's version of *The Phantom.* Aasnes had always been a fan of *The Phantom,* devouring the stories whenever he got to read them. When he discovered a Swedish *Phantom* comic book written and drawn by Swedish artists, he was irritated by the fact that they tried to emulate Barry's style but were never quite matching it. Thus, he sent in his own drawings, which in the end helped to land him his very own comic strip with Bull's Pressetjeneste (Bull's Press Service, the European affiliate of King Features Syndicate) for distribution to Norwegian newspapers. The strip, unfortunately, did not last into the 1980s, but the artist keeps trying. It is not easy to get wealthy drawing comic strips in Norway, however. Therefore Aasnes is holding down a regular job, besides doing what he dreamed of since he could hold a pencil.

W.F.

ABBIE AN' SLATS (U.S.) *Abbie an' Slats* was the 1937 creation of young Al Capp, fresh from his success with *Li'l Abner,* and Raeburn van Buren, an accomplished magazine illustrator, who decided to enter comics partly on the strength of Capp's prophetic assertion that radio would kill the popular weeklies.

Capp wrote the continuities for the first nine years, followed by his brother Elliot Caplin in what the latter thought would be a temporary assignment; Caplin wrote *Abbie an' Slats* until the demise of the strip.

The strip took place in a small village and involved its local citizens, although adventures took them all over the world. Crabtree Corners, the locale, was never firmly placed in the minds of the readers or the creators; van Buren designed the surroundings as an amalgam of a New England fishing village and the small Ozark town that he visited every year of his professional life.

The characters included old spinster Aunt Abbie, who never emerged as a major character but who was always present, like her inspiration, an old schoolteacher of van Buren's—ugly, tough, and bighearted; Slats Scrapple, a ruggedly handsome country boy and well-meaning roughneck; his girlfriend Becky, an attractive dark-haired girl; her sister Sue, providing much of the glamour and romantic interest in later days; and the girls' father Bathless Groggins, one of the great comic creations.

Groggins had a walrus moustache and looked, acted, and presumably, smelled like a bum. His companions, including dumb Charlie, a fisherman, and the decidedly Scottish MacBagpipe, ranged from colorful eccentrics to outright swindlers. Like W. C. Fields, who surpassed Groggins only in malevolence, Groggins could only be loved by his fans. The Sunday page, devoted to humorous continuities separate from the dailies, became Groggins' own territory shortly after the strip's debut.

The story lines through the years were consistently good; the *Abbie an' Slats* world was a masterful mixture of suspense, action, and humor. Reader interest in the United Features' comic was always high, as evidenced by the "resurrection" of Bathless' pal Charlie, who was killed off but returned to the strip because of fan pressure.

"Abbie an' Slats," Raeburn van Buren. © United Feature Syndicate.

Van Buren's art was also a mixture of sophisticated illustration, slick beauty and broad humor. The attractiveness of his work on *Abbie* was due as much to his own senses of humor and adventure as it was to his illustration experience. And the merest excuse let an assortment of pretty girls pass through the panels of *Abbie an' Slats*. His world throbbed with action, beauty, and humor; Becker claimed his sense of fantasy was the best in the comics since Winsor McCay.

Abbie an' Slats began as a daily strip on July 7, 1937, and ended on January 30, 1971. The Sunday began on January 15, 1939, and expired several months before the daily version.

R.M.

ABIE THE AGENT (U.S.)   In the wake of his highly successful *Desperate Desmond*, Harry Hershfield ventured into a completely new area with *Abie the Agent*, launched as a daily strip in the *New York Journal* on Monday, February 2, 1914. Abe Mendel Kabibble, the portly, popeyed, moustached protagonist of *Abie* (earlier a minor character in *Desmond*), was the star of the first sympathetic ethnic comic strip. The Katzenjammers were bumbling Germans, Happy Hooligan and the Yellow Kid were caricatured shanty-town Irish, but Abie was at least as real and related to the actual Jewish world of his time as Abe Potash and Morris Perlmutter of the popular *Saturday Evening Post* series by Montague Glass. Like Glass' team, Abie Kabibble was fiercely enmeshed in the New York business world. A car salesman, or "agent" (he termed himself "President: Complex Auto Co."), Abie feverishly worked every angle to make his sales quota and percentage income. As a vital adjunct to this, Abie played politics in his businessman's lodge and, to a lesser degree, on a ward and city level. More than any other early strip, Hershfield's *Abie the Agent* reflects much of the quality of lower middle-class big-city life of the 1910s and '20s. Later in the strip, Abie makes it, and rises in the social strata. It is also often hilariously funny.

There is little doubt in retrospect that Hershfield found his real niche in *Abie*. The *Desmond/Durham* satire was very inventive and often a graphic delight, but it was essentially pointless for so long sustained a work and wore thin at times, while the potential for humor and human involvement in *Abie* was as endless as that in everyday life. Hershfield himself was obviously happy with *Abie* and continued the strip, as a daily and later as a Sunday page, well into the 1930s. The public of the larger cities seemed to like *Abie* well enough to keep it in profitable print in many newspapers during most of its duration, but it had limited appeal in smaller towns, where *Abie* seemed as exotic as *Krazy Kat*.

Hershfield did not create any memorable characters in *Abie* other than Abie himself, but "that phooey Minsk," a business friend of Abie's; Benny Sparkman, agent for the competing Collapsible Car Co.; and Abie's girlfriend (later wife), Rosa Mine Gold Pearlman, are notable regulars in the strip. Abie's tangled syntax, an amusing element of the strip, was curiously dropped in an offshoot of the comic in the early 1930s called *Kabibble Kabaret*. This later feature, measuring about 1" × 2", was a daily comic page insert of text without art and consisted of make-believe readers' questions ("Dear Mr. Kabibble: Should I marry a blonde or a brunette?") and Abie's reply ("Positively NO!"). Some papers ran it with the strip, others separately.

Hershfield folded his Sunday *Abie* page, the last form of the strip, in 1940. It remained richly enjoyable right up to the last panel, and is one of the major comic strips that deserve to be reprinted complete in permanent form.

B.B.

ACHILLE TALON (France)   *Achille Talon* was created by Greg (Michel Regnier) on February 7, 1963, in the French magazine *Pilote*.

The middle-aged Achille Talon is the archetypal French *petit-bourgeois*: block-headed, pot-bellied, and bloated with self-importance, he talks in common phrases, acts in circles, and always appears as a boorish, superficially educated slob. His pompousness and empty intellectualism have no limits, and while he looks down his large nose upon people in a lower social position than his own, he stubbornly refuses to acknowledge any kind of superiority other than a crassly material one.

"Abie the Agent," Harry Hershfield. © King Features Syndicate.

"Achille Talon," Greg (Michel Régnier). © Editions Dargaud.

Achille's father, Alambic Dieudonné Corydon Talon, whose only goal in life is drinking as many mugs of beer as possible, listens with unbounded admiration and paternal pride to his son's fatuous pronouncements, and often aids and abets him in his wild-eyed schemes. But Talon's neighbor, Hilarion Lefuneste, remains unimpressed by the antics of his friend and often puts him in his place, a defeat that Talon accepts philosophically, in the knowledge that some day stupidity will rise again.

Achille Talon is one of the funniest European strips of the last several decades, as well as a brilliant satire on middle-class smugness and philistinism (and, in this respect, it has been compared to Flaubert's *Bouvard and Pécuchet*). So popular had the character become at one time that in 1975 he gave rise to his own weekly, *Achille Talon Magazine*, which lasted for about one year. Following this failure, his appearances have become scarcer, concentrating on longer stories rather than gags.

M.H.

ADAMS, NEAL (1941-   ) American comic book and comic strip writer and artist born June 6, 1941, on Governor's Island in New York. After studies at the School of Industrial Arts, Adams broke into both the comic book and syndicated strip fields in 1959, drawing features for various *Archie* titles and also working three months on the *Bat Masterson* strip. But his first major comic work came in 1962 when Newspaper Enterprise hired him to draw the *Ben Casey* medical strip. Based on the then-popular television series, Adams drew the strip from its November 26, 1962, start until its July 31, 1966, demise.

Adams then drew Lou Fine's *Peter Scratch* for a month before becoming the artist on National's *Deadman* feature in November 1967's *Strange Adventures*. Written by veteran Jack Miller, the strip dealt with circus performer Boston Brand, who could not achieve eternal rest until he avenged his own murder with a variety of spiritual powers. Although the premise was far-fetched, Miller's hard-hitting realistic dialogue kept the series plausible, and Adams' work made *Deadman* a superlative strip. His drawings were highly realistic and beautifully detailed, and he constantly experimented with page layout and composition.

When *Deadman* ended in February 1969, Adams began to branch out: he drew highly acclaimed stories for Marvel's *X-Men*, National's *Teen Titans* and *Superman*, and helped return *The Batman* to its original "creature of the night" bent. In April 1970, he and writer Denny O'Neil combined to produce the first in a new series for National, the highly publicized *Green Lantern/Green Arrow* feature. The strip broke away from standard comic book fare to tackle the serious issues of the day. Writer O'Neil's stories were hailed as the most advanced in comic books, and Adams' raw realism was rarely seen previously in comic book art. Unfortunately, Adams began missing deadlines, sales did not match the critics' raves, and it was finally cancelled in May 1972 after 13 stories.

Since the demise of *Green Lantern/Green Arrow*, Adams has become a powerful and respected force in the industry. His work has appeared in many National, Marvel, and Warren titles, and he has done considerable advertising work, designed the costumes for the science fiction play *Warp*, ghosted work for several syndicated strips, and been president of the Academy of Comic Book Arts.

J.B.

After working briefly on the *Big Ben Bolt* newspaper strip in the late 1970s, Adams founded Continuity Associates to promote his work in the fields of advertising, commercial art, and comic books. On the latter front he produced a number of titles, including *Crazyman* and *Mr. Mystic*, but clichéd writing and erratic scheduling disappointed many of Adams's fans, and the line was discontinued in the mid-1990s.

M.H.

ADAMSON (Sweden) *Adamson* is the best-known comic strip to come out of Sweden. It was created in 1920 for inclusion in *Söndags-Nisse* ("Sunday Troll"), a Swedish humor weekly. Swedish artist Oscar Jacobsson came up with Adamson, a stout little man who, except for three hairs, has a bald pate. He smokes a cigar continuously while trying to cope with whatever problem is at hand. With *Adamson*, Oscar Jacobsson continued and developed to perfection the tradition of the pantomime strip. This, in fact, earned the strip the title *Silent Sam* when, in 1922, it became the first Scandinavian comic strip to be published in the United States. Jacobsson also succeeded in selling his strip to China and Japan and to many European nations. Selections of his strip were published in Berlin (1925-1928), London (1928), and Paris (1929). In Sweden, where annuals first appeared in 1921, *Adamsons bästa under 25 år* ("The Best from 25 Years of Adamson") was issued in 1944. Earlier, a trip to Greece and Italy in 1925-1926 resulted in a book titled *Adamsons resa* ("Adamson's Journey").

Jacobsson's strip enjoyed an immense popularity thanks to his simple style and his bizarre, original, and witty ideas, which are as fresh today as when they were originally conceived. *Adamson*'s popularity helped the strip survive its creator, who died in 1945. *Adamson* was continued by Danish artist Viggo Ludvigsen, who preferred to work in anonymity. Since 1965 no new *Adamson* strips have been produced, but the old artwork is being revived.

Adamson's witty misadventures, because of their historic importance and international popularity, have resulted in the adoption of the Adamson character as a statuette—a Swedish analogy to the Shazam or Oscar awards—two of which are awarded annually to the best Swedish and foreign comic artists. This is a fitting tribute to the genius of Oscar Jacobsson and to the popularity of *Adamson*, the strip that also boasts the distinction of having been reprinted in one of the first of a line of pocket books in postwar Germany.

W.F.

"Adamson," Oscar Jacobsson. © Consolidated News Features.

ADAM STRANGE (U.S.) Space opera in comic art has always been a syndicated strip proposition. There was Raymond's *Flash Gordon*, Gray's *Brick Bradford*, and even Calkins' and Nowlan's *Buck Rogers*. On the other hand, comic book science fiction has never been done well: The Fiction House group's material was always more interested in scantily dressed ladies with obvious attributes; Orbit's science fiction was uninspired; and EC's work, generally regarded as comic books' best, was predominated by bug-eyed monsters. Even Basil Wolverton's promising *Spacehawk* was destroyed when *Target Comics'* publisher decided it was unpatriotic for Spacehawk to be in space during a world war.

So, it remained for artist Carmine Infantino and writer Gardner Fox to fill the gap when they created *Adam Strange* for National's *Mystery in Space* number 53 in August 1959. The strip's basic premise was simple: earth-bound scientist Adam Strange was struck by a "zeta" beam and instantaneously transported to the planet Rann in the Alpha Centauri galaxy. He instantly fell in love with Alanna, a raven-tressed Rann woman, became enthralled with the Rann civilization, and became a more-or-less permanent resident of the planet. He also adopted a red-and-white jumpsuit and a helmet and became Rann's greatest protector.

All the stories were written by Gardner Fox, who blended considerable scientific knowledge and research with soaring flights of fancy to create the *Adam Strange* adventures. Adam and Alanna, two beautiful people, spent issue after issue of *Mystery in Space* cavorting through the galaxy, solving crimes, protecting both Earth and Rann, and exchanging what appeared to be harmless kisses.

Artistically, Carmine Infantino handled the pencilling and Murphy Anderson handled most of the inking. (Bernard Sachs handled the inking on the first and several early stories.) Infantino utilized a series of impeccable Hal Foster-inspired layouts on the strips and a tight illustrating line to make the feature one of the best-drawn of the early 1960s. Most breathtaking on the feature were his magnificent futuristic cityscapes. Much like comic strip artist Leonard Starr used night city scenes, Infantino drew cityscapes for maxi-

mum drama. They were always in the background, lush and round and beautifully symmetrical.

Adam Strange lost Infantino and Anderson shortly before the end of its run—they were replaced by Lee Elias—and it last appeared in September 1965's 102nd issue of *Mystery in Space*. The feature has been sporadically revived by National (now DC) Comics from the 1970s through the 1990s, but it has never been as successful as it was in former years.

J.B.

ADDISON *see* Walker, Mort.

ADOLF (Japan) Osamu Tezuka's last major work and the one most widely circulated outside Japan, *Adolf* (in Japanese *Adolf ni Tsugu* or "Tell Adolf") was serialized in the prestigious *Shukan Bunshun* magazine between 1983 and 1985. In a torrential story that stretches over more than 1,000 pages, the author displayed the full panoply of narrative devices in a graphic style approximating illustration, though many caricatural distortions and cartoony shortcuts are evident.

The Adolf in question is Adolf Hitler, Fuehrer of Germany, evidence of whose Jewish ancestry has somehow been discovered by a Japanese exchange student in Berlin and sent by him to a correspondent in the Japanese port city of Kobe, thus providing the wellspring for the tortuous plot. In a circuitous way the Fuehrer's fate becomes intertwined with those of two young boys, friends growing up in Kobe and who also happen to be named Adolf: Adolf Kaufmann, the son of a German diplomat, and Adolf Kamil, son of a Jewish refugee couple from Germany. As the tentacles of the Gestapo reach into Kobe to suppress the proof of Hitler's non-Aryan origins and to silence all witnesses, the two young Adolfs are increasingly sucked into the vortex of Nazi insanity. Kaufmann will turn into a leader of the Hitler Youth and later of the S.S., while Kamil will become a dedicated Zionist.

"Adam Strange," Carmine Infantino. © DC Comics.

"Adolf," Osamu Tezuka. © Tezuka Productions.

Looming behind the almost nonstop action involving Hitler's missing birth documents is the awesome shadow of World War II. The plot, reflective of Greek tragedy, does not stop at war's end but continues to engulf the protagonists long after the general madness has ended. Kamil now lives in Israel and is an officer in the army, while Kaufmann fights on the side of the P.L.O. and Black September. At the conclusion, in a highly symbolic gesture, Kamil will kill his childhood friend.

An ardent pacifist, Tezuka posits a revisionist version of the conflict of World War II, blaming it all on Adolf Hitler (as the defendants at the Nuremberg trials also did, to little avail), and somewhat glosses over the willing role played by the great majority of the German (and Japanese) populace in the chronicle of aggression leading up to the outbreak of global war. The author seems to have felt that the Jewish identity (or "Jewish problem," as the Nazis and their sympathizers chose to term it) is at the heart of World War II, and indeed at the heart of most of this century's history. It is revealing to note in this context that of the three principals, the Jewish Adolf is the only one to survive at the end.

Adolf was made into a radio drama in 1993. In the United States it was produced in five volumes published by Cadence Books in 1995-96.

M.H.

ADVENTURES OF PATSY, THE   *see* Patsy.

AGACHADOS, LOS (Mexico)   *Los Agachados* (which can be translated as "Those Who Stoop Down") was created in Mexico by Eduardo del Rio ("Rius") on September 14, 1968, in a twice-monthly comic book format. In the first two issues Rius carried over the characters he had earlier created in his series *Los Supermachos*, but afterwards each story treated a different theme.

"Los Agachados," Rius (Eduardo del Rio). © Rius.

The "agachados" are the Mexican people, the lower classes who take their siestas stooped down on the doorsteps of their churches and whom Rius wanted to politicize through his stories. There are no central characters since it is the people themselves who live and breathe through the pages. In this way each book deals with a relevant theme whose reality is graphically depicted by Rius. He narrates the history of his country, looks at the Spanish and later North American colonialism, and examines Mexico's customs, virtues, and faults. Christ, Lenin, the Olympic Games, the housing problem, Coca-Cola, and the Mexican comics are all themes that the author presents in his strip, in a popular and authentic dialect far removed from classical Castilian. The balloons are integrated within the panels, the layout of each page forms a whole entirely different from the conventional comic strip, and color delineates the different areas in a very personal rendering.

Rius has also written a book inspired by his series, *La Iglesia de los Agachados* ("The Church of the Agachados"). The political, social, and artistic significance of *Los Agachados* have made it the most important comic strip published in Mexico.

L.G.

AGHARDI (Spain)   *Aghardi* was created in Spain by Enric Sio in 1969, and was being published simultaneously in the Italian monthly *Linus* and in the Spanish magazine *Mundo Joven*. The strip relates the expeditions of a group of scientists headed by anthropology professor Samantha Jordan and her assistant Martha, who are united by emotional ties with lesbian undertones. Steve, a photographer, and Jo, a humanities professor, are also in the team. All these characters weave their complex relationships in Mexico, Bolivia, and Peru, the situation reaching its climax in Tibet. Real history is continually intertwined with references to Mayan and Incan legends, especially the one relating to Matreya, the god of the subterranean kingdom of Aghardi.

In this experiment in black and white, Enric Sio relates a story of "realistic fantasy" based on traces possibly left by extraterrestrial beings who visited Earth. His narrative blends adventures and surreal circumstances at one level with well-defined sociopolitical opinions on another level. To this end he uses analytical montages, and the continual inclusion of legends illustrated in the style of old Mayan and Aztec codices.

The texts are written by Sio himself (the first time he has done his own scriptwriting). In this feature, where there can be found many aesthetic innovations, it is well to note that the two main protagonists were inspired by fashion model Veroushka and by singer Guillermina Motta. The difficulty of its language, the dialogues that differ from those ordinarily found in comics of the period, and the ground-breaking montages make *Aghardi* a work of exquisite complexity and beauty.

L.G.

AGUILA, DANI (1928-   )   According to his fellow artists, Dani Aguila is one of the busiest painter-cartoonists around. Born in the Philippines on September 24, 1928, he started to work on his first cartoon strip in 1949, when he was enrolled at the University of the Philippines. He graduated in 1952 with a Bach-

Dani Aguila, "Pinoy Moreno." © Filipino Reporter.

elor of Fine Arts degree. He then began his second strip, called *Student Life*, but he soon departed for the United States to continue his studies. In 1956 he attended graduate courses in mass communications at Syracuse University in New York. Returning to the Philippines, Aguila worked for the Philippine Rural Reconstruction Movement. There he did a cartoon strip called *Kamagong* (the name of a hard, black wood). He said that the name, though ironic, signified strength and uniqueness. The strip was about a rare, white water buffalo.

From 1960 to 1962 he did a series called *Barrio Breeze*, and from 1962 to 1965 he did a strip for *Asian Newsweekly Examiner* called *The Cock and Bull*. It was a political strip that gained an avid following.

After traveling back and forth between the Philippines and the United States, Aguila finally settled in Nashville, Tennessee, where he worked for a local television station as an art director and drew political cartoons for a Nashville periodical. Several of his panel cartoons have won editorial awards and have been included in anthologies. Recently he started a new comic strip for the *Filipino Reporter* (a Filipino-American weekly) called *Pinoy Moreno*. It is a humorous strip dealing with the lighter side of acculturation, integration, and assimilation. He is now back in the Philippines.

While in the Philippines, Dani Aguila was a leading force in the Society of Philippine Illustrators and Cartoonists. He edited a cartoon anthology that included the works of many of the most important names in the Philippine comic book and cartoon fields.

O.J.

AHERN, GENE (1895-1960) Gene Ahern called himself a southerner, as he pointed out that he had been born on the south side of Chicago, in 1895. As a boy, he wanted first to be a comedian, and then a "funny writer." He finally fell in love with comic strips and decided to work at his decidedly unmarked talent until he could make the funny pages. For three years he studied at the Chicago Art Institute, improving his basic technique to minimal competence—but that, as it proved, was unimportant. For Ahern, like Segar, Dorgan, and others, was a man who simply "drew funny": people laughed at his work on sight, regardless of his technical facility.

Gene Ahern, "Room and Board." © King Features Syndicate.

Newspaper and syndicate editors loved him and gave him sports page work in the early 1910s, with the NEA syndicate sending it to Scripps-Howard papers, among others throughout the country. He immediately began developing strip ideas and concepts, such as *Taking Her To The Ball Game* (a 1914 panel series poking fun at women reacting to the mysteries of baseball), *Fathead Fritz* (a dumb rookie on the diamond), and *Dream Dope* (comic panels on sports); the last two were unified under the running panel title of *Squirrel Food*, where Ahern's two longest-lasting characters, The Nut Brothers, Ches and Wal, eventually emerged.

The young cartoonist's big break came in 1923, when NEA began distributing his innovative daily panel, *Our Boarding House*. This often hilarious narrative strip was Ahern's big success with the public, and a Sunday page about the panel's star character, Major Hoople, soon followed. By 1936, Ahern was nationally famous and accepted a contract with King Features to do a variant on *Our Boarding House* for them. This new feature, called *Room and Board*, focused on a Hoople simulacrum named Judge Puffle. Like the Sunday *Boarding House* page's *Nut Brothers* topper, the new

Room and Board Sunday page carried a *Squirrel Cage* half-page about the same kind of characters, adding a new figure: the once-famed bearded hitchhiker with his "Nov Schmoz Ka Pop?" comment. Ahern died on November 17, 1960, and his King Features panel folded.

B.B.

AIRBOY (U.S.) Created by Charles Biro in November 1942, *Airboy* made its first appearance in Hillman's *Air-Fighters* number two. Featuring the exploits of Davy (Airboy) Nelson and his amazing airplane "Birdie," *Airboy* quickly became the premier boy's strip of all time, and, as an aviation strip, it was second only to Quality Comics' *Blackhawk*. Strangely enough, however, Airboy was never the main attraction in *Airboy*. That distinction fell to the plane, Birdie.

Created by a monk named Martier, Birdie was an amazing invention. It had gray, serrated wings that flapped like a bat, two massive 50-calibre machine guns, and unusual hovering abilities and remote-control devices. One of the many wartime patriotic comic features, *Airboy* dealt almost exclusively with Birdie's (and Airboy's) battles against hordes of Fascist-controlled planes. It was not unusual for Birdie to out-maneuver and destroy 50 or 60 Nazi or Japanese aircrafts in one dogfight. And, in fact, these herculean dogfights became the major selling point in *Airboy*. The air-war fantasy motif made the strip an escape from the real and horrible war. *AirFighters* comics eventually became *Airboy* comics in December 1945.

As originally scripted by Biro, personal conflict and interaction dominated *Airboy*. But under later writers, Birdie achieved such an exalted position that artists like Bernie Sachs, Carmine Infantino, and Tony DiPreta

"Airboy," Fred Kida. © Hillman Periodicals.

were hardly drawing people anymore. Fred Kida was the only artist who ever managed to develop the red, yellow, and blue-clad Airboy into a distinguishable character. He depicted Airboy as an older, more mature person and later portrayed him as a soldier-of-fortune rather than a child with a toy. Before these stories, which were always dark and moody, Airboy was a one-dimensional pilot, totally subservient to Birdie's remarkable machinery. Kida drew a majority of the stories between 1943 and 1946, and he is recognized as the strip's definitive artist.

There were very few recurrent villains in *Airboy*, as they were never allowed to develop. Airboy did have one outstanding adversary, Valkyrie, and she soon developed into the comic industry's answer to *Terry and the Pirates'* Dragon Lady. A beautiful and sexually agressive aviatrix, Valkyrie made her debut in November 1943. Bearing a remarkable resemblance to motion picture's Veronica Lake, she and her squadron of "Air Maidens" were originally exponents of the Nazi cause. She adopted a more pragmatic view of the war, however, and was constantly shifting from one side to the other. At times, she'd even change during a story, alternately trying to save and destroy Airboy and Birdie. Her coquettish flirtations were in sharp contrast to Airboy's often adolescent, flag-waving behavior.

The postwar years were troublesome for *Airboy*, however. Having outlived the war they were created to fight, Airboy and Birdie were floundering in a sea of common, everyday crimes. Birdie wasn't made to fight bank robbers, however, and the feature was discontinued in May 1953's *Airboy* number 111.

J.B.

In 1986 Eclipse Comics decided to bring back Airboy, pitting him against some of his old adversaries, such as Valkyrie and Skywolf. With sometimes excellent drawing by the likes of George Evans, Dan Spiegle, and Paul Gulacy, *Airboy* (and its collateral titles) managed to survive until the end of the decade.

M.H.

AIR HAWK AND THE FLYING DOCTORS (Australia) Created by former comic book artist John Dixon, the Sunday page was first published in the Sydney *Sun-Herald* on June 14, 1959. The popularity of the strip over the next four years led to the introduction of the daily strip in May 1963. Both versions are still running, making it the most successful adventure strip to be published in Australia. *Air Hawk* is the name of an air charter service operated by the tall blond ex-fighter ace, Jim Hawk. The charter service is based in Alice Springs, in the heart of the continent. In addition to operating this flight charter enterprise, Jim has been granted the franchise to supply a special Emergency Relief Unit to work in conjunction with the Royal Flying Doctor Service. The unit's function is to relieve any Flying Doctor Base in need of assistance and to be available for special emergencies. Dr. Hal Mathews, who has been seconded by the R.F.D.S. to work with the special unit, is a close friend of Hawk and has been with the strip since its inception. The romantic interest is provided by Sister Janet Grant, a former nurse with the Australian Inland Mission, who is now a full-time assistant to Dr. Mathews.

In Hawk, Dixon has successfully portrayed the tall, lean, suntanned, unflappable Australian of popular mythology and invested him with a better education and more technical skills than his legendary counter-

"Air Hawk," John Dixon. © The Herald and Weekly Times Ltd.

Sandy Highflier, "the airship man," was a young adventurer who roamed the world in his dirigible (made up of a motorboat suspended from a sausage balloon), in search of wrongs to redress and damsels to rescue. His adventures proved more humorous than suspenseful. His airship became tangled in telegraph wires and ran into church steeples, and, at one time, Sandy himself was plucked out of his ship by a mischievous giraffe. Sandy usually managed to outwit his

part. The scripts, written by Dixon, have always been solid with plenty of action, drama, suspense, and good characterization—but fairly conventional (i.e., conservative) in approach, avoiding any contentious areas. *Air Hawk* is played out against the background of cathedral-like ridges, barren landscapes, caverns, rivers, and waterholes of the Outback country. The locations allow for the introduction of native fauna, Aborigines, and their way of life. Dixon captures all these things with graphic authenticity. A great deal of the strip's popularity stems from the amount of time-consuming detail that Dixon depicts on his variety of airplanes—for the strip is, above all, an aviation strip. Apart from satisfying the reader's taste for realistically drawn adventure, *Air Hawk* offers the majority of readers (including the bulk of those in Australia) an opportunity to experience the far-off, exotic frontier of the rugged yet beautiful inland country. Dixon has taken great care to see that the hero has not strayed from his basic role of a flying adventurer.

Soon after the introduction of the daily strip, Mike Tabrett took over the Sunday page under Dixon's guidance. In March 1970, he was replaced by Hart Amos, a former comic book artist and illustrator, whose keen eye for depicting mechanical details almost equals Dixon's. As well as appearing in most Australian states, *Air Hawk* appears in New Zealand, Hong Kong, South Africa, Ireland, Italy, Spain, France, Germany, Sweden, and Argentina. To date, its U.S. appearances have been restricted to *The Menomonee Falls Gazette*, a weekly with limited circulation. Since the late 1970s every Australian artist worth his salt seems to have worked on the strip, including Paul Power, Keith Chatto, and Phil Belbin.

J.R.

AIRSHIP MAN, THE (U.S.) C. W. Kahles produced one of his first comic creations, *The Airship Man*, as a Sunday half-page for the *Philadelphia North American* from March 1902 to October 1903.

"The Airship Man," C. W. Kahles.

enemies, be they bloodthirsty pirates or spear-throwing cannibals, more by luck than by design. Some of his aerial stunts would later find their way into the author's celebrated *Hairbreadth Harry*.

The *Airship Man* stands out among early comic strips as one of the first (if not the very first) attempts at mixing derring-do with humor. As for Sandy Highflier, he deserves a niche of his own as the first air adventurer of the comics.

M.H.

AIRY ALF AND BOUNCING BILLY (G.B.) *The Adventures and Misadventures of Airy Alf and Bouncing Billy* began on the front page of *The Big Budget* number one, a jumbo-size three-in-one comic, 24 pages for one penny. The date was 19 June 1897, and so the edition was also a special one to celebrate Queen Victoria's Jubilee. Alf and Billy went on their bicycles and wound up in prison, a standard payoff for this pair. Tom Browne, then the top British comic artist, created them, and while physically they were fat and thin, resembling his established *Weary Willie and Tired Tim*, they were of a slightly higher class than those two tramps. They also reflected Browne's major hobby, bicycling, and for the year that he drew them, he cycled almost continuously. They even joined the Cycle Scouts section of the Volunteer Army Reserve. Their adventures reflected other aspects of Victorian society, and not only did they make dutiful appearances at the Oxford and Cambridge Boat Races, Henley Regatta, Lords Cricket Ground, etc., they also met such notables as Prime Minister Joseph Chamberlain and Dan Leno, and they ran the Cuban blockade.

Alf and Billy were taken over in 1898 by Ralph Hodgson, who signed himself "Yorick." At first he followed Browne's style closely, even going so far as to draw Alf and Billy meeting their rivals Willie and Tim! But having been made art editor of the *Big Budget*, Hodgson experimented in a number of styles, adding balloons in the American manner and dropping typeset captions. The strip ran until 1908. Many *Alf and Billy* episodes were reprinted in *Victorian Comics* (1975).

D.G.

"Airy Alf and Bouncing Billy," Ralph Hodgson.

AIZEN, ADOLFO (1907-1991) Brazilian editor, born in 1907 in Juazeiro, Bahia. At age 15, Adolfo Aizen moved to Rio de Janeiro, then the country's capital, and in 1933 he started his career as a journalist with *O Malho*. During a trip to the United States, he met the executives at King Features Syndicate and bought the

Brazilian rights to King's properties. In March 1934 he started *Suplemento Juvenil* as a children's supplement to the newspaper *A Noite*, publishing such comics as *Jungle Jim, Flash Gordon, Tarzan, Mandrake,* and *Terry and the Pirates*; it became an instant hit. He later launched *O Mirim* along the same lines. This gave rise to a rival publication, *Gibi*, which became the synonym for comic book (even today children ask for a "gibi" from their newsstand vendor).

In the early 1940s Aizen brought American superheroes to Brazil, with the publication of *Superman* and *Batman*, and later of *Spider-Man* and *Thor*, among others. He also published the Brazilian edition of *Classics Illustrated*; after the title had folded in the United States, he hired Brazilian artists to illustrate the literary works of national authors such as Jorge Amado, José Lins do Rego and Machado de Assis. In the process he nurtured the talents of Andre Le Blanc (a former Will Eisner assistant), Manoel Victor Filho, Ziraldo, and others. In 1950 he published a co-edition of a Disney special with Argentina. This was the start of yet another publishing giant, Editora Abril, the authorized Disney publisher for Latin America, and today one of the largest publishers in South America. At his death in 1991, he was celebrated as the pioneer of comics publishing in Brazil.

A.M.

AKADŌ SUZUNOSUKE (Japan) *Akadō Suzunosuke* was created by Eiichi Fukui in the August 1954 issue of the Japanese comic monthly *Shōnen Gahō*. Eiichi Fukui died suddenly, before he could draw the second story, and was succeeded by Tsunayoshi Takeuchi, who was to draw the strip until its demise.

Akadō Suzunosuke was a young man living in the time of the samurais. He was trained in the Japanese art of fencing ("Kendō") at a small school in the country. Recognized as a promising swordsman by his mas-

"Akadō Suzunosuke," Eiichi Fukui.
© Shōnen Gahō.

ter Oshinosuke Yokomura, Suzunosuke became a pupil of the famous Chiba in Edo (the former name for Tokyo). Gentle and honest, Suzunosuke worked hard at his craft and earned the respect of his schoolmates, including that of his chief rival, Rainoshin Tatsumaki, whom he defeated in a sword contest and who later became his friend.

Suzunosuke (whose full name is Suzunosuke Kinno, but who received the nickname Akadō because of the red shield—"akadō"—which he uses) fought against brigands, plunderers and other villains (Namiemon Kuroshio, Kaiomaru, Madara-seij in, Naoto Maka, etc.), whom he invariably defeated by his intelligent tactics and his superior swordplay (which includes his favorite technique, the deadly "shinkügiri" or "vacuum cut").

Akadō Suzunosuke has been made into a radio program, a television series and a number of animated films. In 1958 an Akadō festival was held in the Hibiya concert hall in Tokyo. Tsunayoshi drew his character to the accompaniment of a theme song that later became a hit recording. *Akadō Suzunosuke* was discontinued in the December 1960 issue of *Shōnen Gahō*.

H.K.

AKATSUKA, FUJIO (1935-   ) Japanese comic book artist, born September 1935 in China. After the Pacific War (World War II) his mother brought him back to Japan. Following graduation from high school, Fujio Akatsuka was employed by a chemical company; he hated it and in his spare time drew a number of comic strips, which he sent out to magazines. In 1955 he made his debut with a girl strip, *Arashio Koete*, which met with scant success. To support himself, he worked as an assistant to Mitsuteru Yokoyama from June 1955 to January 1958. Akatsuka describes these years as the most miserable of his life.

Finally Akatsuka was able to sell a gag strip to the monthly *Manga Ō*: it was *Namachan* (1958). In 1962 he followed with his first popular success, *Osomatsukun* (in which he brought to life some of his most famous characters: Iyami, Chibita, Dekapan, Hatabo, etc.). In 1962 he also created his most famous girl strip, *Himitsu no*

Akko chan. From this time on, Akatsuka produced one successful strip after another: *Otasukekun* (a humor strip, 1963), *Shibire no Skatan* (another humor strip, 1966), *Ijiwaru Ikka* ("The Spiteful Family," 1966), *Tensai Bakabon* (a humor strip again, and one of his best works, 1967), *Moretsu Ataro* (a 1967 humor strip in which he created some new characters such as Kemunpasu, Beshi, the Mad Policeman, Nyarome, and others), and *Waru Waru World* (1974).

Akatsuku's greatest merit was to uphold and renew the humor strip tradition at a time when the continuity strip was in its heyday. Next to Osamu Tezuka, he created the greatest number of popular comic characters, and he is, without a doubt, the greatest humor cartoonist working in Japan today. Many of his works (notably *Osomatsu-kun, Tensai Bakabon, Moretsu Ataro* and *Himitsu no Akkochan*) have been adapted into animated films. Akatsuka's graphic style is simple and basic, his characters are not superheroes, but antiheroes, and his stories are grounded in comedy, slapstick and nonsense. He has also promoted the work of other Japanese artists through his Fujio Productions; as Frederik Schodt wrote in *Manga! Manga!* (1983), "He is helping transform the humor of Japanese comics and, indirectly, of Japanese society."

H.K.

AKIM (Italy) In the period between 1950 and 1970, the *Tarzan* comic books and comic strips were only sparsely distributed in Italy. This situation offered a golden opportunity to unscrupulous imitators, and a swarm of spurious editions sprang up, all trying to take advantage of the success enjoyed by E. R. Burroughs' jungle hero in movie theaters all over Europe.

Among the many *Tarzan* imitations, only one became very popular and enjoyed wide circulation: *Akim*, conceived by Augusto Pedrazza and published for the first time in a 32-page comic book in the collection "Albo Gioello," by Edizioni Tomasina on February 10, 1950. In the first episode (which was palmed off as true fact to the readers), the origin of the character was given in lines identical to the story written by Burroughs. Here are some of the opening lines:

"Akim," Augusto Pedrazza. © Tomasina.

". . . Son of the British Consul in Calcutta, Count Frederick Rank. During the journey back to England, the ship bearing Count Rank and his family sinks, due to the dereliction of a sailor: the only survivors are Mrs. Rank and her son Jim. Washed ashore on an unknown land, the mother builds a shelter for her son, but a panther tears her to pieces. But, as the panther is carrying the child into her den, a gorilla attacks the panther and the wounded beast is compelled to drop the child. The curious gorilla picks the child up."

Some 16 years later (so the story continues) a strapping young fellow is swinging from treetop to treetop: his name is Akim, the white ape. Of course he speaks the language of the animals and is respected and obeyed by all of them. Later Akim will befriend two other apes, Kar and Zug, and meet Rita, a white girl with whom he promptly falls in love; Akim also has a young ward whom he protects like his own son.

The only difference with the Tarzan saga is that Akim and Rita are not bound in wedlock (as are Tarzan and Jane). As for the rest, the plots totally follow the Tarzan stories, especially the movie scripts. There is the impact caused by civilization, whether in the jungle or in New York (to where Akim journeys), the love contest for Akim, and the stereotyped distinctions between good people and villains. Even the environment and the physical features of the characters are not very dissimilar, apart from the drawing style, which in the Italian version was always hurried and barely adequate (this was primarily due to Pedrazza's enormous output).

After more than 1,000 issues in comic books and one-shots, *Akim* disappeared from Italian newsstands, but continued being published abroad. In fact, Akim enjoyed his own comic book in France, which was drawn by the indefatigable if mediocre Pedrazza, although the texts were written for a while by Roberto Renzi. This version also eventually ended.

G.B.

ALACK SINNER (Argentina / Spain / Italy / France)

Alack Sinner is a prime example of the growing internationalization of comics, as well as one of the most innovative creations of the last 20 years. The brainchild of Argentinian-born José Muñoz and Carlos Sampayo working in Spain, it first appeared in the pages of the Italian magazine *Alter Alter* in 1975. Both authors had been raised on Dashiell Hammett and Raymond Chandler novels and on Humphrey Bogart movies, and they strove to re-create the dark atmosphere and bleak outlook of their early inspirations.

Scriptwriter Sampayo set his thriller in the New York of his imagination (only in 1981 did he visit the city for the first time). Alack Sinner, the nominal protagonist, was initially an ex-cop turned private investigator whose caseload included blackmail, kidnapping, and attempted murder. For a while he dropped out of the gumshoe business to become a taxi driver, but he later returned to his true calling. In the course of his business, he encountered other lost souls, including Sophie, a pathetic and engaging figure (and the protagonist of a later series of her own), whose lover he would become and whose daughter he would father. All the characters socialize, argue, deal, pair off, or collide at Joe's Bar, a sort of crossroads of the netherworld, a meeting place for society's outcasts. In that context even the antihero's name, so redolent of an Adamic fall from grace, seems to point to some cosmic disjunction.

"Alack Sinner," José Muñoz and Carlos Sampayo. © the authors.

Sampayo's narrative is uncannily matched by Muñoz's artwork—sulfurous, brutal, and unsparing. Employing only black and white with no halftones, Muñoz is able to conjure up images of bleak despair with a dispassionate minuteness that belies their white-hot intensity. As the critic Oscar Zarate noted, "Every visual element, even the smallest one, is a protagonist that fights to be listened to, becoming a threatening presence that haunts you."

Alack Sinner was greeted enthusiastically almost from the moment it came out. The series was snapped up by the French monthly *A Suivre* immediately after *Alter Alter* folded in 1980. In the United States, it has been published by Fantagraphics under the pared-down title *Sinner*, and it has been a great influence—even down to the title—on Frank Miller's critically acclaimed *Sin City*.

M.H.

ALAN FORD (Italy)

Published for the first time in July 1969, *Alan Ford* is the most important phenomenon that the Italian comic industry has recorded in recent years.

From the inception, *Alan Ford* has enjoyed tremendous success and wide distribution, due to the imaginativeness of its authors, Max Bunker (Luciano Secchi) for the text, and Magnus (Roberto Raviola) for the drawing, who have created a comic book of high humor and picaresque adventure, as well as a satire on our dehumanizing society.

Alan Ford, the first existential nonhero in the history of Italian comics, was for years the only specimen

"Alan Ford," Luciano Secchi and Roberto Raviola. © Editoriale Corno.

of his kind. Built on solidly constructed texts, *Alan Ford* displays its rich fantasy in each of its 120-page comic books. Alan Ford, the handsome but shy and luckless protagonist, is a member of the shady secret organization known as TNT and is entrusted with the weirdest missions by his boss, the deathless Numero Uno. Numero Uno is an old man confined in a wheelchair who has lived through the ages and never lets anyone forget it. Bob Rock (modeled on Magnus) is the frustrated number-two man, resentful and petulant; the Cariatide (modeled after Bunker) is the symbol of the eternal bureaucrat; Il Conte (the Count) is the professional burglar, indispensable to any organization of the kind; Grunf is a nostalgic of the old times of freebooting adventure; Geremia is the perennial complainer; and the two animals Cirano and Squitty round out the zany outfit.

The TNT members are so hung up physically and psychologically that they always prove unable to successfully complete any assignment. Caught in awkward situations, tripped up by their own schemes, Alan Ford and his associates display the resignation of all losers. In the end we forgive them their shortcomings because they are no different from those of every inhabitant of this planet. *Alan Ford* remains a big seller in Italy, having reached issue number 300 in 1995.

G.B.

ALBERTARELLI, RINO (1908-1974) Italian cartoonist and illustrator, born in 1908 in Cesena. After many experiences in disparate fields—painter, ceramist, store clerk, actor, set designer—Rino Albertarelli went to Milan at the age of 20. There he met Antonio Rubino, who gave him the opportunity to work for the children's weekly *Il Balilla*. After military service, Albertarelli began working with several publishers, Paravia and Vallardi among them. His works also appeared in the magazines *Viaggi e Avventure* and *Cartoccino dei Piccoli*, and he assumed the editorship of the latter from 1933 to 1935. Starting in 1936, he published his first continuing comic stories: for Argentovivo he realized *I Pirati del Pacifico*, and for *L'Audace* he created *Capitan Fortuna* and *Big Bill*. In 1937 Albertarelli started working for Mondadori, bringing out his most famous cre-

ations: *Kit Carson, Gino e Gianni, Baghongi il Pagliaccio* ("Baghongi the Clown"), *Il Dottor Faust, Mefistofele, Un Gentiluomo di 16 Anni* ("A Gentleman of 16"), and *Gioietta Portafortuna*, all of which were published in the large-circulation weeklies *Topolino* and *Paperino*, along with his adaptations of Salgari's novels, the long saga of *Il Corsaro Nero* ("The Black Corsair") paramount among them.

In the meantime, Albertarelli had broadened his field to include satirical magazines such as *Il Bertoldo, Marc'Aurelio, Settebello, Il Galantuomo*, and *Fra Diavolo* and had become a member of the editorial staff of *Le Grande Firme*. In 1942 he was recalled to the army and, when the war ended, he tried his hand at a stage farce, *Il Simulatore*, written in collaboration with Pepino De Fillippo. In 1946 he resumed his Salgarian work, illustrating many of the master's stories for the periodical *Salgari*. These were practically his last comic stories for children and were drawn from 1946 to 1948.

Albertarelli experimented next with romance comics for the publisher Cino del Duca in 1948, and these works were published in the French magazine *Nous Deux*. After some collaboration with foreign publishers, Albertarelli devoted himself fully to illustration for didactic, religious, and western articles and stories. His work was published in *Successo, Historia, Tempo, Settimo Giorno, Visto*, and *Marie-Claire*. An important series of his wash drawings was published by Dardo in 1965. Only recently did Albertarelli come back to comic art, producing the series *I Protagonisti* for Daim Press, a collection of monographs of famous personages from Custer to Billy the Kid, all of them scrupulously documented. His sudden death on September 21, 1974, prevented Albertarelli from completing this work.

G.B.

ALCALA, ALFREDO P. (1925-   ) Filipino comic book illustrator and cartoonist, born August 23, 1925, in Talisay, Occidental Negros, Philippines. Alcala dropped out of school at an early age to pursue his first love, drawing. He started out painting signs. After a year he got a job working for a wrought-iron shop designing chandeliers, table lamps, hat racks, and garden furniture. At one time he designed a church pulpit. He copied and studied the works of Harold Foster's *Prince Valiant* and Alex Raymond's *Flash Gordon* until the early hours of the morning. However, it was Louis K. Fine (Lou Fine), the artist of *The Black Condor, Uncle Sam, The Dollman*, etc., who most influenced Alcala.

In October 1948, Alcala's first comic book illustration appeared in *Bituin Komiks* ("Star Comics"). By November of the same year he was illustrating for the largest publishing house in the Philippines: Ace Publications. They started out with two comic books titled *Filipino Komiks* and *Tagalog Klassiks*, and after a few years they expanded to two more titles: *Espesial Komiks* and *Hiwaga Komiks*. These books were published twice a month, and Alcala drew for all of these simultaneously. The stories that Alcala drew were serials that ran for several months. Their themes varied from superheroes to melodramatics, from comedy to fantasy. Because of his versatility, Alcala never had any problems adapting to these different stories. He is considered one of the fastest illustrators in the Philippines and has been known to work for 96 hours straight without sleep. Alcala always does his own pencilling, inking, and lettering. He very rarely uses an assistant.

As Alcala progressed, he studied American illustrators such as Howard Pyle, N.C. Wyeth, Dean Cornwell, Robert Fawcett, J.C. Leyendecker, and others. One of the strongest influences on Alcala was the great British muralist Frank Brangwyn.

In the early 1970s an American editor went to the Philippines to look over some of the work of the Filipino artists. Alcala was one of the first to be praised. Since then he has done work for two of the largest comic book publishers in the United States, D.C. National and Marvel Publications. He has also contributed to *Captain Marvel* and *House of Secrets*; in the late 1970s and early 1980s he also illustrated the *Rick O'Shay* and *Star Wars* newspaper strips.

M.A.

"Alfredo," Moco (Jørgen Morgenson and Cosper Cornelius). © PIB.

ALFREDO (Denmark) *Alfredo* is one of the European strips that enjoys worldwide fame because it is a pantomime strip with a universal appeal. The American title for the strip is *Moco* (Los Angeles Times Syndicate), a signature that combines the names of its artist/writers Jørgen Mogenson and Cosper Cornelius. The Danish comic strip *Alfredo* conquered a worldwide audience by following the example of H. Dahl Mikkelsen's *Ferd'nand* and Oscar Jacobsson's *Adamson*, which had long since proved the old adage that silence (especially that of pantomime) is golden.

Jørgen Mogenson had already embarked on a career as painter and sculptor and Cosper Cornelius had chosen the life of jazz musician when they got together in 1940 to devote their time to *Hudibras*, a satirical magazine founded by Cornelius as a forum for talented "crazy" artists. Mogenson's early work had one character that suited that idea fully: the Mad Artist. The Mad Artist's misadventures appeared in the form of a pantomime comic strip. Whatever the Mad Artist did became reality: When he is chased through the desert by a lion, a fat man he draws in the sand springs to life and serves as a decoy. The surrealistic strip had already won international renown when Mogenson decided to end it before he ran out of ideas. The pantomime style, however, was carried over into *Alfredo*, on which he and Cornelius have cooperated since the 1950s. Their collaboration is rather unusual. Mogenson and Cornelius each do three daily strips per week without comparing notes or sketches. Surprisingly enough, they never come up with the same gags. This method of collaboration leaves enough time for other pursuits.

Mogenson draws another comic strip, *Poeten*, starring a writer and his family.

Alfredo, however, stars a black-haired, round-headed, moustachioed man who, although married to a domineering wife, has never given up flirting. Alfredo is shown in many different jobs, places, and epochs of history. He is the perennial Everyman living out everyone's fantasies. As such he has endeared himself to his readers and has become a perennial success.

W.F.

"Alix," Jacques Martin. © Editions du Lombard.

ALIX L'INTRÉPIDE (Belgium) *Alix l'Intrépide* ("Alix the Fearless") was created by Jacques Martin in October 1948 for the Belgian weekly *Tintin*.

Alix is the son of a Gaul chieftain, Astorix but has been adopted by the Roman governor Honorus Galla, a friend and faithful lieutenant of Julius Caesar. This situation provides a built-in conflict of loyalties within Alix, which Martin knows how to put to good dramatic use. At the same time Alix's most persistent enemy is the Greek Arbaces, ambitious and cunning, and an ally of Caesar's enemy Pompey.

At first Alix was a lone wolf pursuing his own dreams and aspirations, but in 1949 he met the young Egyptian Enak and the two struck up a lasting friendship, in spite of misunderstandings and vicissitudes.

Alix has been pursuing his adventures almost uninterruptedly since 1948 from one end of the Roman Empire to the other; his exploits have carried him from Rome to Scythia, from Egypt to the German *limnes*. He has fought against the callous directives of the Roman Senate and the grand designs of Parthian and Egyptian usurpers, and he has even had to repress mutiny within the ranks of his own Gaul mercenaries.

Jacques Martin has been able to maintain the epic sweep of Alix's adventures for over a quarter of a century, without compromising historical authenticity or tampering with factual accuracy. *Alix* is an outstanding adventure strip depicted with an almost archaeological knowledge of the period. The adventures of Alix have been reprinted in book form by Editions du Lombard and Editions Casterman. The success of the series has continued unabated to this day and has given rise to a number of exegeses, notably *L'Odyssée d'Alix* (1987).

M.H.

ALLEN, DALE   *see* Saunders, Allen.

ALLEY OOP (U.S.)   Created by Vincent T. Hamlin and distributed by Newspaper Enterprise Association (NEA), *Alley Oop* premiered on August 7, 1933, as a daily strip, which was followed by a Sunday version on September 9, 1934.

Alley is a caveman, uncivilized and invincible in the tradition of Popeye (like Popeye he has gigantic forearms and tremendous strength). Mounted on his faithful pet dinosaur Dinny, he brings order to the Kingdom of Moo, which is going to pot under the inept leadership of King Guzzle (in turn, Guzzle is bedeviled by his scheming grand vizier, Foozy, and nagged by his wife, Queen Umpateedle). Oftentimes Alley must go and fight against Moo's many outside enemies, as well as against its unruly subjects. His martial feats and bullheaded sense of duty are only matched by his unswerving devotion to his sweetheart Oola, a piquant brunette whom he spends a good part of his time fighting over.

In 1939 Hamlin, tiring of all this prehistoric folderol, introduced two new protagonists: Professor Wonmug, inventor of a time machine, and his demented assistant Oscar Boom. In short order Alley and Oola found themselves transported to the 20th century (Alley's dinosaur was later to follow). In a series of screwball adventures, Hamlin made good use of the device: he had his hero meeting Cleopatra, fighting in the Crusades, crossing swords with 17th-century pirates, and rescuing settlers from attacking Indians. Alley Oop has also made a few reappearances in the Land of Moo, where his compatriots, cantankerous and rowdy as ever, seem unperturbed by all his comings and goings.

In 1971 Hamlin retired, and the strip was taken over by his former assistant Dave Graue, who did a credible job of continuation and preserved most of the feature's original flavor. Since 1993 *Alley Oop* has been drawn by Jack Bender, while Graue still continues to provide the scripting.

Alley Oop has been entertaining its readers for over 60 years now, and much of the credit must go to V. T. Hamlin's great vision. His strip has remained consistently imaginative both narratively and graphically (some of *Alley Oop*'s Sunday pages of 1936 through 1940 are models of innovative layout and skillful use of color) and must be ranked as one of the best comic creations to come out of the 1930s.

Alley Oop has been reproduced in comic books, and in 1960 it inspired a popular song of the same name.

M.H.

ALLY SLOPER (G.B.)   The first British strip hero (or rather antihero), Alexander Sloper F.O.M. ("Friend of Man"), Ally for short—his name is a pun on the Victorian poor man's dodge of sloping off down the alley when the rent man is in sight—was born in the pages of *Judy*, a weekly cartoon and humor magazine clearly modeled on *Punch*. His first adventure, "Some of the Mysteries of Loan and Discount," a full-page strip, was published on August 14, 1867. It was drawn, somewhat crudely, by Charles Henry Ross, who was not known for his artistry. Ross was a popular literary hack who could reel off "penny dreadfuls" by the yard but who preferred wordplay of a humorous variety. Helping him with the inking, and taking over completely once the series was established, was Marie Duval, a French teenager whose real name was Emilie de Tessier, otherwise known as Mrs. Charles Henry Ross. Established from the start was Sloper's character, that of a seedy con man forever hatching new get-rich-quick schemes doomed to failure. So was his partner in crime Isaac Moses, otherwise known as Ikey Mo.

Sloper soon became a weekly fixture in *Judy*, and this resulted in the world's first comic book, a paperback reprint, *Ally Sloper: A Moral Lesson*, published in November 1873. The first original periodical to feature Sloper was the annual almanac *Ally Sloper's Comic Kalendar*, and 13 almanacs were published between December 1874 and 1887. Then came *Ally Sloper's Summer Number* (1880-1884); *Ally Sloper's Comic Crackers* (1883); and the ultimate triumph, the weekly comic paper *Ally Sloper's Half-Holiday*. This ran from May 3, 1884, to May 30, 1914, changed its title to *Ally Sloper* from June 6, 1914, to September 9, 1916, was revived as *Ally Sloper's Half-Holiday* again from November 5, 1922, to April 14, 1923, then turned up later as two one-shots in 1948 and 1949. There was also the annual extra edition, *Ally Sloper's Christmas Holidays* (1884-1913), and a short-lived weekly, *Ally Sloper's Ha'porth* (January 23 to March 21, 1899).

"Alley Oop," Vincent Hamlin. © NEA Service.

"Ally Sloper," Charles Ross and Marie Duval.

Ross benefited little from this exploitation, as he had sold all the copyrights to Gilbert Daziell, the former engraver turned publisher. However, it had made Ross the editor of *Judy* magazine along the way; and his son, Charles Jr., wrote pieces for the *Half-Holiday* under the guise of Tootsie Sloper. Tootsie was a member of the enlarged Sloper Family of Mildew Court, created for the *Half-Holiday* by W. G. Baxter. This inspired cartoonist died suddenly, at an early age, of alcoholism. Ally was taken over by W. F. Thomas, in similar style, and Thomas was to draw the strip into the 1920s.

Ally was also the first strip hero to be merchandised. There was the Sloper Keyless Watch, the Sloper Insurance Scheme, the F.O.S. ("Friend of Sloper") award with his colored certificate, the Sloper Pipe, the Sloper Club with bronze medallion, and the Sloper China Bust. He was also "toned down" for coloring books for children, had popular songs written about him, and was portrayed in early films.

D.G.

ALMA GRANDE (Mexico) *Alma Grande* ("Great Soul"), subtitled "El Yaqui Justiciero" ("The Justice-Fighting Yaqui"), was created in 1961 by the writer Pedro Zapiain, with illustrations by José Suárez Lozano, as a weekly comic book. As is usually the case with this type of Mexican comic book, the action goes on indefinitely without regard to chronological niceties, and without allowing the reader a moment of respite.

Alma Grande is the titular hero, a half-breed Yaqui and Caucasian, who has been brought up in the wild Yaqui Valley in Sonora, where he also experiences a great deal of his adventures, in the company of his friend "the Swede," the inseparable Culebra Prieta ("Black Serpent") and Marcelino. His sweetheart, the schoolteacher Alice, often provides Alma Grande with cause for alarm, being continually the target of the villains. These villains form a whole rogues' gallery, filled with psychopathic brutes. They are headed by Count Cieza, Alma Grande's mortal enemy, and by the beautiful and sadistic nyphomaniac Laura (who resembles movie actress María Felix), as cruel as her father, Colonel Venegas, ever was.

The epic flavor is constantly present in the scenarios written by Zapiain and Rafael Arenas, and in the drawings done by Suárez's successors, the illustrators Othon Luna, R. R. Zambrano, Angel José Mora, and Ricardo Reyna.

"Alma Grande," José Suárez Lozano. © Novedades.

Two movies were based on the strip: *Alma Grande, el Yaqui Justiciero* ("Alma Grande, the Justice-Fighting Yaqui," 1965), and *Alma Grande en el Desierto* ("Alma Grande in the Desert," 1966).

L.G.

"Alphonse and Gaston," F. B. Opper. © International Feature Service.

ALPHONSE AND GASTON (U.S.) A super-polite team of comic Frenchmen created by Fred Opper for the Hearst Sunday pages in the early 1900s, *Alphonse and Gaston* first appeared there early in 1902, initially as a weekly half-page gag strip with a descriptive subtitle, then with the addition of implicit or actual week-to-week continuity. The two leads (plus their Parisian friend, Leon, who entered the strip on July 13, 1902) traveled out West, then around the world through 1902 and 1903. Characterized by their flamboyant 19th-century French dandy clothing and their highly affected good manners ("You first, my dear Alphonse!" "No, no—*you* first, my dear Gaston!"), Alphonse and Gaston (and Leon, although he was rarely involved in the exchanges of *politesse*) were often trapped in brutal mishaps as the result of their undue attention to social proprieties in the face of an undeterred menace.

An original comic strip concept in the United States, *Alphonse and Gaston* became an immense hit with comic section readers and could have run for years as an individual strip had the Hearst Sunday space not been so limited. Opper's interest in trying new strip concepts, however, relegated Alphonse, Gaston, and Leon to occasional appearances in his other strips after 1904 (most notably, *Happy Hooligan* and *Maud*). Revived as feature characters in newspaper advertisements for a few months in the 1940s, the Frenchmen otherwise faded from the comic page with fewer appearances in Opper's work through the 1920s and early 1930s.

Surprisingly overlooked for film adaptation, the characters had one book of their own (*Alphonse and*

"American Splendor," Harvey Pekar. © Harvey Pekar.

Gaston, N.Y. American & Journal, 1905) as well as appearances in several Happy Hooligan and Maud titles of the same period. They are immortalized in the American idiom, however, as a universally understood symbol of excessive politeness.

B.B.

AMAZING MAN (U.S.) *Amazing Man*, alias *A-Man*, was created by Bill Everett and made its first appearance in Centaur's *Amazing Man* number five in September 1939. Although the character was slated to have a short run with a lackluster house, he has become one of the most fondly remembered heroes of the early days of comic books.

Amazing Man was really John Aman. According to his origin, the Tibetan " 'Council of Seven' selected an orphan of superb physical structure, and each did his part to develop in the child all the qualities of one who would dominate the world of men." Aman stayed with the council until he was 25, at which time he passed a grueling series of tests to earn his freedom and powers. He was also given the ability to turn into green mist. Dubbed the Amazing Man, Aman returned to America to battle crime. In one of the most interesting plot lines ever to appear in comics, Amazing Man was also forced to fight a psychological war with one member of the Council, The Great Question, who constantly bombarded Aman with telepathy. While most

comics were sticking to pedestrian villains, *Amazing Man* was the only strip using mental battles.

In several early adventures, Aman even abandoned the traditional superhero garb, opting instead for a simple, double-breasted blue suit. He eventually switched to trunks and crossed suspenders, and added a sidekick, Tommy, the Amazing Kid, in August 1941.

Creator Bill Everett handled the first two years of *Amazing Man*, and many consider his work on the strip superior to his *Sub-Mariner* material. He left the feature in 1940, however, and Paul Gustavson and Sam Glanzman produced the bulk of the remaining stories.

The *Amazing Man* feature ended after the 27th issue of *Amazing Man* in February 1942. The character also appeared in several issues of *Stars and Stripes* during 1941.

J.B.

AMERICAN SPLENDOR (U.S.) Harvey Pekar's work as an elevator operator, sales clerk, photocopier, and hospital file clerk provided the ideal background for his tales of grimly commonplace life in *American Splendor*. An occasional writer on jazz and other aspects of popular culture for such publications as *The Jazz Review*, *Downbeat*, and *Evergreen Review*, Pekar began composing realistic stories for underground comic books in 1975, with his contribution to *Bizarre Sex*, followed by *Flaming Baloney, Flamed-Out Funnies, Snarf,* and *Comix Book* in 1976. He has never been a fan of fantasy or superhero comics, he reports, but writes as he does in an effort "to push people into their lives rather than helping people escape from them."

Pekar's interest in the comic strip was first inspired by the work of pioneer underground cartoonist and fellow jazz fan Robert Crumb, whom he met in 1962 and about whose work he wrote articles for the *Journal of Popular Culture* in 1970 and *Jazzworld* in 1971. Self-described as "having no discernible skill as an illustrator" himself, Pekar called on Crumb and other comic book artists to draw the stories he wrote. He published his first independent collection of contemporary slices of life under the ironic title *American Splendor* in 1976, which included the artwork of Crumb and others, and he has produced collections annually ever since. The first 15 collections were published and distributed at his own expense, but as his initial audience has grown, his work has appeared in more prestigious trade imprints.

Doubleday issued two large volumes in paperback under their Dolphin imprint, *American Splendor: The Life and Times of Harvey Pekar* (1986) and *More American Splendor: From Off the Streets of Cleveland Comes . . .* (1987), and *New American Splendor Anthology* appeared in 1991. The strip has become a cult classic but has entered the American mainstream sufficiently to bring Pekar invitations to appear on national television talk shows.

After nearly two decades of recording the small irritations and frustrations of everyday life in his annual installments of *American Splendor*, Pekar and his wife Joyce Brabner collaborated on a poignant account of the writer's 1990 recovery from cancer. The 252-page novel, *Our Cancer Year* (1994), movingly drawn by Frank Stack, achieved great power through Pekar's characteristic focus on the small details of their ordeal. In his fragmentary one-page vignettes as well as his longer, more ambitious narratives, Pekar is unsparing in the light he throws on the littleness of life. An actor, and often the protagonist, in most of his modest dramas, he is merciless in his depiction of his own weakness. *American Splendor*'s unsparing candor and clarity of vision have contributed a new note to American comics and prompted critic R.C. Harvey to describe the series in *The Art of the Comic Book* (1996) as a "beacon for those who sought to make comics intimate and personal and therefore individually expressive in ways not hitherto attempted."

D.W.

AMOK (Italy) In the wake of the superhero comic books that the American troops brought with them to Italy, many Italian cartoonists were influenced by their American colleagues and produced characters that were similar in theme and artwork to those of the American comic scene. So, partly as imitations of the superheroes, partly as nostalgic remembrances of The Phantom, a whole slew of masked crime-fighters appeared in the months following the end of WWII; few of these are still remembered today.

Amok (subtitled "Il Gigante Mascherato"—the Masked Giant) is certainly one of the most celebrated. It appeared for the first time on the newsstands on October 17, 1947. It was written by Cesare Solini and drawn by Antonio Canale (who were respectively signing their work with the pen names "Phil Anderson" and "Tony Chan"), and it was published by the

Milanese firm of Agostino della Casa. The more than 50 books that told of the adventures of Amok, an Indian crime-fighter engaged in a war to the death against the evil "Scorpion" gang, met with immediate success. Amok and his inseparable companions, the newspaperman Bill Davidson, Amok's comic sidekick, and Kyo, Amok's faithful panther, soon became part of the comics' mythology.

The Scorpion band (which had stolen the treasure of the "Moon Pagoda" and kidnapped the beautiful Nikita) was pursued by Amok through ominous jungles and sinister cities as far as Sambaland Lake. After countless adventures, perils, fires, and gunfights, Amok, with the help of his friends and of his fiancée Edmea, finally put an end to the murderous Scorpion's depredations.

The last stories of the series were published by Dardo in December 1948 and written by Franco Baglioni. Two special issues, printed in full color and written by Giovanni Bonelli, the celebrated author of *Tex Willer*, were produced especially for the French publisher Sagédition, which had bought the rights to the strip. *Amok* was also published in Spain, Argentina, and Turkey.

G.B.

ANDERSON, CARL THOMAS (1865-1948) The renowned creator of the bald-headed, mute little boy who was the hero of *Henry*, Carl Thomas Anderson, was born on February 14, 1865, in the Norwegian district of Madison, Wisconsin, to immigrant parents. He took his first schooling in Janesville, Wisconsin, and continued it, after a family move, in Beatrice, Nebraska, where he became a carpenter's apprentice. Leaving school early, he traveled around the Middle West, working in planing mills. An expert cabinetmaker by age 25, Anderson invented a patented folding desk that is still being manufactured. After reading a correspondence school pamphlet promoting cartooning, he traveled to Philadelphia, where he enrolled in the Pennsylvania Museum and School of Industrial Art. To support himself, he took a job on the *Philadelphia Times* in 1894, drawing fashion pictures for $12.00 a week. In the late 1890s he was asked by Arthur Brisbane of the *New York World* to come to Manhattan to draw for the *World* Sunday pages. There he created a short-lived strip called *The Filipino and the Chick* before he was "raided" by Hearst's *Journal* and put to work on a strip called *Raffles and Bunny* for the *Journal*'s Sunday section. In 1903 he produced *Herr Spiegelberger, the Amateur Cracksman* for the McClure Syndicate.

Anderson's early work failed to catch the public fancy, however, and he turned to freelance work in the early 1900s, doing gag cartoons for *Judge, Life, Puck,* and *Collier's* over the next few decades. His income dwindled as his markets collapsed or changed, and, hit by the Depression like many others, Anderson finally left New York in 1932 to return to Madison, where his father was dying, determined to return to cabinetmaking. Teaching a night class in cartooning while he altered his sights, he made one final stab at a new market, sending the first rough sketches of a panel series about a scrawny-necked, egg-headed boy named Henry off to the *Saturday Evening Post*. The editors loved them, began to run them every week on the last page of text in the magazine, and demanded more. From 1932 through 1934, *Henry* appeared every week in the *Post*, where he was noticed by W. R. Hearst, who contacted Anderson in Madison and asked for a Sunday half-page and a daily strip based on the character. Anderson obliged and was signed by King Features. The public, already engaged by the *Post* series, was delighted by the new strip, and it was an enormous success over the next two decades. In 1942 Anderson was forced to retire because of ill-health and turned his feature over to his assistants, Don Trachte and John Liney. A lifelong bachelor, Anderson died in Madison on November 4, 1948. The strip was continued beyond his death by his assistants for some time.

B.B.

Lyman Anderson, magazine illustration.

ANDERSON, LYMAN (1907-1993) American illustrator and cartoonist, born May 4, 1907. Anderson studied at the Chicago Art Institute and graduated in 1928, when he moved to New York and enrolled at the Grand Central Art School to study under top illustrator Pruett Carter.

In 1929 Anderson began illustrating for pulp magazines—displaying his versatility in crime, science-fiction, love, and western titles—for various publishers, while pursuing his studies.

In the early 1930s Major Malcolm Wheeler-Nicholson, a publisher, conceived *New Fun*, a comic book. Anderson worked on the first two issues and left shortly before the magazine folded.

An associate on *New Fun* was Sheldon Stark, who, in 1934, contacted Anderson as a possible artist for a strip he was designing for King Features Syndicate, based on Edgar Wallace's detective stories. *Inspector Wade* was the result, and the collaboration appeared in daily newspapers later that year. Wade was the quintessential detective, a pipe-smoking case-solver, sophisticated and calm. Anderson's pulp style was well suited to the story line.

Anderson continued to study illustration with Harvey Dunn and Walter Biggs during his work on *Wade* (which he left in July 1938 to the pen of Neil O'Keefe). Top-flight illustration and advertising work followed, and later Anderson became a staff instructor with Famous Artists School in Westport, Connecticut. He retired, doing only occasional work; some of his illustrations appeared in the revived *Saturday Evening Post*. He died on May 30, 1993, at his home in Connecticut.

R.M.

ANDERSON, MURPHY (1926-   ) American comic book and comic strip artist, born 1926 in Asheville, North Carolina. Influenced by many of the slickest artists in the field—including Will Eisner, Lou Fine, and Alex Raymond—Murphy Anderson's only real training came at the Art Students League. He broke into comic books in 1944 at the Fiction House group, pencilling and inking strips like *Suicide Smith* (1944), *Sky Rangers* (1946), and *Star Pirate* (1944-1947). And it was here he received his only writing assignment, handling a minor Fiction House feature entitled *Life on Other Worlds*.

When Dick Calkins retired from the long-running *Buck Rogers* syndicated strip in 1947, Anderson assumed the artistic duties. Not quite the craftsman and innovator Calkins was, the young artist was a better draftsman and illustrator. His smooth, fine-line work on the 25th-century space adventure strip was among the best work the feature sported in its run. Anderson left *Buck Rogers* in 1949 but returned for another stint on the strip in 1958 and 1959.

After Anderson's first go-round on *Buck Rogers*, he returned to comic books in 1950 and drew for a number of houses, including Pines (1950-1953, science fiction), Marvel (1950, horror), St. John (1953, weird), Ziff-Davis (1950-1953, science fiction), and finally National. Joining the latter in 1950, he was with the company for years, primarily as their top-flight inker. He joined penciller—later publisher—Carmine Infantino on two strips of note, *Adam Strange* and *Batman*. Handling the former in the late 1950s and early 1960s, Anderson was the perfect choice for this science-fiction strip. He complemented Infantino's pencils, and together they produced the slickest, prettiest, and best-received science-fiction strip of the era. In 1964, when *Adam Strange* editor Julius Schwartz was handed the faltering giant *Batman*, he again called on penciller Infantino and inker Anderson. Together they broke away from the sometimes grotesque Kane-Robinson style and produced a slicker, more pristine Batman than had ever been seen before. This interpretation became so popular that an Infantino-Anderson drawing graced the cover of the *Batman* anthology published by Crown in 1971. After Infantino was promoted in 1966, Anderson went on to ink Gil Kane on *Green Lantern* and *Atom*, and eventually teamed with veteran penciller Curt Swan to revamp still another National giant, *Superman*. This Swan-Anderson rendition, clean, straightforward, and exciting, may well be the most popular style ever imposed on the "Man of Steel."

Anderson also had an illustrious career at National as a penciller. Between 1960 and 1964, he drew the *Atomic Knights* feature, a well-received "after-the-nuclear-holocaust" strip, and between 1963 and 1967, drew *Hawkman*. He and Joe Kubert, a more detailed and stylized artist, made the strip one of the finest illustrated of the 1960s. His work on one of the Spectre revivals in 1966 was also highly regarded. He retired from comics to devote more of his time to commercial art, to which end he founded Murphy Anderson Visual Concepts in the late 1980s.

J.B.

Oskar Andersson, "Mannen som gör vad som faller honom in."

ANDERSSON, OSKAR EMIL (1877-1906) Oskar Emil Andersson, Swedish cartoonist and comic artist, was born January 11, 1877, in Stockholm, Sweden. He grew up in Ekero near Stockholm. His father worked in the Royal Mint, and so did Andersson after he had finished school. He had plans to get an education in furniture designing, but his talent at drawing led him down another path. At the age of 20 Andersson tried selling his first cartoons to *Söndags-Nisse* (Sunday Troll), a Swedish humor weekly of the time. Realizing Andersson's talent, the editors of *Söndags-Nisse* employed him as a regular contributor. Oskar Andersson's initials, O.A., served as his pseudonym, which is still as well known as it was in his time.

O.A. read all the American comics he could lay his hands on: *Little Bears, The Yellow Kid, The Katzenjammer Kids*. In 1902, he created for *Söndags-Nisse* his now-legendary *Mannen som gör vad som faller honom in* (The man who does whatever comes to his mind), a comic strip some 20 episodes of which were published between 1902 and 1906. The man who does whatever comes to his mind is a kind of sour-faced libertarian living out his every whim in a protestation of man's free will against morals and mechanization. Thus, when it stops raining, he simply drops his opened umbrella to the ground; he pulls a folded car out of his coat pocket when he wants to go for a ride; he cuts off his fingers after shaking hands with a person he dislikes; or watches a dynamiting site at close proximity while others warn him from a safe distance. The latter incident is one of the few in which O.A. employed speech balloons.

Besides *Mannen som gör vad som faller honom in*, O.A. also drew *Urhunden* (the story of a prehistoric dog and his prehistoric owner in modern surroundings) and a large number of cartoons for *Söndags-Nisse*. He also made book illustrations. His pen-and-ink drawings show that he was a master of perspective and employed various styles. They also show a predilection for satire, irony, black humor, and morbid self-destruction. O.A.'s life ended in suicide on November 28, 1906. According to his own wishes, his headstone simply reads "Har vilar sig O.A." (Here rests O.A.).

W.F.

AND HER NAME WAS MAUD (U.S.) Fred Opper's classic kicking-mule strip, *And Her Name Was Maud* (a play on "and her name was mud"), technically began publication under that title as a Sunday page-topper with Opper's *Happy Hooligan* on May 23, 1926, consisting of two rows of about four panels each. Actually, however, Maud the mule was a feature character in many of Opper's Sunday page episodes going well back into the early 1900s, where her appearances about 12 times a year were interspersed between the occasional entries of Alphonse and Gaston and the more frequent appearances of Opper's chief character, Happy Hooligan (although all of these characters or a combination of them could be grouped together in a weekly episode from time to time).

Maud was a mule on the farm of a bespectacled, white-whiskered, patch-elbowed old tiller of the soil in a flat black hat named Si and his bun-haired wife, Mirandy, who first appeared on the comic page on Sunday, July 24, 1904 (although Si himself had appeared before as "Uncle Si" in Opper gag sequences before 1900). Si has just purchased Maud in the opening half-page episode for $10.00 and is showing his new barnyard acquisition off to Mirandy (who says nothing but a reiterated "Land Sakes Alive") when Maud first demonstrates her kicking proclivities by belting Si across a half acre of farmland, then emits the first of her many classic "Hee Haw's!"

The genius behind the concept of Maud lay in Opper's draftsmanship: the drawing of the grinning, demonic mule (whom Si cannot resell to anyone, try as he can) provokes a certain chuckle in the reader on every appearance, no matter how repetitive or flat the basic gag situation may be. Later, the mule does as much good for Si and Mirandy as she does harm, by kicking various undesirables off the farm, booting Si's car out of the way of a speeding freight train, etc., and becomes a fixture on the farm for some 30 years to come.

Dropped by Opper in the 1910s when the artist wanted to concentrate on continual weekly series about other characters, Maud was revived in May 1926, to run weekly until her final appearance in the Sunday pages in the early 1930s (most papers dropped the strip with the episode of August 14, 1932), when Opper went into semi-retirement. A classic figure in American graphic art, Maud deserves a sizable contemporary anthology to complement her now rare, early book appearances in such collections as *Maud*, *Maud the Mirthful Mule*, and *Maud the Matchless*, all before 1910.

B.B.

ANDRAX (Germany) *Andrax* is one of a number of German comic strips produced in Spain for Kauka comic books. Starting in No. 27/1973 of *primo*, just nine issues after the debut of *Kuma*, *Andrax* may well be the most interesting of the German adventure comics to come out of that year. Earlier reprints of adventure comics from the pages of the Spanish comics magazine *Trinca* helped establish contact with Spanish artists of the Bardon Art Studio. One of the ideas the editorial offices toyed around with was that of a science-fiction or fantasy series. It was proposed to Spanish artist Jorge Bernet, who, together with Miguel Cusso, came up with *Andrax*.

Andrax is a kind of modern Rip Van Winkle. In 1976, during the Montreal Olympics, he is still known as Michael Rush, decathlon winner supreme. The somewhat mad, wheelchair-bound professor Magor considers him to be the perfect specimen for his experiment and has him kidnapped. Rush is injected with a serum that is to keep him in suspended animation for two thousand years, so he can wake up as Andrax in a new, perfect civilization.

But Andrax does not wake to a super-civilization where peace reigns supreme. Instead he finds a desolate planet Earth that has returned to barbarism, presumably after a nuclear holocaust. His experience as a decathlon athlete comes in handy whenever he encounters giant rats or barbarian hordes. He wins in hand-to-hand combat with Holernes, who has dreams of world rule (which are soon tempered by Andrax's views about society and justice).

H. G. Wells, Isaac Asimov, Theodore Sturgeon, and Richard Matheson are some of the literary influences that helped create the *Andrax* myth, which holds up extremely well, both story and art wise, compared to similar fantasies of life in a post-holocaust future. The stories are fast-paced and offer splendid visuals with easy-flowing lines, perfect mastery of anatomy, vast landscapes, perfect staging and lighting. There is the slightest hint of Frank Robbins in the facial expressions of the Andrax characters, but that is where the likeness ends, as Bernet has a powerful style all his own.

Andrax has proved extremely popular. Besides being featured in *primo*, the series also appeared in *Action Comic* albums, in the digest-sized *Super Action*, and in 1975 became one of three series alternating in the revamped *Action Comic*, a continuation of *primo* after that comic book was discontinued in 1974. The feature ended in 1981, some time after Rolf Kauka had sold his company.

W.F.

ANDREASSON, RUNE (1925-   ) Rune Andreasson, Swedish writer/artist, born August 11, 1925, in Lindome, is now living in Göteborg-Viken. After graduation from high school, Andreasson attended theater school in Göteborg for three years. But, after several roles in the theater and films, he started working mainly on comics. He had been working as a self-educated comic strip artist ever since he was in high school, his earliest strip, *Brum*, being published in the weekly *Allers*, starting in January 1944.

Andreasson's best-known feature, *Lille Rickard och hans katt* ("Little Richard and his Cat"), began in Stockholm's evening newspaper, *Aftonbladet*, on December 23, 1951, and has since been exported to other countries. Like all of his comic strip work, *Lille Rickard och hans katt* is chiefly aimed at children. The idea for this strip dated back 10 years to a time in high school when, during English lessons, Andreasson read a story titled "Dick Wittington and his Cat." Andreasson had drawn some 80 pictures inspired by the story. They served him well when he created his own boy hero who roams the world, his tiny cat at his side.

Also for children, Andreasson created the little bear, Bamse, and Pellefant, the blue-skinned kid elephant. *Bamse* was very successfully transplanted to television in 1973. Since then a new series of *Bamse* films has gone into production, and *Bamse* is also available in albums, coloring books, etc. Pellefant started appearing in his own monthly comic book in 1965. Pellefant is a small, blue toy elephant with a tiny orange mouse as his best friend. They live in a world of living toys, acting out their humorous little adventures to their young readers' delight. With a little bit of their own magic they usually succeed in outsmarting an evil wizard who occasionally tries to make short work of Pellefant because he cannot stand his good nature.

Pellefant, like all of Andreasson's work, is distinguished by a clear style with firm lines and enough uncluttered space for perfect color reproduction. Andreasson, who, by his own admission, has been influenced by the work of Walt Disney and Charlie Chaplin, has devoted his time to writing and drawing mainly for the youngest readers. He has also freelanced for Swedish television as a writer.

W.F.

ANDRIOLA, ALFRED (1912-1983) American cartoonist, born in 1912 in New York City. In 1935, after dropping out of the Columbia University School of Journalism, Alfred Andriola started working in the studio of Noel Sickles and Milton Caniff as secretary and man Friday (not as an assistant, as often stated). In October 1938, with the help of Caniff and Sickles (who assisted on the writing and drawing respectively), he started his first comic strip, *Charlie Chan*, based on the famous detective created by Earl Derr Biggers, for McNaught Syndicate. After the demise of the strip in March 1942, he took over *Dan Dunn*, which he drew and scripted for one year.

In 1943 Andriola created *Kerry Drake*, an original detective strip, for Publishers Syndicate. Under the pseudonym of Alfred James, and in collaboration with Mel Casson for the drawing, he created in 1957 the short-lived girl strip *It's Me Dilly*. Andriola died of cancer on March 29, 1983, in New York City. One of the most articulate practitioners (some would say exploiters) of the newspaper syndicate system, he succeeded in creating four different strips for which he received credit without hardly ever having worked on any of them. After his death it was learned that he had not drawn a speck or written a line in decades; *Kerry Drake*, the feature he had promoted exactly 40 years earlier, survived him by only a few weeks.

M.H.

ANDY CAPP (G.B.) On August 5, 1957, a truculent little layabout, cloth cap too big for his head, was kicked out of the Boilermaker's Arms and landed in the new Northern Edition of the *Daily Mirror*. The single-panel cartoon, signed Smythe (Reginald Smythe), came to the National Edition less than a year later (April 14, 1958), and shortly after spread to the *Sunday Pictorial* (May 8, 1960). This little Northerner, with his cigarette, his beer, his bets on the dogs, his mate Chalky, and his long-suffering missus Florrie, not only touched a chord common to Cockneys and Scotsmen alike, but soon touched the world. Russia printed him in *Izvestia*, the Swedes put him in a monthly comic book called *Tuffa Viktor*, and the Americans not only syndicated him in his daily strip form, they asked for a colored Sunday strip too! He appears in 34 countries in 13 dif-

"Andy Capp," Reginald Smythe. © *Daily Mirror Ltd.*

ferent languages, and if Andy himself isn't surprised, his creator, who became Britain's richest strip cartoonist, is.

Smythe was born in Hartlepools, Yorkshire (1917), son of a boat builder. He left Galleys Field School at the age of 14 to become a butcher's boy, and then enlisted in the army as a regular soldier. A machine gunner during WWII, he joined the post office after demobilization and began freelancing single gags to *Reveille* and the *Mirror's* joke page. The first "Andy" was little more than an extension of this daily gag cartoon, given a semblance of character continuity. Reprints include the hardback *Cream of Andy Capp* (1965), regular paperback series from 1958 to date (32 books by 1974), and the *Laugh Again with Andy Capp* reprints series (1968). Andy's son is featured in the children's comic *Buster* (May 28, 1960, to date). Having now reached the 40th anniversary mark, *Andy Capp* is still going strong on both sides of the Atlantic.

D.G.

ANGEL, THE (U.S.) When Timely published *Marvel Comics* number one in November 1939, most eyes were focused on the trail-blazing *Human Torch* and *Sub-Mariner* features, although Paul Gustavson's *The Angel* also made its debut there. The feature was unique in several ways: The Angel sported an almost-never-seen mustache; he had no appreciable superpowers, save the ability to cast an angel shadow as he disappeared victorious; and he had no secret identity, being known only as The Angel in or out of costume. On the other hand, he did have a yellow and blue superhero suit, incongruously topped by an outstretched eagle emblazoned upon his chest attire.

The feature began as a direct steal from Leslie Charteris' Saint character, and the first story was unabashed plagiarism of *The Saint in New York*. The Angel soon became involved in a series of "weird" tales, however, which made him one of the first heroes to prowl the supernatural beat. Because of these aberrations, it was also an offbeat strip: The Angel, sometimes in uniform, sometimes in a business suit, would battle some eerie menace with only his physical prowess, would be ultimately victorious, and would then cast that curious angel shadow as he disappeared. If nothing else, these stories were a change-of-pace diversion from the more standard fare offered by the *Human Torch* and *Sub-Mariner* features.

Artistically, Gustavson handled the strip in his fast-paced, no-nonsense style. Most of his panels were long shots, Gustavson having no use for frills or tricky layouts. He handled the feature until 1942, but George Mandel (1941), Al Avison (1941), Simon and Kirby (1940), and Carmine Infantino (1945-1946) also drew stories.

The Angel appeared in the first 79 issues of *Marvel Mystery* (formerly *Marvel Comics*) until December 1946, and in the first 21 issues of *Sub-Mariner* (Spring 1941 to Fall 1946). The character was briefly revived from 1985 to 1987 in Marvel's *X-Men* line of comic books.

J.B.

ANGLO, MICK (1916-   ) British cartoonist, writer, editor, and publisher, born Maurice Anglo in Bow, London, on June 19, 1916. Educated at the Central Foundation School, he then studied art at the John Cass Art School in the city. He did professional artwork, fashion sketches (1936), then freelancing in commercial art to 1939, when he was conscripted into the army. He drew his first cartoons for *Seac*, the official army newspaper for South East Asia Command (1942), and then for Singapore papers (1945). Upon demobilization, being seven years behind the times, he abandoned designing for advertising agency work. Anglo began writing fiction and created *Johnny Dekker*, a detective story in the style of Damon Runyon, whom he greatly admired. He drew the cover for *The Siamese Cat*, whereupon the publisher, Martin & Reid, suggested that he try strips for their children's comics. After a few pages signed "Mick," he was given a complete comic to draw: *The Happy Yank* (1948).

An admirer of the American school of comic art as well as of crime fiction, he soon abandoned his primitive humor style for frankly imitative superheroes. After a short period with a comic art agency run by Eric Souster and Jack Potter, he became editor of the comics put out by Paget Publications. To their weeklies *Premier* and *Comic Wonder* he added *Wonderman*, featuring *Captain Justice*, a *Superman* figure, which ran for 24 issues between 1948 and 1951.

When Martin & Reid expanded comic publication in 1949, he took on their editorial work, opening his own studio in Gower Street, and soon the "Gower Studios" imprint began to appear on a long list of independent comics. His best productions here were the full-color photogravure series, *Frolicomic* and *Jolly Western* (1949), and cartoonists working at Gower included Bob Monkhouse and Denis Gifford. Clients included Barrett Publishing (*The Sheriff, Bumper Comic*) and Timpo Toys (*Pioneer Western*). When Paget discontinued publishing, L. Miller & Son became clients, then separate clients, as Arnold Miller left his father to set up the Arnold Book Company (ABC Comics). For Arnold, Anglo created the monthly *Ace Malloy* (1951) and the weekly *Space Comics* (1953), featuring *Captain Valiant*, a character who caught on sufficiently enough to warrant heavier merchandising. For Miller, Anglo took over a number of established American titles, continuing (with English and Spanish artists) series such as *Jim Bowie, Annie Oakley,* and *Davy Crockett*. When Miller, who was the British agent for Fawcett Publications, had to cease publication of the weekly *Captain Marvel Adventures*, Anglo replaced this with *Marvelman*, who quickly became the number one British superhero. *Young Marvelman* replaced *Captain Marvel Junior*, and *Marvelman Family* replaced *The Marvel Family*. These were Anglo's most successful comic books, running from 1954 till 1963.

Under "Anglo Comics," he published his own series of comic books, mostly revised versions of earlier Miller strips—*Gunhawks, Battle, Captain Miracle,* and *T.V. Heroes* (1960-61)—then continued the American *Gilbert* on *Classics Illustrated* for Thorpe & Porter. From 1967-68 he edited his best weekly, *T.V. Tornado*, which ran 88 issues for City Magazines. Next he served as editor of *Look & Cook* magazine, as a compiler of cookbooks and *Striker Annual*, and as a ghostwriter to comedian Tommy Cooper, while continuing to work in comics as editor of several Picture Library series of war comics, translated from the Spanish. He retired during the 1980s.

D.G.

ANIBAL 5 (Mexico) *Anibal 5* was created on October 1, 1966. Although lasting a total of only six comic books, it represented in its time a major renovation of the Mexican comic. Its greatest contribution came from the scriptwriter, Alexandro Jodorowski, writer, draftsman, actor, and stage and movie director, who produced stories filled with innovations in the fields of fantasy and science fiction. His illustrator was Manuel Moro, an artist with traditional style, a fine line, and a taste for the erotic.

Anibal 5 was a cyborg, a human being who had miniature electronic devices inserted into him, making him an exceptional being. His arms were rifles, his pupils television cameras, and his ear lobe concealed a receiver. His mortal enemy was Baron de Sader, and in this titanic struggle, Anibal 5 was pitted against mulewomen, killed on five separate occasions, reincarnated in several animals, imprisoned inside a woman's womb, and witness to the invasion of the world by mummies.

Expressive inventions thrived in the strip, such as lipstick that allowed the wearer to launch kisses into space, or the resurrection of the incomplete remains of Attila, Hitler, Napoleon, Genghis Khan, and Al Capone. (Anibal 5 was modeled after movie actor Jorge Rivero.)

L.G.

ANITA DIMINUTA (Spain) *Anita Diminuta* ("Tiny Anita") was created on April 2, 1941, in the first issue of the girl's weekly *Mis Chicas*, where it remained until 1950. Its author was the illustrator Jesus Blasco (who also wrote the scenarios), and the 12 very long adventures of *Anita* that he published in *Mis Chicas* made his little heroine into the mascot of the magazine.

Anita was a little blonde orphan girl who lived in Illusion Land with her old grandmother and her teddy bear Mateo. Her friends were the Genies of the Woods; Soldatito (who introduced himself as "Andersen's little lead soldier"); Payasito the clown; and the cat Morronguito, with whom she fought Carraspia the witch and the wizard Caralampio, as well as assorted sorcerers, pirates, and spell-casters. Her wanderings blended traditional fairy tales and Oriental magic stories, thereby

"Anita Diminuta," Jesus Blasco. © Chicos.

conjuring an imaginary world in which Anita, dressed like a modern little girl, blissfully moved, oblivious of the anachronisms that surrounded her. Her adventures were at once tender and cruel; on occasion she found herself in terrifying circumstances from which she would always escape with the help of her friends. The tenderness was mostly obvious in the episodes published in the annual almanacs, while the strip took on a decidedly humorous character in the pages published by the magazine *Gran Chicos*.

Anita Diminuta's success was such in Spain and Portugal that its author published two *Anita* books, a doll was named after the character, and it was made into a radio program.

On October 1, 1974, *Anita Diminuta* was revived in *Chito* magazine, where it was set in modern times in a series of "hippie" comic strips. It ceased publication in the 1980s.

L.G.

ANMITSU HIME (Japan) *Anmitsu Hime* ("Princess Anmitsu"), created by Shōsuke Kuragane, made its first appearance in the May 1949 issue of the Japanese monthly *Shojo*. The strip was born out of the creator's concern for the children of Japan, most of whom were deprived of food, clothes, or parental affection (because of the losses suffered in World War II). Kuragane wanted to show these children that these deprivations were only temporary and that Japan would one day return to the old days of plenty.

Anmitsu Hime was therefore set in the Edo era, and all the characters' names related to food items: Anmitsu (boiled beans, bean paste sweetened with syrup), her father Awano Dangonokami (dango is a Japanese-style dumpling), her mother Shibucha (astringent tea), her English teacher Kasutera (sponge cake), her little friend Manjū (a kind of Japanese jelly cake), her page Amaguri-nosuke (amaguri is a sweet roast chestnut), her maids Anko (bean paste), and Kinako (bean flour), etc.

Anmitsu was a tomboy whose pranks enlivened the castle of Amakara (amakara means sweet and pun-

"Anmitsu Hime," Shōsuke Kuragane. © Shōjo.

gent), where she lived with her parents and entertained her friends with all kinds of festivities during which they were served the utmost delicacies and where the guests wore the most gorgeous clothes. It was a simple but romantic and optimistic fairy tale, which enchanted the young readers (and their parents) and made them forget the rigors of the day.

As Japan steadily recovered from her postwar prostration, there was no need for *Anmitsu Hime*, and the strip was finally discontinued in April 1954. During its lifetime it had proved popular enough to inspire several motion pictures as well as a TV series.

H.K.

APARTMENT 3-G (U.S.) Beginning daily and Sunday publication on May 8, 1961, *Apartment 3-G* was the product of author Nicholas Dallis; Harold Anderson, head of Publishers Syndicate; and artist Alex Kotzky.

The main characters are three young career women (3-G is an obvious derivative of "three girls"): Lu Ann Powers, schoolteacher; Tommy Thompson, nurse; and Margo Magee, secretary. Lu Ann married in the strip, but her husband, Gary, was and remains an MIA in Viet Nam, which provides ongoing suspense and pathos.

The girls' neighbor, Professor Papagoras, is a college professor, a dead ringer for Ernest Hemingway, and as the girls' best friend, trusted advisor, and sometimes protector, he provides a counterpoint personality. Other characters are short-term: those moving in and out of the apartment building, workmates, or would-be boyfriends.

Kotzky's art is slick and breezy, and his characters are handsome without being academic, as in other story strips. Likewise, Dallis' stories flow easier than in his other efforts, *Rex Morgan, M.D.*, and *Judge Parker*. *Apartment 3-G* concentrates on the characters and their personalities, rather than emphasizing heavy plot developments. In this way, 3-G appears less substantial than other story strips, but its characters are definitely more human than their counterparts in the other straight strips. Humor is also frequently introduced as a plot element.

The space crunch in newspapers has forced Kotzky's rendering to include more close-ups; this has been a coincident advantage to 3-G's scheme of accentuating character identification. (The title of the strip was briefly changed to *The Girls of Apartment 3-G*.)

R.M.

Due to protests from women's groups, the strip reverted to its original title in 1977. Dallis died in 1991, and Kotzky assumed complete authorship of the feature, which he maintained on an even keel, with very few changes. After his death in September 1996, it was taken over by his son, Brian Kotzky, who had been assisting his father since the early 1990s. *Apartment 3-G* is now being distributed by King Features.

M.H.

A. PIKER CLERK (U.S.) Clare Briggs (later famed for *Mr. and Mrs.* and *When a Feller Needs a Friend*) was just beginning his cartooning career on the new Hearst *Chicago American* and *Examiner* papers in 1903 as a sports, feature, and editorial cartoonist when editor Moe Koenigsberg decided that a continuing sports-page comic strip might keep the fickle afternoon newspaper audience of the time buying the *American* rather than seesawing back and forth between that paper and its

"A. Piker Clerk," Clare Briggs.

chief rival, the afternoon *Daily News*. The final sports edition of the *American* was the edition to be moved by this innovative device, and so Koenigsberg and Briggs devised a feature about a fanatically dedicated horse player named A. Piker Clerk, to be prominently featured in the sports section of that edition.

This much seems to be agreed upon by published sources and by reference to the *American* of the time. From this point, however, written accounts and the actual files seem to disagree. Koenigsberg, for example, states in his 1941 autobiography, *King News*, that he and Briggs started the strip in 1904, while the San Francisco Academy of Comic Art files of both the *American* and *Examiner* for 1903 contain episodes of the *Clerk* feature. Koenigsberg states that he innovated the idea of a day-to-day comic strip years before Bud Fisher launched *Mutt and Jeff* in the *San Francisco Chronicle* of 1907, yet the Academy files of the *American* and *Examiner* show only two *Clerk* runs of even three successive days in all of 1904, while gaps of three days to a month between episodes are frequent. (*Mutt and Jeff*, on the other hand, ran six days a week every week from its initial appearance.) It is apparent that Koenigsberg grasped the idea of using a weekday comic strip to bring readers back for the next day's paper, but since the strip's "suspense" was based on whether or not Clerk's hot horse tip would pay off in the next day's race (actual racing horses in actual races were used), the strip tended to be published only during major track seasons. The strip probably died of public apathy, although Koenigsberg claims that Hearst himself suppressed the strip as "vulgar" shortly after it had been launched and had given an upwards boost to the *American's* circulation. This is a good story, but obviously untrue, since *A. Piker Clerk* was published for over a year and a half in a straggling, desultory manner before it was finally dropped on June 7, 1904, with Clerk making a farewell appearance as a minor figure in a general Briggs sports cartoon of that date. *Clerk*, then, was not "the first daily strip," as has been claimed, nor was it in any way a strip novelty in its

time except in its advocacy of horses for gamblers, being a true "first" in that limited field. It is not even an important Briggs work (although it is possibly his most curious undertaking), nor a memorable strip in any other way. No book collection exists, and—of course—it ran only in the *Chicago American* and *Examiner* during 1903 and 1904. It is, perhaps, best left there.

B.B.

APPLE MARY   *see* Mary Worth.

AQUAMAN (U.S.)   *Aquaman* was created by writer Mort Weisinger and artist Paul Norris and made its first appearance in November 1941's *More Fun* number 73. The character was National's response to Timely's phenomenally popular *Sub-Mariner*.

Aquaman was the son of a marine scientist who had discovered the secrets of underwater living. He was also the leader of the lost continent of Atlantis. His duties, as described in his premiere adventure, were to "swim forth to keep the freedom of the seas in tropic and arctic waters alike."

Aquaman lasted in *More Fun* through January 1946's 107th issue and then moved to *Adventure* comics starting with April 1946's 103rd issue. During this time, Aquaman used the secret identity of Arthur Curry. This cover didn't last long, however, and Aquaman now appears solely as the sea monarch.

Despite a horde of authors, *Aquaman* was never a fascinating feature. The addition of Aquaman in *Adventure* number 269 did little to help, and the feature was dropped from *Adventure* after the 284th issue. The strip was finally given its own title in January 1962, and it was only there that the strip began to take on several interesting aspects. Mera was introduced in Aquaman 11 and Aquaman married her in issue 19, one of the infrequent comic book marriages. A child was born in the 23rd issue, aptly christened Aquababy. The series ended after the March 1971 issue of *Aquaman* number 56. The character is a charter member of the Justice League and has also appeared on television in animated cartoon form. The first series of *Aquaman* comic books ended in 1978. The title was briefly revived by DC Comics in 1986, and again in 1989. A second monthly series was attempted in 1991, but it only lasted for 13 issues. Undaunted, in 1994 DC Comics launched a third series, which has managed to survive so far.

J.B.

ARABELLE LA SIRÈNE (France)   Jean Ache (Jean Huet) created *Arabelle la Sirène* ("Arabelle the Mermaid") on May 2, 1950, for the French daily newspaper *France-Soir*.

Arabelle, the last representative of the legendary race of mermaids, is discovered in the course of a marine expedition by the American professor H. G. W. Bimbleton. After a surgical operation that gives her two (shapely) legs, Arabelle becomes indistinguishable from the host of other pretty comic strip girls, except in the water, where she is capable of accomplishing the most extraordinary stunts. Jean Ache makes generous use of Arabelle's aquatic abilities in his strip, sending her to find sunken treasures, to rescue floundering ships, or to fight a band of undersea pirates. In the course of her adventures Arabelle is accompanied by her pet monkey Kouki and by her boyfriend Fleur Bleue (Blue Flower), who often has to rescue the adventurous mermaid from the clutches of her enemies.

Arabelle was discontinued by *France-Soir* in 1962 but made her reappearance in the short-lived *Illustré du Dimanche*. After a long absence, *Arabelle* surfaced again in the pages of the Belgian weekly *Tintin* in 1972 but, after only two adventures, the strip was dropped the next year. The little mermaid surfaced again in 1976 in a new adventure in *Tintin-Selection* but only lasted into 1977. She was used in a number of commercials, however, until the creator's death in 1985.

Arabelle la Sirène was not without a pixieish charm, in spite of the conventionality of its plots and its unimaginative drawing style. In the 1950s its popularity ran high, and a number of the strip's episodes have been reprinted in book form by Denoël.

M.H.

ARAGONÉS, SERGIO (1937-) Mexican-American comic book and magazine cartoonist, born in 1937 in Spain. At the age of six months, because of the Spanish Civil War, the family relocated to a French refugee camp and, several years later, moved to Mexico City. Aragonés grew up as a compulsive doodler, creating endless streams of cartoons for his friends. In 1953, one of these friends sent some to the Mexican humor magazine, *Ja Ja*, which bought them, beginning the appearance of Aragonés' work in various Mexican magazines, including a weekly page in *Mañana*. Aragonés went to architectural school and enrolled later in a mime workshop set up under French pantomimist Marcel Marceau. For a time, Aragonés worked as a clown, and he credits his mime training as a major influence on his cartooning, most of which consisted of wordless gags.

In 1962, with very little money, Aragonés went to America and made the rounds of New York publishers, trying—and failing—to sell his cartoons to small magazines. Advised to start at the top, Aragonés went to *Mad* magazine and had no trouble selling a two-page spread of astronaut cartoons. The feature, which ran in *Mad* number 76, marked the beginning of Aragonés' affiliation with *Mad*, and he quickly became one of its star artists. In addition to various cartoon features, Aragonés did "marginal" cartoons, which *Mad* printed in the corners of pages throughout each issue. Aragonés also began contributing to other magazines, illustrating books and designing storyboards for cartoon specialties.

In 1967, Aragonés began doing work for National Periodical Publications (DC). He drew pages of his pantomime cartoons, which ran as comedy relief in DC's ghost comics, worked on some stories for those books, and collaborated on the scripts for a short-lived western strip, *Bat Lash*.

Sergio Aragonés is probably the fastest cartoonist in the world. He works directly in ink, with rarely any preliminary pencil work, using a fountain pen to put down his visual ideas. His specialty is large mural-cartoons, which generally consist of immense crowd scenes, filled with countless gags, and he is constantly trying to top himself on these. His work remains very cartoony, virtually always in pantomime, and is highly regarded by most for its range of subject matter and expression.

M.E.

Aragonés created his most popular character, Groo the Wanderer, in the pages of *Destroyer Duck* in 1982. One of the innumerable parodies of *Conan*, *Groo* soon gathered a vociferous coterie of fans, and the title has managed to stay afloat to this day, despite sophomoric humor and ham-handed writing, on the strength of the artist's very funny and appealing drawing style.

M.H.

ARCHIE (U.S.) *Archie* was created by artist Bob Montana and made its first appearance in December 1941 in the 22nd issue of MLJ's *Pep*. The strip was an instant success and eventually became one of the most famous comic features in the world. By the next winter, *Archie*

"Archie," Dan DeCarlo. © Archie Publications.

number one had been published, and MLJ knew its future lay with *Archie* and not with its superhero line. The MLJ group was eventually retitled Archie Publications, dozens of spin-off magazines appeared, and *Archie* was soon a syndicated newspaper strip as well.

Archie was and is the consummate American humor feature: it portrays the teenagers of the day, as the adults apparently see them. Stereotypes abound and multiply. First and foremost, there is Archie Andrews himself, the "typical high school student." Then there are the dozens of narrowly defined supporting characters: Jughead, who loves hamburgers more than girls; Reggie, Archie's rival, complete with slick black hair; Betty and Veronica, Archie's girlfriends who vie for his attention; Moose, the dim-wit football hero; and dozens of others too numerous to mention.

It is impossible to judge the influence the *Archie* feature has on its young audience. Aimed at juveniles, the strip has never strayed from the "basic" American principles, whatever they may be. And it has only minutely changed to fit the drastically altered mores of an American civilization 50 years removed from the strip's first appearance. For this reason—their "wholesomeness" to parents of American children—*Archie* and spin-offs have always been the most consistently high-selling comic books on the market. In short, they are a tremendously saleable anachronism.

Naturally, this high-powered appeal has not been lost on the publishers, and *Archie* has made appearances in every possible form. In addition to a whole line of *Archie* comic books—*Jughead* (1949), *Betty and Veronica* (1950), *Pals and Gals* (1951), and *Joke Book* (1954) are just a few of dozens—there have been paperback books, religiously oriented comic books, toys, games, merchandising material, and just about every other conceivable commercial gimmick. There has been one sort of Archie cartoon program or another on television since 1968. When the series peaked in 1969, comic book sales on *Archie* alone surged over a million copies a month while the other best-sellers barely managed 300,000. There was even a "bubble-gum" rock-and-roll group from the program called the Archies, and they recorded several hit songs. This television success matched the earlier radio success—when the *Adventures of Archie* ran for nine years after World War II.

Archie, like *Batman*, *Superman*, and a small handful of others, has transcended comic books into pure Americana. There will, it often seems, always be an Archie. It is as inevitable as death and taxes.

J.B.

King Features Syndicate started distributing *Archie* as a newspaper strip in 1947. The cast of characters and setting remained virtually unchanged from the comic book version, but the relatively greater freedom enjoyed by newspaper features has allowed Bob Montana to go beyond the mere teenage antics of Archie and his gang into somewhat more believable situations.

Following the creator's death in 1975, Dan DeCarlo, who had been working on the comic-book version since 1961, wrote and drew the *Archie* newspaper strip until 1993. Since that time it has been done by Henry Scarpelli, later joined by Craig Boldman. Archie is still going strong in 1997, both in comic books being published under the banner of Archie Comics and in news-

"De Argonautjes," Dick Matena. © PEP.

paper strips (with Creators Syndicate having taken over from King Features).

M.H.

ARGONAUTJES, DE (Netherlands) *De Argonautjes* ("The Little Argonauts") is one of the comic series that ushered in a new era of the Dutch comic strip. The introductory episode appeared in 1968 in the Dutch comics weekly *Pep*, in issues number 3 through 23. *Pep* began publication on October 6, 1962, but had mainly featured foreign comic material, especially Walt Disney strips and features from the pages of *Tintin*. In 1964 strips from *Pilote* were added. But in 1968 *Pep* decided to bring in more Dutch comic art. That was to the advantage of Dick Matena, who had received a thorough schooling in comic art at the Mart en Toonder studios, and who was already successful with *Polletje Pluim*, an animal strip published in the women's magazine *Prinses*. *De Argonautjes*, written by L. Hartog van Banda and drawn by Matena, immediately established Matena as one of the foremost artists among the new school of Dutch comic artists.

Strongly influenced by *Astérix* and the Belgian school, Matena displays an energetic style with good layouts, the right amount of animation, a firm, flowing line, a balance of black and white, and considerable care for detail. *De Argonautjes* takes the reader back to the times of the ancient Greeks, when two young argonauts do their best to make short work of Greek mythology—for example, by involving King Tantalus in a tantalizingly funny tale, having a run-in with Hypocrite during the Olympic games, or trying to beat each other and a lot of curious people to open Pandora's box.

While continuing work on *De Argonautjes*, Matena started alternate series to provide for a change of pace in the pages of *Pep*. In 1969 he started *Ridder Roodhart* (scenario by L. Hartog van Banda) and in 1970 turned writer/artist for *De Grote Pyr* (retitled *Peer Viking* for publication in Germany), before also starting to write scenarios for Dino Attanasio's *De Macaronis*.

Pep's change of policy went one step further in 1969 when it was decided that Geillustreerde Pers, the publishers of *Pep*, should have their own stable of comic artists. *De Argonautjes* was only one of the harbingers of new things to come out of the Netherlands.

W.F.

ARMAN EN ILVA (Netherlands) The innovative science-fiction strip *Arman en Ilva* was created in 1969 by scriptwriter Lo Hartog van Banda and illustrated by artist The Tjong Khing. Hartog van Banda and Khing had previously collaborated on *Iris* (1968), which con-

ONZE AGENTE HELENE IS ONTIJDIG GELIKWIDEERD_ GA LIGGEN

"Arman en Ilva," The Tjong Khing. © Marten Toonder.

stituted an introduction to *Arman en Ilva*. Distributed by Marten Toonder Studio, the strip was widely published in daily newspapers all over Europe.

In an eerie and disturbing world of the future where wars between planets are continuous and existence a constant peril, the young Arman and his blonde girlfriend Ilva serve as troubleshooters for Earth. Along their way they meet mad potentates, crazed rulers, ruthless space pirates, and a slew of seductive secret agents of both sexes who invariably (but in vain) try to kill them when they cannot seduce them.

Banda's scripts—ambiguous, ironic, searching—were well served by Khing's unique style, a harmonious blend of action-packed composition and a decorative, sinuous Oriental line. The teamwork of Banda and Khing assured the success of *Arman en Ilva*, but early in 1975 it was learned that Khing had been replaced on the strip by Gerrit Stapel, a competent, but uninspired, draftsman. In his hands the strip did not survive the decade.

M.H.

ARRIOLA, GUS (1917-) With a Mexican rooster perched sadly on his oversized military cap, the lean, hungry-looking guy with curly black hair cradled a chihuahua against his chest with one arm, looked straight out of the comic strip panel at a million readers, and said a dolorous farewell to each and every one. Gustavo Montano Arriola, born in July 1917, was an eminently draftable 26 years old in the fall of 1942, and he had been tagged by Uncle Sam for immediate service. His new daily comic strip, *Gordo*, launched one year earlier, was being shot down in flames. Arriola had to put in his basic training, and there would be no time for strip work. So Arriola drew himself woefully engulfed in his new uniform in the last panel of an episode dated October 28, 1942—which would be the last panel of the daily *Gordo* for the duration—surrounded himself with the characters he had created over the two years of the new strip (from the sveltely plump Gordo himself and the bosomy Widow Gonzales to Gordo's elfin-eared nephew Pepito and the strange mountain of flesh called Goblin), blew a plume from

Gordo's cocked hat out of his way, and thanked his *nuestros buen amigos*, "each one," for their "eenterest," and promised to "be back real soon." He also sounded a topical note in knocking "that dorty jork—Heetler!!"

Arriola was speaking in the *patois* English of his characters—much subdued in later years—but what he said was correct. He was back "real soon," with a Sunday half page on May 2, 1943, never to leave the comic strip scene again. What the young draftee was doing, of course, was managing to do a weekly strip and his military duties as an animator in the air force. (After his discharge in 1946, he resumed the daily strip as well.) Circumstances were varied for strip artists drafted in wartime; Fred Lasswell, working on *Leatherneck Magazine*, managed to find the time to draw both the daily and Sunday *Barney Google*, for example. Arriola, however, was unique in World War II in closing down a major new strip completely until he was able to get it under way again.

Born in Arizona, Arriola moved to Los Angeles at an early age and grew up in the shadow of the great animation studios. From high school he moved into the MGM cartoon story department in the mid-1930s. Other animation work followed, and then Arriola sold the concept for *Gordo* to United Features in 1941. The local color and folk pageantry of Mexico had had very little exposure on the comic page, and it proved a natural for strip use as handled by the young artist. Moreover, Arriola drew funny; his character and situation ideas were fresh, and grew naturally out of the setting and populace of Mexico. Despite the wartime break in continuity, the strip's popularity mounted through the 1940s, until *Gordo* became one of the most widely published and read strips in the country. The author decided to retire in 1985.

A winner of numerous awards in his field, Arriola moved to the Monterey peninsula, where he periodically advertised (via the *Gordo* strip) his fabulous recipe for beans with cheese and pursued artistic interests beyond his strip work. He occasionally still departs for explorative trips into Mexico with his wife, Mary Frances, and son Carlin, where they presumably at least touch base with a drink at Pelon's before driving to Monterey or flying down to the Hotel of Parrots in Yucatan.

B.B.

ASHITA NO JOE (Japan) *Ashita no Joe* ("Joe Who Aims to Win Wonderful Tomorrow") was created by Asao Takamori (script) and Tetsuya Chiba (drawing) in January 1968 for the weekly magazine *Shōnen*.

The protagonist of the strip, Joe Yabuki, was a lonely boy in a strange land. One day Joe met former boxer Danpei Tange, and it changed his whole life. Tange trained Joe as a professional boxer, and the strip took a realistic and even naturalistic turn as it followed Joe's career. Unlike American boxing strip heroes, Joe did not always win and was even knocked out on occasion. But he doggedly fought on, finally meeting his old reformatory school rival, Tooru Rikiishi, who knocked Joe out after an especially vicious grudge fight. Rikiishi, however, died from the weight loss he had sustained in order to be able to meet Joe in his category. After Rikiishi's death, Joe went into a slump and lost his title to Tiger Ozaki.

Coming out of his depression, Joe started to fight again, winning match after match, until he got a chance to fight the world bantamweight champion Jose

"Ashita no Joe," Tetsuya Chiba. © Shōnen.

Mendoza. Mendoza proved too strong for Joe, who exhausted himself and died in the ring. Joe's death also signaled the end of the strip (May 1973).

Joe's popularity had been very great but was eclipsed by that of his hated rival Tooru Riikishi. After the latter's death, a farewell ceremony was held in his memory in the Kodansha boxing hall on March 24, 1970. A gong sounded the count of 10, after which a minute of silent prayer was observed. During the prayer people could be heard sobbing from all corners of the hall.

Ashita no Joe has also inspired a series of animated cartoons.

H.K.

ASPIRINO Y COLODION (Spain) Alfonso Figueras created *Aspirino y Colodion* on June 6, 1966, in issue 234 of the comic magazine *El Capitan Trueno*, from which it passed the next year to the weekly *DDT*.

With *Aspirino y Colodion* the author paid homage to the old comedies of the silent cinema and to the American humor strips of the 1920s, by successfully reconstructing a whole atmosphere long since lost, but not forgotten. The two protagonists are a pair of inventors: Aspirino, ancient and bearded, and Colodion, young and completely crazy. They both devote their time to inventing the most extravagant devices, and to complicating each other's life, in a constant struggle to top each other, with innocence on the part of the older savant, with sly goofiness on the part of the younger. They come up with the most outrageous inventions, to the great amazement of Adolfo, the guard who vainly tries to restore a little sanity into the relations between the crazy pair.

In this humor series falls and fights are rife, punctuated with onomatopoeias, and, when the two inventors get involved in one of their interminable quarrels, they disappear under clouds of smoke, re-creating the spirit, grace, and subtlety of such comic masterpieces

as *Krazy Kat* and *Happy Hooligan*. It is no longer being published, but the characters live on in reprints.

L.G.

ASSO DI PICCHE (Italy) The immediate postwar period saw a proliferation of Italian masked avengers dressed in close-fitting tights. One of those was Asso di Picche ("Ace of Spades"), whom his creator Hugo Pratt modeled after Eisner's *Spirit*. Written by Mario Faustinelli and published in the collection "Albi Uragano," *Asso di Picche* first appeared at the end of 1945.

The newsman Gary Peters is in actuality the "Ace of Spades," a mysterious justice-fighter and the nemesis of evildoers everywhere. Dressed in tights and a yellow cloak complete with his emblem, an ace of spades, the hero fights in the company of his fiancée, Deanna Farrel and his assistant, the Chinese Wang. The Ace of

"Asso di Picche," Hugo Pratt. © Editrice Sgt. Kirk.

Spades' most dangerous enemies were the Gang of the Panthers, and the Club of Five, a sinister organization plotting to take over all the world's resources. The Ace of Spades' last adventure, against an organization of Nazi criminals, was unfortunately interrupted by the disappearance of *Asso di Picche* in 1947.

The stories were well plotted and well written, with the emphasis more on suspense than violence. Hugo Pratt's style, still heavily influenced by the American comic strip and comic book artists, was to gradually come into his own, and foreshadows his later creations.

In addition to *Asso di Picche*, the "Albi Uragano" published many other comics in the three years of their existence and revealed to the public the talents of such authors as Alberto Ongaro, Dino Battaglia, Damiano Damiani, Giorgio Bellavitis, and Mario Leone.

Some of the adventures of the Ace of Spades were reprinted in 1967-69 in the monthlies *Sgt. Kirk* and *Asso di Picche*.

G.B.

ASTÉRIX (France) Created by René Goscinny (text) and Albert Uderzo (art), *Astérix le Gaulois* ("Asterix the Gaul") appeared for the first time in issue number one of the French comic weekly *Pilote* (October 29, 1959).

Astérix is a diminutive, moustached Gaul who lives in a little village in Armorique (the ancient name for Brittany), the last holdout in a country overrun by the Romans. Made invulnerable by the drinking of a magic potion concocted by the druid Panoramix, Astérix, helped by his loyal companion, the dim-witted but strong Obélix, and by his fellow villagers, is able to keep Julius Caesar's Roman legions at bay. (The Romans are invariably depicted as dumb, cowardly, rapacious, and gullible.)

Starting from this basic premise, the authors soon were enlarging on the theme by having the duo of Astérix and Obélix travel to Cleopatra's court, to the Olympic Games, and to Britain, without departing from the belief that everything is better, more beautiful and more rational in Gaul (i.e., France). The heroes' constant refrain: "Ils sont fous, ces Romains!" ("They're crazy, those Romans!"—or Britons, or Teutons, as the case may be) gives some indication of the author's smug assertion of xenophobic superiority.

There are a few good things in *Astérix* (the clever use of balloons, drawing that is clean and uncluttered, and some genuinely funny situations), but the basic plot is tiresome, and Goscinny's endless stream of bad puns and chauvinistic asides make this quite unpleasant as a strip. *Astérix* was incredibly popular in the France of the 1960s (at the height of de Gaulle's *politique de grandeur*), so much so that even the respected newsweekly *L'Express* had a cover story on the strip, but its decline in the 1970s was as precipitous as its rise had been meteoric. Following Goscinny's death in 1977, Uderzo continued to produce *Astérix* solo (averaging one adventure a year). He has toned down some of its more egregious faults, and the series, now published by the author under the Albert René imprint, remains extremely popular in France and in Europe to this day.

Astérix has been reprinted in book form by Dargaud, and the success of the books has also been phenomenal (although not in the United States, where they failed both as hardcover books and as paperbacks). Two feature-length animated cartoons, *Astérix le Gaulois* and *Astérix et Cléopatre*, were produced in the 1960s

"Astérix," René Goscinny and Albert Uderzo. © Editions Dargaud.

and early 1970s by Belvision. An Astérix theme park opened with great success near Paris in 1989.

M.H.

ATLAN (Germany) *Atlan* is to Perry Rhodan what Spock is to Captain Kirk. Yet, Atlan is not just another member of the cast of the *Perry* comic book or the *Perry Rhodan* novels; he is also the star of his own line of novels and for some time was the backup feature of *Perry Rhodan—Bild* (Numbers 1 to 27) and of *Perry* (Numbers 1 to 36). These stories gave the history of Atlan from around 8000 B.C. to his meeting with Perry Rhodan in 2040 A.D. Although interesting enough in plot, *Atlan* was not very artistically stimulating at the time. This was drastically changed when *Perry* expanded to 48 pages with No. 106, once again to share the spotlight with *Atlan* in his solo adventures. Now the visually pleasing artwork was done by Massimo Belardinelli from the Giolitti shop in Rome, Italy. Belardinelli, who also has drawn some of the backgrounds for Alberto Giolitti's artwork on *Turok Son of Stone* and *Star Trek*, did a magnificent job of putting the scripts of Dirk Hess into striking pictures. The fact that Belardinelli seems to favor the John Buscema style of drawing comics has no doubt helped the strip's popularity but accounts only for part of the feature's fascination.

Atlan, a native of the planet Arkon and admiral of the space fleet of Arkon, is stranded on Larsaf-III (Earth) when the Druuf, a fifth-dimensional warrior race, wipe out the Arkon colony on Atlantis. Atlan is given a cell activator by the Immortal of Wanderers to endow him with immortality. Seeking refuge in the only base left to him, a bubble-house on the bottom of the Atlantic Ocean, Atlan rests in suspended animation awaiting spaceships from Arkon or ventures forth to speed up the progress of humanity, the sooner to be able to leave Earth for his home planet. Thus he becomes witness to and aide in humanity's struggle from the Stone Age to modern civilization.

Time and again he is confronted by alien beings who are out to destroy or conquer humanity, yet Atlan always succeeds in averting disaster and in speeding up progress. Picking up ideas expounded by von Däniken, Charroux, et al., *Atlan* turns them into a kind of feasibly realistic "sword and sorcery" saga from Earth's past, with technological explanations for whatever "sorcery" occurs. The demise of the *Perry* comic book in 1975 also stopped the further exploits of *Atlan*.

W.F.

ATOM, THE (U.S.) National's original feature entitled *The Atom* was a long-lived but rather pedestrian strip created by artist Ben Flinton and writer B. O'Connor for October 1940's *All-American* number 19. Actually five-footer Al Pratt, The Atom, had an unusually powerful body and, as was the custom of the day, used it to fight crime. He donned his almost mandatory costume in his second appearance, and it was the most unique facet of the feature. It had short leather trunks, leather wrist bands, a blue mask and cape, and a yellow tunic open to the navel.

The story line was never particularly inventive, as the Atom spent most of his time beating up criminals startled by the great strength in his tiny body. Most of these macho scripts were written by O'Connor (until 1942) and Ted Udall (1942-1946). Artistically, Ben Flinton was sloppy and uneven, and he had an unfortunate "talent" for drawing incredibly ugly women. He handled the artwork until 1942, passing it on to the more competent Jon Kozlak (1946-1948) and Paul Reinman (1947-1949).

The Atom survived in *All-American* until April 1946's 72nd issue and appeared with the Justice Society in *All-Star* from Winter 1941's third issue to March 1951's 57th issue. The feature also made sporadic appearances in *Flash, Comic Cavalcade,* and several other titles.

National launched a second Atom character in October 1961's *Showcase* number 34. This Atom was scientist Ray Palmer, who, finding white dwarf star material, constructed a device that allowed him to change his size and alter his weight.

The stories—mostly by John Broome and Gardner Fox—concentrated on scientific plots and subplots. The writers concentrated heavily on the Atom's ability to transport himself through telephone lines. There were several well-received "time pool" stories, and Chronos, the strip's major villain, was also scientifically based. Almost all of the artwork was handled by penciller Gil Kane and inkers Side Greene and Joe Giella. Kane's artwork was tight and clean, just a notch below his stellar material for the *Green Lantern* strip.

The *Atom* feature got its own book in July 1962, and it lasted 39 issues before merging with *Hawkman* and then finally folding in November 1969. The character also appears regularly in the Justice League of America.

J.B.

In 1983 the Atom was brought back to comic books by Gil Kane and Jan Strnad in the *Sword of the Atom* miniseries. The character again came back in 1988 for a somewhat longer run in *Power of the Atom*, which lasted for 18 issues into 1989.

M.H.

AVENGERS, THE (U.S.) *The Avengers* was created by writer Stan Lee and artist Jack Kirby and made its first appearance in Marvel's *The Avengers* number one for September 1963. Originally consisting of Thor, Iron Man, The Wasp, The Hulk, and Ant-Man, there was almost immediate upheaval when The Hulk went his own way. But in the fourth issue, Captain America was revived and joined the group; for a long while, the newly revived Captain dominated the action. By the 16th issue, however, there were further upheavals: the remaining original members resigned and Captain America re-formed the group around Hawkeye, Quicksilver, and the Scarlet Witch. Over the years, there were more switches and identity changes, most often in Henry Pym, who was Ant-Man, then Giant-Man, then Goliath, then Yellowjacket.

Artistically, many fine illustrators handled the strip over the years. Jack Kirby produced the first eight issues and Don Heck drew the next few dozen, followed by John Buscema, Sal Buscema, Gene Colan, and Bob Brown. All did credible jobs, most notably John Buscema. Three writers have handled the bulk of *The Avengers* stories. Editor Lee handled almost all of the group's first three dozen issues; he was followed by Roy Thomas, who scripted 70 consecutive stories. Next, Steve Englehart took over as the writer.

Because of the large number of cast changes and frequent artist switches, the feature has gone through several different periods, many not resembling that which had gone before. However, the unquestionable peak of the series came with five 1972 issues. Written by Thomas, who had just become the book's editor, and drawn by Neal Adams, a long serial was started. Involving dozens of characters invented by Stan Lee over the years, Thomas consistently wrote top-notch stories with a most unusual sidebar: The Scarlet Witch had fallen in love with The Vision, a red-skinned humanoid, much to the chagrin of her brother, the quick-footed but slow-witted Quicksilver. Artist Adams' dazzling pencils and superb layouts are among the best work of his illustrious career.

J.B.

In the last 20 years the series has experienced a number of ups and downs, and its quality has varied widely, depending on the teams that were working on the title at the time. It fared best at the hands of John Byrne, Sal Buscema, and George Perez.

M.H.

AWAY, CAESAR *see* Caesar, Kurt.

AYERS, RICHARD (1924-) American comic book artist born in Ossining, New York, on April 28, 1924. After service in the Army Air Corps during World War II and attending the Cartoonists and Illustrators School, Dick Ayers began his comic book career in 1947 as the pencil artist on M.E. Comics' *Funnyman* feature. From that feature, the young Ayers worked on a number of diverse strips, including the comic book version of comedian Jimmy Durante. But his major work at M.E. was production of several Western features: the white-outfitted *Ghost Rider, Bobby Benson and the B-Bar-B Riders* and the *Calico Kid.* He also worked on one of the few important superhero strips of the 1950s, *The Avenger*, the first superhero feature initiated under the comics code. Ayers remained with M.E. until 1956, and during this time also drew for Charlton (1953-1955, humor strips), Prize (1951), and St. John (1956).

But the bulk of Ayers' comic book work came for the Timely/Atlas/Marvel group, which he joined in

1951 as an inker for the newly revived *Human Torch* strip. Most of his work with Marvel during the 1950s was done on Western material. Utilizing a clean and uncluttered style, which made him equally competent as a penciller or an inker, Ayers worked on such Marvel Westerns as *Rawhide Kid, Outlaw Kid, Wyatt Earp* and *Two-Gun Kid*. None of them were well written, but Ayers' art was always above average, especially for the often-inferior Atlas line.

When Marvel ushered in the Stan Lee-Jack Kirby "Marvel Age of Comics," Ayers worked on the whole range of creations. Over the years, he has pencilled and inked such diverse strips as *Captain America, Hulk, Combat Kelly, Rawhide Kid* (a revived and revised version of the earlier feature), and *Ka-Zar*. In addition, Marvel started a new *Ghost Rider* feature—one that bore only a superficial relation to M.E.'s earlier strip—and Ayers again handled the art. Undoubtedly, however, Ayers' best work in the 1960s came in conjunction with inker John Severin on the *Sgt. Fury*

war book. A title that alternately ranged from the sublime to the ridiculous—one month's release portrayed Fury as a torn-shirted superman seemingly impervious to harm and the next brought a superhuman, superfallible character—Ayers' and Severin's artwork was consistently top-notch. Both were masters at portraying some of the horrors and pain of war, something that was rare for comic books.

Ayers has made only one foray into syndicated strip art; in 1959 and 1960, he inked Jack Kirby and Wally Wood's *Skymasters* space feature.

J.B.

Ayers confirmed his position as the foremost Western artist with his illustrations for *Jonah Hex* in the early 1980s. He has also taught at the Joe Kubert School of Cartoon and Graphic Art and given classes at the Guggenheim Museum. After an absence of several years, he returned to comic books in 1996 with *Dr. Wonder*, a thriller.

M.H.

BABY SNOOKUMS   *see* Newlyweds, The.

BACKER, HENK (1898-1976)   Henk Backer, Dutch comic artist and illustrator, was born December 15, 1898, in Rotterdam. For five years he studied at the Academie voor Beeldende Kunsten en Technische Wetenschapen (Academy of Fine Arts and Technical Sciences). In 1921 it was he who started the tradition of Dutch comic strips.

Comic strips and picture stories had been well known in the Netherlands thanks to imported materials. The newspaper *De Telegraaf* published *Jopie Slim en Dikkie Bigmans* (an English import) when, in 1920, Backer offered them his services without success. Backer had more luck in 1921 when he offered his own strip to the *Rotterdamsch Nieuwsblad* ("Rotterdam News"). On April 1, 1921, Backer's first strip, *Yoebje en Achmed* ("Yoebje and Achmed"), appeared. The strip is generally considered to be the first Dutch comic strip, despite persistent rumors that there might have been earlier Dutch efforts to enter the comics field. Done in the European tradition of child-oriented comic strips, *Yoebje en Achmed* presented the narrative below the pictures. The second strip by the 22-year-old Backer started that same year in *Voorwaarts* ("Forward"), the Social Democratic party newspaper. The strip was called *Hansje Teddybeer en Mimie Poezekat* ("Johnny Teddybear and Mimi Pussycat"), and reprints in book form started appearing in 1922. While obviously written (by Jet van Strien) and drawn for juvenile readers, adults also enjoyed the strips.

After becoming staff artist for *Rotterdamsch Nieuwsblad* in 1923, it did not take long before Backer started a new comic strip, *Tripje en Liezebertha*. Backer continued doing this strip until he retired in December 1963. *Tripje en Liezebertha* charmed the public, and many persons stood in line to buy the first *Tripje* book published in 1924. The strip's popularity was used to endorse a number of products.

While continuing *Tripje en Liezebertha*, Henk Backer also did a number of other comic strips, such as *Adolphus* (in 1930), for *Rotterdamsch Nieuwsblad*. Henk Backer's seemingly simple style breathed an amazing life into dolls and toys, making for comic strips ideally suited for children while also charming the young-at-heart with their dreamy fantasies. He died in Eemness, the Netherlands, on June 5, 1976.

W.F.

BAKER, GEORGE (1915-1975)   Born in Lowell, Massachusetts, on May 22, 1915, George Baker, creator of the famed *Sad Sack,* was raised in a middle-class merchant's family, who moved to Chicago in time for Baker to attend Roosevelt High School before he took on the usual budding cartoonist's variety of jobs: truck driver, cleaner and dyer assistant, salesman, office clerk, etc. Finally he landed his first art job: drawing pots and pans for an advertising artist at $7.00 a week.

His cartooning ability improved, and in 1937 he contacted the Walt Disney Studios in Burbank for a job. Hired after he completed the usual Disney trial mail assignment, he left Chicago for good, taking the train to California and a career in animation.

After four years with Disney, he was inducted into the army in June 1941 and quickly developed—through experience—his basic concept of the browbeaten little infantry private he called the Sad Sack (based on the old army term for a worthless soldier: "a sad sack of s--t"). S. Sack, as Baker's hero dolefully signed himself, became an almost instant hit when his weekly, black-and-white strip adventures (related in double rows of unmargined panels) began to appear in *Yank,* the U.S. Army service magazine, in May 1942. (In fact, the *Sad Sack*—already a widely reprinted winner of a commercial contest for soldier cartoonists a few months earlier—was the first permanent feature selected for the still unpublished magazine in the spring of 1942.)

The Sack's fame ballooned; he shared G.I. pinup space beside Ann Sheridan and Betty Grable; he forced chuckles from second lieutenants and guffaws from generals; he was read by the hundreds of thousands of copies in his first book, *The Sad Sack,* a collection of the *Yank* strip episodes published by Simon & Schuster in 1944, and reprinted as an Army Overseas Edition; and finally he made the U.S. newspaper syndication scene when Consolidated News Features, Inc., began to circulate the *Yank* episodes as a limited daily series in February 1945.

Phased out in *Yank* by the end of the war in 1945, *The Sad Sack* was launched as a newspaper comic strip through Baker's own organization on May 5, 1946, becoming the basis for a movie starring Jerry Lewis in 1960 and the focus for a series of comic books that still appear (drawn by other hands). Baker, who had become a sergeant by the time of his army discharge, moved to Los Angeles in 1946 and formed Sad Sack, Inc., through which he merchandised Sad Sack artifacts

George Baker, "The Sad Sack." © *George Baker.*

of all kinds. Hospitalized at the Alhambra Medical Center on the campus of the University of California at Los Angeles for cancer, Baker died there on May 8, 1975, a few days short of his 60th birthday.

B.B.

BALD, KENNETH (1920-) American comic book and comic strip artist, born in 1920 in New York City. Kenneth (Ken) Bald graduated from Pratt Institute in New York and immediately started working in the comic book field. He was first with the Binder shop, then moved to the Beck-Costanza studio. His credits for this period (1941-43) include, either under his own name or under the pen name "K. Bruce": *Captain Marvel* and *Bulletman* for Fawcett; *Doc Strange* for Pines; *Doc Savage* for Street & Smith; *Black Owl* for Prize; and *Captain Battle* for Gleason.

In 1943 Bald was called to serve in the Marine Corps. He fought in New Guinea and New Britain and served as an intelligence officer in Okinawa and Peking before being discharged with the rank of captain in 1946.

Back in civilian life, Ken Bald resumed his career as an advertising and comic book artist, drawing romance comics for Marvel and doing illustration work. In 1957 King Features Syndicate asked him to draw the newly created *Judd Saxon*, about a young executive on his way up in the business world. In 1963 he abandoned *Saxon* to illustrate the comic strip version of *Dr. Kildare*, which was then a hit television series. In 1971, in addition to his work on *Kildare*, he took up the drawing of *Dark Shadows* (also based on a TV show), but the strip was dropped the following year. After *Dr. Kildare* was discontinued in 1984, he went into retirement in Florida, briefly resurfacing in 1996 to write the preface for the reprint book of *Dark Shadows* newspaper strips.

M.H.

"Una Ballata del Mare Salato," Hugo Pratt. © Editrice Sgt. Kirk.

BALLATA DEL MARE SALATO, UNA (Italy) Hugo Pratt's *Una Ballata del Mare Salato* ("A Ballad of the Salty Sea") made its appearance in the first issue (July 1967) of the comic monthly *Sgt. Kirk*. After *Sgt. Kirk* folded in 1970, the strip went on to *Il Corriere dei Piccoli*.

The story relates the adventures of two adolescents, Cain and Pandora, who are brother and sister searching for their father among the islands of the Pacific Ocean. The action takes place during World War I, and the two youngsters are confronted with German submarines, British spies, and, most dangerous of all, the dreaded old pirate Rasputin and the faceless "Monk." They also meet an enigmatic adventurer, Corto Maltese, who puts them under his protection. (Corto Maltese later became the hero of another of Pratt's comic creations.)

In a climate reminiscent of Robert Louis Stevenson's and Jack London's novels of the South Seas, Pratt succeeds in telling a superb story, at once dramatically gripping and visually exciting.

M.H.

"Banana Fish," Akimi Yoshida. © Akimi Yoshida.

BANANA FISH (Japan) Moving swiftly from the steamy jungles of Vietnam to the asphalt jungle of Manhattan, *Banana Fish* is one of the more entertaining thrillers to come out of the Japanese *manga* tradition. The work of Akimi Yoshida (a woman), it blends the conventional manga style with the West's more illustrative comic-book line. Taking as its starting point the words "banana fish" uttered by an American G.I. gone berserk, it centers on a conspiracy involving the Mafia, America's military establishment, and some of its political leaders, all related to a potent, mind-altering drug called banana fish.

The hero of the piece is a young street punk turned avenging angel who goes by the name of Ash Lynx. Spurred by the drug wars going on all around him and enraged by the fact that his brother (who happens to be the run-amok soldier we meet at the beginning of the tale) has been rendered useless by the drug, he takes on all comers, from a female Chinese gang leader to the homicidal head of the Corsican Mafia, Papa Dino (coincidentally his former homosexual lover). Ash Lynx is helped in his monumental task by a few honest New York City cops and by a young visitor from Japan named Eiji. The story takes place in a nightmarish New York, much inspired by Yoshida's repeated viewings of 1940s American *films noirs*; it is, as Fred Schodt notes in his study *Dreamland Japan*, "a hard-boiled action thriller filled with killings and blood."

Yoshida's blood-curdling saga (it runs to more than 3,000 pages) was serialized in (of all places) the girl's magazine *Shojo Comics* from 1985 to 1995. *Banana Fish* remains unpublished in the U.S., but excerpts have appeared in Europe.

M.H.

BANANA OIL (U.S.) Milt Gross's first really popular comic page feature, *Banana Oil*, began as a daily gag sequence of four panels in the *New York World* in late 1921. Not a strip, the feature had no continuing characters; its daily anecdotes were linked by the climactic, mocking cry of disbelief uttered by an observing figure in each: "Banana oil!" In a typical example, a timid little man is shown assiduously reading a text on jujitsu, which tells him of various simple systems of leverage that will render an opponent "helpless and entirely at your mercy." Immediately thereafter he is depicted cornered in an alley by an enormous holdup man brandishing a large gun. The little guy glances shrewdly at his encouraging text—and in the following panel is deep in his grave, from which a mournful but sarcastic "Banana oil!" is heard.

Picked up by a number of the more sophisticated metropolitan dailies around the country, *Banana Oil* was a popular hit, and the term itself moved into gen-

eral usage for the better part of the decade, dying in the 1920s, together with such other popular phrases of that epoch as "hootch," "flapper," and "bathtub gin." (Oddly, it remains unmentioned in the three volumes of H. L. Mencken's *American Language*.) A softcover book collection of *Banana Oil* appeared in the mid-1920s and went into several printings, while a number of lapel pins and other artifacts celebrated the phrase.

In 1926 *Banana Oil* became a Sunday feature, running as a four-panel gag across the top of the new Gross weekly strip, *Nize Baby*, while Gross undertook a new daily strip, *The Feitlebaum Family* (which became *Looy, Dot Dope* a few months later). Continuing in the top-strip position when the Sunday *Nize Baby* was replaced by *Count Screwloose of Tooloose* in early 1929, *Banana Oil* was finally dropped in 1930 when Gross left the *New York World*'s Press Publishing Company for King Features.

B.B.

BANCKS, JAMES CHARLES (1895-1952) Australian cartoonist, born in 1895 at Hornsby, New South Wales, the son of an Irish railway worker. On leaving school at the age of 14, he worked for a finance company as a clerk/office-boy/lift driver. Unhappy with the drudgery of his job, Jimmy Bancks decided to become an artist, and his first drawing was accepted by *The Arrow* in 1914. This encouraged Bancks to submit drawings to *The Bulletin*, which not only accepted them but also offered him a full-time job at $16 per week. He accepted the offer and remained with *The Bulletin* until 1922. During this period he took art lessons from Datillo Rubbo and Julian Ashton and began supplying freelance cartoons to the *Sydney Sunday Sun*. In 1921 the veteran editor Monty Grover suggested that Bancks draw a strip about the adventures of *Gladsome Gladys*, under the title of *Us Fellers*. It didn't take very long for Bancks to tire of *Gladys* and, in its place, to create a strip based on one of the minor characters, *Ginger Meggs*—which was to become Australia's best-known and most-loved comic strip.

"Banana Oil," Milt Gross. © Milt Gross.

Around 1923, Bancks created the first Australian daily strip, *The Blimps*, for the *Melbourne Sun*, but the strip was dropped when this paper was swallowed up in a Murdoch-Fink takeover in 1925. At the suggestion of Sir Keith Murdoch, Bancks drew a single daily panel called *Mr. Melbourne Day By Day*, for the *Melbourne Sun-Pictorial*, which ran for many years under the pens of Len Reynolds and Harry Mitchell.

Apart from writing the book for a musical comedy, *Blue Mountain Melody*, in 1934 and several newspaper columns in 1939, Bancks devoted most of his time to *Ginger Meggs*, which, as well as appearing all over Australia, had become the first Australian strip to be syndicated overseas and was appearing in England, France, South America, and the U.S. There was a large demand for *Ginger Meggs* material and merchandise. In 1924 the first colored annual was produced, and these volumes continued to be published annually for the next 35 years. There were *Ginger Meggs* dolls, badges, school blotters, calico wall decorations, and many other items. *Ginger* even became the subject of a stage play and a pantomime.

In February 1951 Bancks repudiated his $160 per week contract with Associated Newspapers Ltd. (*Sunday Sun*) on the grounds that they had violated his contract by failing to run *Ginger Meggs* on the front page of the comic section. The resultant Equity Court decision ruled in favor of Bancks and, as the result of a new contract with Consolidated Press Ltd., *Ginger Meggs* became a permanent feature on the front page of the comic section of the *Sunday Telegraph*.

Jimmy Bancks was noted for his kindness and good humor, as well as for the scholarship he established to assist young black-and-white artists to study overseas. While his drawing ability improved with maturity, his draftsmanship and fidelity of line never reached the same high level as many of his contemporaries—yet his humor and wit-without-cruelty placed him in a class of his own. His sudden death from a heart attack on July 1, 1952, left a void that has never been filled.

J.R.

BANDE DES PIEDS-NICKELES, LA see Pieds-Nickeles, Les.

BANGER, EDGAR HENRY (1897-1968) British cartoonist Edgar Henry Banger was born in Norwich, Norfolk, on February 27, 1897. His father ran a photographic studio and his uncle was an art teacher. He was educated at Cambridge House but had no formal art training. He drew sports cartoons for *Eastern Daily Press* before doing full-time freelance work in children's comics. His first strips were published in *Chips*, *Butterfly*, and *Comic Cuts* during 1926, and his first full page was a red/black serial *Tubby & Trot* on the back of *Crackers* in 1927. In 1933 he began contributing to the new group of weeklies published in Bath, edited by Louis Diamond, eventually becoming their top artist. For them he did *Rattler* (1933), *Dazzler* (1933), *Chuckler* (1934), *Target* (1935), *Rocket* (1935), *Sunshine* (1938), and *Bouncer* (1939). With their abrupt discontinuation, Banger joined D. C. Thomson and created the colored cover strip *Koko the Pup* for their new weekly *Magic* (July 22, 1939). When paper shortages finished this comic, he joined the new independent publisher Gerald G. Swan and created many characters in two-page and even four-page episodes, a departure from the traditional 6 to 12 panels that were the average for Brit-

ish strips. He also tried an adventure series, *Rockfist the Jungle Ruler* (1940), but was better with a touch of humor, as with his serial secret agent *Slicksure* (1940). When Swan changed format from comic book to "traditional" after the war, Banger drew strip covers for all titles and returned to his happiest style, the "nursery" comic, with *Kiddyfun* (1945). He remained outside Amalgamated Press for the rest of his career, working on J. B. Allen's *Sun* (1947), the *Fido* series (1950), and dozens of Paget titles, including one he drew entirely himself, *Surprise*. His last work was *Funny Folk of Meadow Bank*, detailed panels in color that filled the center spread of *Sunny Stories* (1955). Although he signed his strips "Bang," he pronounced his name "Bainjer." He died in 1968, aged 71.

His characters include: 1926: *Curly Crusoe*; *Willie Write*; *Enoch Hard*. 1927: *Boney & Stoney*; *Dinah Mite*; *Cheekichap the Jap*. 1929: *Diary of a Bad Boy*. 1930: *Stanley the Station Master*. 1931: *Oggle & Woggle*; *Bob Stay*. 1932: *All Sorts Stores*. 1933: *Teddy Turner & his Television*; *Percival the Perky Page*. 1934: *Jimbo the Jungle Boy*. 1935: *Dudley Dudd the Dud Detective*; *Boney Prince Charlie*. 1936: *Freddie & His Flying Flea*. 1937: *Sandy Cove*. 1938: *Fatty Fitt*. 1939: *Sheriff Sockeye*. 1940: *All at Sea*; *Coal Black Jones*; *Exploring*; *Over There*; *Baffels*; *Stoogie*; *Chubb & Tubb*; *Tornado Tom*. 1945: *Lollipop Gnomes*; *Kiddyfun Circus*. 1946: *Tip & Topper*. 1947: *Addy*. 1948: *Rollicking Ranch*. 1950: *Tropical Tricks*. 1951: *Wanda the Wonder Girl*. 1955: *Funny Folk of Meadow Bank*.

D.G.

BARA see Herzog, Guy.

"Barbarella," J. C. Forest. © J. C. Forest.

BARBARELLA (France) Jean-Claude Forest created *Barbarella* for the French *V-Magazine* in 1962. This tale of a scantily dressed (when dressed at all), sex-loving blonde astronaut met with instant success (as well as with the ire of the French authorities, who banned the book version). Of this same book version the reviewer for *Newsweek* was later to write: "Cruising among the planets like a female James Bond, Barbarella vanquishes evil and rewards, in her own particular way, all the handsome men she meets in outer space. And whether she is tussling with Strikno the sadistic hunter or turning her ray gun on weird, gelatinous monsters, she just cannot seem to avoid losing part or all of her skin-tight space suit.''

The ballyhoo generated by *Barbarella* should not obscure its merits. The first outstanding space-heroine of the comics since Godwin's Connie, Barbarella went through a string of harrowing adventures, from her sexual encounters with assorted weirdos (including a robot) to her explorations of bizarre worlds, all of them told with tongue-in-cheek relish by J. C. Forest. Forest's line is elegant, perhaps too elegant, and somewhat brittle, but he remains a master at the evocation of disquieting places (the city of Sogo, for instance) and of haunting faces (Barbarella herself, the Black Queen.)

As mentioned above, *Barbarella* was reprinted in book form, by the French publisher Eric Losfeld, in 1964. In turn, the book was translated into an American version by Grove Press in 1966. In 1968 Roger Vadim directed a screen adaptation of *Barbarella* with Jane Fonda in the title role. Following the release of the movie, Forest tried unsuccessfully to revive *Barbarella* several times (in France in 1969, in Italy in 1970). In 1981 Barbarella made a comeback of sorts in the pages of the humor monthly *L'Echo des Savanes*; in this episode Forest wrote only the script, leaving the drawing to Daniel Billon. It did not meet with great success, and the liberated heroine has not been heard from since that time.

M.H.

BARBIERI, RENZO (1940-   ) Italian writer, editor, and publisher, born March 10, 1940, in Milan. Renzo Barbieri decided on a writing career very early in life: at the age of 15 he had his first story, "La Perla Nera" ("The Black Pearl"), published in the *Dick Fulmine* comic book. Then for Dardo he wrote a number of Western stories, which were published in the comic books *Ranch* and *El Coyote*. He also assumed the writing of the successful strips *Nat del Santa Cruz*, *Sciuscia*, and *Il Piccolo Sceriffo* ("The Little Sheriff"), created by Tristano Torelli and continued by Bubi Torelli and Giacomo Dalmasso. For the Genoan publisher De Leo, Barbieri authored a number of stories published in the monthly *Avventure Western* and other publications.

Barbieri's first novel, *Vitellini in Citta*, was published in 1954 by Maccari. From 1956 to 1966 he wrote short stories for the magazine *La Notte* while continuing his collaboration with a number of Milanese publishers. Then, for Dardo, he wrote the scripts for a number of comic books: *Tornado*, drawn by Giuseppe Montanari; *Billy Rock*, by Sandro Angiolini; and *Timber Jack*, by Pietro Gamba.

Meanwhile, in partnership with Gino Casarotti, Barbieri had founded his own publishing house, Edizioni del Vascello, but his attempt was unsuccessful; some time later he tried again with Editrice Sessantassei, specializing in comics for adults. His first creations were *Isabella* and *Goldrake*, drawn by Sandro Angiolini and Giuseppe Montanari, and both were huge popular successes. A year later, in 1967, he took a partner and changed the name to Edizioni RG, while substantially adding to the two previous collections. In 1972 he left RG, and during the next year he established Edifumetto and GEIS, two publishing firms. One specializes in comics for adults, the other in comics for children, thus covering the whole spectrum. For his adult publications, Barbieri wrote racy adaptations of famous fairy tales, the best of these being *Biancaneve* ("Snow White"), drawn by Leone Frollo.

In addition to his involvement in comics, Renzo Barbieri has written regularly for the fiction page of the *Corriere d'Informazione* and is the author of 10 published novels. He is still active in both fields, although his output has somewhat diminished.

G.B.

BARKS, CARL (1901-   ) Long the anonymous artist and author of the *Donald Duck* pages in *Walt Disney's Comics and Stories* (between April 1943 and March 1965), and creator of the renowned Uncle Scrooge McDuck, Carl Barks was born in 1901 in Oregon. Randomly educated, he held a variety of jobs, from cowboy to logger, steelworker to carpenter, until he decided to make use of his long-noticeable ability as a cartoonist to freelance in that area. After six years of this, he signed on as an apprentice animator at the Walt Disney Studios in Burbank in the mid-1930s, shortly after Donald Duck himself had gained public prominence through his animated cartoon success. After six months in animation, Barks was transferred to the studio story department, where he sketched in panel outline narrative ideas for the animated cartoons. He had the good luck to be assigned to outline the story for a projected Donald Duck feature-length movie in the late 1930s, to be called *Donald Duck Finds Pirate Gold* (or possibly just *Pirate Gold*). Knocked out of the running by the spectacular success of *Snow White* and *Pinocchio* (which turned Disney's fancy to other prepublished film sources at the time), the Donald feature was salvaged in part by being utilized as the basis for a one-shot, 64-page comic book printed by Dell Publishing Co., Disney's non-newspaper comic strip outlet. Drawn by Barks and a Disney artist named Jack Hannah (each doing successive pages), the *Donald Duck Finds Pirate Gold* comic book of 1942 was a considerable success—so much so that when Barks left the Disney studios in late 1942, tired of studio pressure and routine, he was made an offer by Dell (also known as Western Publishing Co., and K. K. Publications) to draw an original *Donald Duck* feature story in strip form for *Walt Disney Comics and Stories*.

Prior to 1943, the bulk of the *WDC&S* content had consisted of reprinted newspaper comic strips featuring Mickey Mouse, Donald Duck, and other Disney characters. Now these were running short, and the editorial decision was made to fill the pages with original stories and art. Accordingly, Barks was given story control of his continuing *Donald Duck* feature and 10 pages of six panels each per monthly issue. At about the same time, Barks was asked to do another *Donald Duck* 64-page one-shot for 1943, this one to be entirely Barks' work. Called *Donald Duck and the Mummy's Ring*, this work convinced Barks' Dell bosses that they had a considerable talent on their hands. So did the reader response to the *Mummy's Ring* issue and the *Donald Duck* strips in the monthly magazine.

Barks' assignments mounted through the years, until he was doing a number of complete magazine stories and lead stories for Disney character books together with his monthly *Donald* stint every year. In December 1947, he capped his previous success by inventing Uncle Scrooge McDuck, as a character in a *Donald Duck* feature magazine entitled *Christmas on Bear Mountain*. Scrooge was reintroduced as a regular character in Barks' *Donald Duck* work, and in March 1952 he appeared as the lead character in his own feature magazine: Uncle Scrooge in *Only a Poor Old Duck*. From then until his retirement from active drawing in 1965, Barks' Duck comic work won thousands of devoted fans, who finally ferreted out his identity from Disney studio and Dell publishing secrecy (their policy was to use only the Disney name for all published material featuring Disney characters) and bombarded him with appreciative letters. In response to this acclaim, Barks began to produce a series of remarkable oil paintings for his fans, based on familiar scenes and covers from his Dell Duck artwork of the past. At the same time, repeated pleas from Dell persuaded Barks to write scripts for other artists on the magazine staff, a task he gave up in 1973 to devote himself to personal pursuits and art interests.

He retired to Goleta, California, not far from the sea upon which he once sent Donald Duck in high adventure, and from which he received such deserved critical and popular success.

B.B.

Barks came out of retirement in the mid-1970s at the urging of his many admirers. In the last 20 years he has been turning out numerous paintings based on his comic-book covers and has even written and/or drawn an original story or two for the anthologies of his work that have kept appearing since that time.

M.H.

"Barnaby." Crockett Johnson (David Leisk). © Crockett Johnson.

BARNABY (U.S.) *Barnaby* was created by Crockett Johnson (David Johnson Leisk) for Marshall Field's experimental New York newspaper *PM*. After the strip's debut in April 1942, Field's Chicago Sun-Times Syndicate distributed the strip.

Carl Barks. "Uncle Scrooge." © Walt Disney Productions.

Barnaby is a youngster graced with a fairy godfather, but the makings of a cute nursery tale are irretrievably shattered as the character of the fairy godfather manifests himself. Mr. O'Malley is, simply, a cross between Little Nemo's Flip and W. C. Fields; even on the rare occasions when he makes a concerted effort to work his magic for good (instead of good mischief), he leaves an incredible wake of disaster, confusion, and trouble—all from which he walks away contentedly, usually benignly lecturing Barnaby on a totally unrelated and often irrelevant subject.

The boy is a blonde towhead who manages to elude the frustrations of living neither in the real, nor in the fairy, world totally. He can, on the one hand, befuddle gangsters, but he can never convince his perplexed parents that Mr. O'Malley really does exist. There are many times when a meeting almost takes place, but O'Malley inevitably and absentmindedly misses each opportunity.

Also in the strip are Barnaby's parents, the Baxters, who can never fully resign themselves to the fact that their son lives matter-of-factly in the fairy world, and so seek counsel with an endless string of child psychologists. Aunt Minerva is a brief visitor who readily believes in Barnaby's friends. Those friends include a sandman who always sleeps late; Gus the Ghost, afraid of his own shadow; Davy Jones, a nautical shade in 1890's bathing suit; and Gorgon, the talking dog.

Barnaby was an instant hit in critical terms, but it never enjoyed widespread sales. It shared the fate of other intellectual-appeal strips—it was cherished by an influential and loyal few.

Johnson's emphasis in the strip was clearly literary rather than artistic, and shortly before his death he listed to this author his major inspirations and influences: Robert Benchley, Dorothy Parker, Donald Ogden Stewart, Max Beerbohm, the old *Life* magazine, the *New Yorker* humorists, and films such as those of Frank Capra. He admitted to no special fondness for any other comic strip in his life.

His concern with *Barnaby* was to "tell a rather brighter story"; and to further his zany but reserved stories he decided to typeset the lettering "to allow for 60 per cent more words." The neat machine lettering fit in well with the stark, simple, unshaded drawing of the strip. The virtual lack of action accentuated its literary emphasis.

In spite of the critical acclaim and the artistic success of *Barnaby*, a waning concentration and other interests led Johnson to turn the strip over to others in late 1946. Jack Morley, a commercial artist, copied Johnson's style closely, and Ted Ferro, a writer for radio's comic soap opera *Lorenzo Jones*, were able to approximate the flavor of the feature until its demise in 1952 (when Johnson returned to write the concluding continuity).

In mid-passage *Barnaby* shifted syndicates from the Sun-Times to Bell. Henry Holt published two books—*Barnaby* and *Barnaby and Mr. O'Malley*—the first of which has been reprinted by Dover. An ill-fated attempt by Johnson and the Hall Syndicate in 1962 to revive *Barnaby* with the same characters and even the same early sequences (the Hot Coffee Ring was updated to the Hot Credit Card Ring) was a disappointment. Peter Wells worked on the art, but the project died after a few episodes. (Also short-lived was a *Barnaby* Sunday page around 1950.)

In spite of the troubles incumbent upon any effort that avoids broad appeal in strips, *Barnaby* was an artistic masterpiece. It contained some of the cleverest and most literate writing in comics and was extremely engaging. In the best tradition of comics since Opper, Johnson created a clever situation—a device, a basic conflict—and worked variations upon it. His characters were real, his humor very much in the tradition of his idols Benchley and Capra: zany but never out of hand, broad but always sophisticated. This experimental presentation was so unique and appropriate that it has never been employed since by any other artist.

Minor merchandising ventures included Mr. O'Malley dolls and a television cartoon. Johnson maintained that the best of the *Barnaby* strips never saw light of re-publication; the "lost" strips are surely classics of strip art that fans can look forward to with anticipation.

R.M.

"Barney Baxter," Frank Miller. © King Features Syndicate.

BARNEY BAXTER (U.S.) Frank Miller's *Barney Baxter in the Air* (later *Barney Baxter*) appeared as a daily strip on December 17, 1936, followed by a Sunday version on February 21, 1937. The feature was distributed by King Features Syndicate. (A local version of the strip had been running in a Denver newspaper since 1935.)

Barney Baxter represented the quintessence of the pilot-turned-adventurer in the tradition of the thirties—clean-cut, fair-haired, and freckle-faced, he was forever ready to hop into his plane and answer the latest call of adventure. Thus we find him successively fighting kidnappers in North America, rescuing the heir to the throne of Bronzonia from the clutches of foreign agents, and helping the police capture a gang of bank robbers. In the course of a forced landing in Alaska he meets Gopher Gus, a grizzled gold prospector who will become his trusted assistant and the strip's comic relief. Together they go adventuring to the far corners of the earth, leaving behind Barney's long-suffering sweetheart Maura.

With the coming of World War II Barney and Gus enlist in the RAF, later transferring to the U.S. Air Force. In 1942 they bomb Tokyo, just days ahead of General Doolittle. By the end of 1942, Miller having enlisted in the Coast Guard, *Barney Baxter* passed into the hands of Bob Naylor, who turned the strip into one of the most racially stereotyped of the war comics: yellow-skinned, fang-toothed Japanese were forever torturing war prisoners and blonde, white-skinned female civilians while shouting "Banzai!" By 1948 the strip's appeal had declined so severely that Frank Miller was called back to salvage it. In a misguided attempt to bring it up to date, Miller tried to turn *Barney Baxter* into a science-fiction strip, but he did not succeed and the strip folded in January 1950.

While it never had the quality of *Scorchy Smith* or the renown of *Tailspin Tommy*, *Barney Baxter* was still one of the more interesting aviation strips of the 1930s and 1940s, because of solid draftmanship and the flair for accurate detail.

M.H.

BARNEY GOOGLE (U.S.) *Barney Google* was born of a love affair between Billy De Beck and the American sporting scene. Originally, Barney had nothing to do with sports, or even the name he later made famous. He emerged out of De Beck's inkwell as one of several harassed spouses featured in a daily and Sunday strip De Beck was doing for the *Chicago Herald* in 1916. Called *Married Life*, this feature, without continuity or even regular characters, focused on the bickering between men and their wives. But one lean, cadaverous figure appeared more often than any other. With his bulbous nose and bushy moustache, he went under a number of names at first, such as Willis and Thomas (never a last name); finally he came to be called Aleck. His wife, whose physical appearance changed frequently, had no permanent name before Pauline was casually used in 1917. By this time, De Beck had dropped the other married couples to concentrate on Aleck and Pauline, and *Married Life* acquired a fairly large syndicated following.

When the *Herald* was sold to Hearst in 1918, De Beck and *Married Life* went along. But De Beck gained an additional plum: the new *Herald-Examiner* sports page, where his first sports cartoon appeared on May 7, 1918. *Married Life* continued to run on the *H-E* comic page every day, but it was plain that De Beck's heart was in his sports work. His cartoons here for the next year are graphically and humorously among the finest sports cartoons of all time. *Married Life* was finally dropped, with the last episode appearing March 13, 1919. De Beck's sports work continued for a few more months and then—on the *Herald-Examiner* sports page for June 17, 1919—the first daily sequence of a strip called *Take Barney Google, For Instance* appeared.

Changed the following week to *Take Barney Google, F'Instance*, the new strip featured the old Aleck of *Married Life* under the Google moniker; married to a woman markedly different from the Pauline of *ML*, and named Lizzie; and with a daughter named Gwennie. The theme was entirely sports-oriented. Barney was almost totally uninterested in family life, spending most of his time around prize fighters, race track touts, horses, baseball diamonds, et al. Still tall and lean, Barney was carefully shortened by three feet over two years as De Beck began to develop the comic potential in his new character. At the same time, his wife's stature increased, until by 1920 she was literally the "wife three times his size" of the Billy Rose "Barney Google" song. At this time Barney devoted all his interest to a racehorse named Spark Plug (carefully draped with a blanket so his knock knees wouldn't show), and lost his unhappy home. Although Barney's wife, the "Sweet Woman," took him back more than once afterward, De Beck's pint-sized hero was never again to know routine domestic horror; he had taken his horse to the road forever, to become the comic strip's first picaresque figure.

Barney's popularity increased in the 1920s. The public was delighted by the exploits of the feisty, top-hatted little guy—especially the readers of the nation's sports pages, where *Barney* usually ran, and was quite different than the standard comic page fare. Over the next 15 years, Barney won and lost fortune after fortune (and Sparky himself); tried other horses (Pony Boy, etc.); raced an ostrich named Rudy; managed a prizefighter named Sully; wooed heiress after heiress; became involved in murders, hijackings, flagpole-sitting, rum-running, secret societies, and opportunistic trips to Cuba and Europe; and finally undertook a flight from the law deep into the Kentucky woods in 1934, which introduced readers to Snuffy and Lowizie Smith (or Smif) and effectively closed Barney's stage-center career on the comic page.

Snuffy, originally somewhat more rambunctious and obnoxious than the milder fellow of Fred Lasswell's present-day strip, captivated the public as much as Barney had done a decade earlier, running away with the strip and De Beck until his hitch in the service during World War II (he was one of the first comic characters in uniform). In 1942 De Beck died, and assistant Fred Lasswell took over the strip. Barney was eventually reduced to the status of a visitor to Snuffy's hill home, and this is how he appears in the strip today. Spark Plug is gone, with Sully, Rudy, and the rest, although all are unforgettable and unforgettable.

In the 1920s Barney Google was the subject of a hit song, "Barney Google with the Goo-Goo-Googly Eyes" by Billy Rose and Con Conrad, and the hero of a series of movie shorts. In the 1960s he was adapted to the television screen in animated form.

B.B.

"Barney Google," Billy DeBeck. © *King Features Syndicate.*

Dan Barry, "Flash Gordon." © King Features Syndication.

Lasswell has successfully continued the strip (now officially called *Barney Google and Snuffy Smith*) to this day, adding new characters such as Little Tater, Elviney, Lukey, and the hound dog Ol' Bullet along the way. A *Barney Google and Snuffy Smith* anthology was published in 1995 by Comicana Books and Kitchen Sink.

M.H.

BARRY, DANIEL (1923-1997) American comic strip and comic book artist, born July 11, 1923, in Long Branch, New Jersey. Daniel (Dan) Barry attended Textile High School and the American Artists' School, where he studied under Ralph Soyer and Osato Kuniyushi.

In 1941 Dan Barry met cartoonist George Mandel, who started him on a comic book career. Among other features, Barry drew *Airboy* for Hillman, *Blue Bolt* for Novelty, and *Doc Savage* for Pines; he also wrote some of the *Blue Beetle* stories for Holyoke. In 1943 he was drafted into the air force, and while on duty did *Bombrack*, a comic strip for the 20th Air Force magazine. He was discharged in 1946. Barry immediately resumed his comic book career, freelancing for Fawcett (*Commando Yank, Captain Midnight*), Gleason (*Daredevil, Crimebuster*), Hillman (*The Heap*), Marvel, and National, among others. At the same time he did advertising work, and in 1947-48 he drew the *Tarzan* daily strip.

In 1951 he was asked by King Features Syndicate to revive the *Flash Gordon* daily strip (after a seven-year hiatus). At the end of 1967, following Mac Raboy's death, he took over the *Flash Gordon* Sunday strip, leaving the dailies to his former assistant Ric Estrada. He left *Flash Gordon* entirely in 1990. Afterward he worked mainly in comic books; his contributions to the many *Indiana Jones* titles published by Dark Horse were particularly notable. He died in late January 1997.

Dan Barry was a versatile artist who, in addition to his work in the comics, had exhibitions of his paintings both in the United States and abroad. A depend-able artist, smooth and polished, he seemed to lack the spark of true creativity, however.

M.H.

BARRY, LYNDA JEAN (1956-   ) A cartoonist who has helped broaden and deepen the range of comic art, Lynda Barry brings to her work a unique vision. The trenchant blend of pathos and humor in her *Ernie Pook's Comeek*, exploring, as she has written, "the torments, dreams, and awakenings of childhood," has been described in the *Washington Post Book World* as "almost literature—literature that culminates in an unbearably poignant insight."

Raised in Richland Center, Wisconsin, in a racially mixed working-class neighborhood, Barry grew up with a sense of social disorientation, which provided a rich source for her creative work. From 1974 to 1978 she studied art at the progressive Evergreen State College in Olympia, Washington, where she began drawing a strip entitled *Spinal Comics*, which depicted men as horny cacti in pursuit of women. Published in the school newspaper, which was edited by her schoolmate Matt Groening, of *Life in Hell* and *The Simpsons* fame, the strip went on to appear in other college and alternative newspapers for several years.

A technically accomplished artist, Barry supported herself as a painter and illustrator after her graduation from college, winning a Seattle Design and Advertising Silver Award for illustration in 1985, while continuing to draw cartoons. In 1980 a mention of her work in an article written by Groening brought her to the attention of the editor of the alternative weekly newspaper *The Chicago Reader*, who offered her a slot for a strip then called *Girls & Boys*. A collection, *Girls & Boys*, was later published in Seattle.

As Barry's strip, renamed *Ernie Pook's Comeek* in 1984, appeared in an increasing number of papers (winning an Excellence in Journalism Award for Cartooning in 1986 and published in more than 60 weekly papers by 1990), it broadened its cast of characters and the range of painful topics it addressed, incorporating parental infidelity, romantic betrayal, homosexuality,

Lynda Barry, "Boys and Girls." © Lynda Barry.

and teenage drug addiction, alcohol abuse, and sex into its ongoing story. Published collections include *Big Ideas* (1983), *Everything in the World* (1986), *The Fun House* (1987), *Down the Street* (1988), *Come Over, Come Over* (1990), and *My Perfect Life* (1992).

In 1984 Barry created a coloring book of female nudes accompanied by a text in which an adolescent girl bitterly examines the impossible male ideal of female beauty; entitled *Naked Ladies! Naked Ladies! Naked Ladies!*, it enraged both puritans and feminists but found a large audience. Barry's novel *The Good Times Are Killing Me*, published in 1988, dealt movingly with the problems of teenage friendship between races and brought its author a new and larger audience. Described in the *New York Times* as "a funny, intricate and finally heartbreaking story [that] exquisitely captures an American childhood," it became a play that ran successfully in Chicago and New York.

Fame as a novelist, playwright, and National Public Radio commentator has not diminished Barry's reputation as a cartoonist. Drawn in a deliberately crude style befitting its adolescent narrative voice, *Ernie Pook's Comeek* enjoys popularity among the adult as well as adolescent audiences.

D.W.

BARRY McKENZIE (G.B.) This strip is the modern version of the innocent abroad, Australian style. Barry McKenzie, broad-beamed and broad-brimmed Australian from the outback, arrived in London in 1967 as a two-bank strip in the weekly satirical paper *Private Eye*. The strip, written by Australian comedian and female impersonator Barry Humphries, is seen by some as a modern *Pilgrim's Progress* of Swiftian satire and venom; others see it as crudely drawn and worthless. (The artist is Nicholas Garland.) Barry McKenzie's attitude may be gauged by his cover comment on the first collection of his strips published in paperback: "Jeez! If you poor old Poms read this you'll flaming well read anything!" The book contains a useful dictionary of Australian

slang terms as used in the strip, *Glossary of McKenzie-isms*. This includes such classics as "Technical or Yawn" (one of 10 terms for being sick) and "Point Percy at the Porcelain" (translated as "to drain the dragon"). The first book, *The Wonderful World of Barry McKenzie* (1968), was followed by *Bazza Pulls It Off* (1972), and the strip was turned into a feature film *The Adventures of Barry McKenzie* (1972). Humphries scripted and also played Barry's aunt, Edna Everidge, and Barry Crocker played Barry McKenzie. The anti-hero still pursues his raucous adventures to this day.

D.G.

BARRY, SEYMOUR (1928-) American artist and brother of Dan Barry, born March 12, 1928, in New York City. Seymour (Sy) Barry studied at New York's School of Art and Design and upon graduation went to the Art Students League while working as an assistant to his brother Dan.

In the late 1940s and early 1950s Sy Barry freelanced, mainly as an inker, for such comic book companies as Gleason, Marvel, and especially National, where he worked on such features as *Johnny Peril, Rex,* and *Phantom Stranger*. He also did commercial illustrations for various companies and dabbled in watercolors. In the late 1950s he again assisted his brother with the inking of *Flash Gordon*. This put him in contact with the King Features editors, who asked him to take over *The Phantom* after Wilson McCoy's death in 1961. After drawing the adventures of the Ghost-Who-Walks for over 30 years—longer than any other artist—he retired in 1995.

Sy Barry has a clean, flowing line and a flair for composition, and his work on *The Phantom* has earned him much praise.

M.H.

BATEMAN, HENRY MAYO (1887-1970) British cartoonist, caricaturist, and illustrator, Henry Mayo Bateman was born in Australia on February 15, 1887. Brought to England almost immediately, he was educated at Forest Hill House, studying art at Westminster and New Cross Art Schools under Frederick Marriot, and in the studio of Dutch painter Charles Van Havenmaet.

Of a humorous bent, he "studied" comic drawing by copying from *Comic Cuts* and *Ally Sloper's Half-Holiday*, and sold his first cartoon to *Scraps* at age 16 (1903). He graduated to *The Tatler* the following year, then moved to *Punch*. Influenced by the clean lines of Phil May and Tom Browne and the purely visual strip cartoons of the Frenchman Caran d'Ache, Bateman evolved a totally new style in 1911. "Going mad on paper," he called it, drawing people as they felt, rather than as they looked. Thus, the embarrassment in his famous cartoon *The Guardsman Who Dropped It on Parade* was the ultimate of embarrassment, and the behavior of *The Boy Who Breathed on the Glass at the British Museum* (1916), wherein a breath led to arrest, trial, jail, and a defiant last, aged gasp upon the sacred glass, was the ultimate in revenge. This strip took 31 pictures to tell. It was something completely new to English magazines, and old volumes of *Punch* spring to life as his spreads come into view—the day in the life of *The One Note Man* that takes 58 pictures to tell; the 48 pictures that illustrate the tragedy of *The Plumber*; then, in contrast, great double-page spreads in full color for some single

Henry M. Bateman, "The Men Who Broke the Tube." © H. M. Bateman.

moment of life, such as *The Man Who Dared to Feel Seasick on the Queen Mary.*

Bateman died in February 1970, fortunately living to see, and contributing a lively sketch to, Michael Bateman's book celebrating his work, *The Man Who Drew the 20th Century* (1969). Bateman's own collected works and books include: *A Book of Drawings* (1921); *More Drawings*; *A Mixture*; *Rebound*; *Brought Forward*; *Burlesques*; *Colonels*; *Suburbia Caricatured*; *Adventures at Golf*; *Considered Trifles*; *Himself* (1937); and *The Evening Rise* (1960).

D.G.

"Batman," Bob Kane. © National Periodical Publications.

BATMAN (U.S.) When National Comics realized their success with *Superman*, editor Whitney Ellsworth

assigned artist Bob Kane to create a new hero. Working with writer Bill Finger, Kane created *Batman* for the May 1939 issue of *Detective Comics* number 27. Unlike his predecessor, The Batman had no super powers—he was just a normal human being with a keen mind and strong body. He traveled the alleys of Gotham City by night, striking fear into the hearts of criminals with his unique, batlike cape and cowl. In his civilian identity, The Batman was millionaire Bruce Wayne, who, as a child, vowed revenge on all criminals because of the murder of his parents. Wayne soon took a ward, Robin, The Boy Wonder, a young circus performer named Dick Grayson who was also orphaned.

The earliest *Batman* stories were among the most unique in comics. The Batman was portrayed as a relentless manhunter dedicated to the eradication of crime. He would play on criminals' fear of the night and exploit his batlike appearance. He could be vicious—he shot more than one man—and his amazing abilities overwhelmed the common hoodlum. In short, The Batman was an avenging vigilante. He was never depicted as the *bon vivant*, talk-of-the-party crime fighter; rather, the early *Batman* strips presented him as a slightly unsavory character.

This dark, mysterious mood was greatly cultivated and well portrayed in the 1940s and early 1950s. The writing was handled by top-notch scripters like Gardner Fox, Jack Schiff, Bill Woolfolk, Otto Binder, and especially Bill Finger. Artistically, the bulk of the stories fell to Bob Kane's assistant, Jerry Robinson. His version quickly became definitive and the character soon began to appear in a variety of National books, including *World's Finest*, *All Star*, *Batman*, and others. This early *Batman* also produced some of comicdom's most remembered villains. First and foremost, there was Robinson's pasty-faced Joker, the homicidal "clown prince of crime." Also in the parade of unique, inventive adversaries were The Penguin, an overstuffed, umbrella-toting snob; The Riddler, a crazed criminal who gave clues before he attacked; the murderous Two-Face, an insane former district attorney with a deformed visage; The Catwoman, a feline lover who fell in love with The Batman; The Scarecrow, a schoolteacher gone mad; and the incomparable Tweedledee and Tweedledum, two emigrants from Lewis Carroll's *Alice in Wonderland*.

But during the mid-1950s, many of the original creators left the strip, and this ushered in a low point in the *Batman* feature. Saddled with new and outlandish characters like Bathound, Batwoman, Batgirl, and Bat-Mite, and crippled by poor science-fiction scripts about monsters, robots, aliens, time travel, and crackpots, *Batman* quickly slumped in sales and popularity. In 1964, however, editor Julius Schwartz and artists Carmine Infantino and Murphy Anderson concocted The Batman's "New Look." The change in art style and the new, more detective-oriented editorial direction returned much of the character's flavor. By 1966, however, the *Batman* television program brought in a new series of changes, all of them "campy" and in complete disregard of the character's former traits. The camp look disappeared by 1970, and artists like Frank Robbins, Neal Adams, Jim Aparo, and Walt Simonson provided interesting new variations on the "Dynamic Duo."

Batman also reached into other media, too. There were two movie serials in the 1940s, *Batman* and *Batman and Robin*, starring Lewis Wilson and Douglas

Croft. There have also been two *Batman* newspaper strips (1943 and 1966), a radio program, and a 1971 Crown anthology, *Batman from the Thirties to the Seventies*. In 1966, ABC-TV premiered *Batman*, starring Adam West as Batman and an array of major stars as villains, including Burgess Meredith (Penguin), Cesar Romero (Joker), Frank Gorshin (Riddler), and Victor Buono (King Tut). This program unleashed a torrent of *Batman* material, including two paperback novels, a cartoon collection, and literally thousands of novelties.

J.B.

The notoriety of the title attracted a number of outstanding practitioners to the Batman banner, and those have included (among the artists) John Byrne, Walt Simonson, Gene Colan, and Berni Wrightson, and such writers as Jim Starlin and Alan Moore. It was Frank Miller, however, who as artist/writer introduced in 1986 a new, older Batman, self-doubting and disillusioned, in *The Dark Knight Returns*. This "dark and gritty" interpretation has been followed almost slavishly by those who came after Miller and has become as much of a worn-out cliché as the dashing crime fighter of yore.

The media has been very good to the Batman mythos in the last 10 or so years. There was the phenomenally successful 1989 *Batman* movie, with Michael Keaton in the title role, followed (to date) by three popular sequels: *Batman Returns* (1991), *Batman Forever* (1995), and *Batman & Robin* (1997). There has also been a third *Batman* newspaper strip (1989-91), and an animated version was produced for television by the Fox network in 1992.

M.H.

BATTAGLIA, DINO (1923-1983) Italian cartoonist, born in 1923 in Venice. Dino Battaglia was a member of the team who established the famed periodical *Asso di Picche* ("Ace of Spades") at the end of 1945. For *Asso di Picche* (which was the first Italian magazine of the post-war period) Battaglia produced the *Junglemen* strip (after an introductory page by Giorgio Bellavitis), which was later taken over by Hugo Pratt. After *Junglemen*, Battaglia created the sea-adventure strip *Capitan Caribe* for an Argentine publisher.

In the early 1950s Battaglia drew a few episodes of *Pecos Bill* (with texts by Guido Martina), and for Edizioni Audace he did a series of adaptations from the classics, as well as the Western *El Kid* (1955), later continued by Calegari and D'Antonio with scripts by Bonelli. Around that time Battaglia hit his full stride, producing illustrations for English publishers and creating a number of adventure strips for *L'Intrepido* and the Catholic weekly *Il Vittorioso*.

Starting in 1962, Battaglia became one of the most active contributors to the *Corriere dei Piccoli* and later to the parent *Corriere dei Ragazzi* as well. There he successively created *La Pista dei Quattro* ("The Trail of the Four," a Western, 1964), *Ivanhoe* in 1966, and his two most famous creations, both of them science-fiction strips, *I Cinque della Selena* ("The Five of the Selena," 1966) and the sequel *Cinque su Marte* ("The Five On Mars," 1967). He also did illustrations, mostly for juvenile stories and novels.

In February 1968 the illustrated monthly *Linus* published Battaglia's strip adaptation of a short story by Fabrizio Gabella. Starting in August of the same year, Battaglia did his famous series of adaptations from tales by Matthew Shiel, Edgar Allan Poe, Herman Melville,

H. P. Lovecraft, and others, which won Battaglia wide acclaim. Also looming very large in the Battaglia corpus are his 10 interpretations of the Devil, which he drew for the essay *Il Diavolo*. Battaglia also contributed to the *Messaggero dei Ragazzi*, notably *Frate Francesco* ("Brother Francis"), which he produced in collaboration with his wife Laura (1974).

Dino Battaglia was awarded the Phénix (France) for "best foreign artist" in 1969, and the Yellow Kid (Italy) for "best Italian artist" in 1970 at Lucca. He died in Milan on October 4, 1983.

G.B.

BATTAGLIA, ROBERTO (1923-   ) An Argentine cartoonist of Italian origin, Roberto Battaglia was born in Buenos Aires in 1923. Battaglia, about whose early life little is known, is famous for his comic creation *Mangucho y Meneca*, started in 1945 (under the title *Don Pascual*) in the children's magazine *Patoruzito*.

A draftsman with a fine sense of design and a supple line, and endowed with a very personal sense of humor, Battaglia is the creator of other comic strips, all done for the publisher Dante Quinterno: *María Luz*, *Martín a Bordo*, and *Orsolino Director*.

L.G.

BAXENDALE, LEO (1930-   ) British cartoonist Leo Baxendale was born in October 1930 in Whittle-le-Woods, Lancashire. He received a grammar school education; as an artist he was self-taught. His first job was at the Leyland Paint and Varnish Company designing paint labels. After national service in the Royal Air Force as a catering clerk (1949-1950), he worked on the art staff of the *Lancashire Evening Post*, where he drew sports and editorial cartoons, designed advertisements, and wrote and illustrated his own series of articles.

Inspired by his own reading of *Beano* as a boy, he tried his hand at some strips for that weekly comic and was immediately accepted. His first original character was *Little Plum Your Redskin Chum* (October 10, 1953), followed by *Minnie the Minx* (December 15, 1953). This latter character was intended as a female counterpart to *Dennis the Menace*. His specialty appeared to be mischievous kids, cemented by his creation of a large panel of riotous mayhem in the style of *Casey Court* called *When the Bell Rings* (February 13, 1954). This became a full-page strip, and its name was changed to the more familiar *Bash Street Kids* (December 1, 1956). Later it became a two-page color spread. A similar gang of juvenile delinquents was created for a new D. C. Thomson comic, *Beezer*, and was christened *The Banana Bunch* (January 21, 1956). A determination to extend himself became clear with a new strip, *The Three Bears*, which began in *Beano* on June 6, 1959. These voracious beasts, Pa, Ma, and Teddy, developed from the zany bears that had popped up in Little Plum's neck of the woods.

Although all the strips thus far mentioned are still running in Thomson comics, Baxendale himself has not drawn any since 1963. He abandoned them to create an entire weekly comic for Odhams Press, *Wham* (June 20, 1964). For this he devised the characters, modeled them, scripted their adventures, and drew and colored the main ones: *Eagle Eye Junior Spy*, *The Tiddlers*, and *General Nitt and His Barmy Army* (all two-page spreads). Other characters included *Danny Dare*, *Biff*, *Georgie's Germans*, and *Footsie the Clown*. The comic was as revolutionary as *Eagle* had been in the 1950s, and a com-

Leo Baxendale, "Little Plum." © D.C. Thomson.

panion, *Smash*, was launched (February 5, 1966). For this he provided *Grimly Feendish*, *Bad Penny*, etc.

When I.P.C. absorbed Odhams and Fleetway, Baxendale joined them and created such characters as *The Pirates* (1967), *Mervyn's Monsters* (1968), *Big Chief Pow Wow* (1969), *Sam's Spook* (1970), *Nellyphant* (1972), *Sweeny Toddler* (1973), and *Snooper* (1974). He stopped working for British comics in 1975 and stopped drawing altogether in 1992, due to what he characterized as "wonky eyesight."

The most imitated artist in British comics today, Leo Baxendale is the modern equivalent of Roy Wilson in the 1930s and Hugh McNeill in the 1940s.

D.G.

B.C. (U.S.) Cartoonist Johnny Hart's *B.C.* was refused by five major syndicates before finally being accepted by the Herald-Tribune Syndicate (later absorbed by Publishers-Hall Syndicate). The first daily strip appeared on February 17, 1958, followed by a Sunday version on October 19 of the same year.

Around the strip's titular "hero" (B.C., the "average caveman," not far removed from the typical suburban-dweller, meek, gullible and unimportant) a weird assortment of prehistoric characters endlessly mope around, passing their time in mindless errands or on subtle speculations about the world's progress and the future of civilization. Their discussions are often fuzzy, carried out, as they are, by such creatures as Wiley, the dirty, one-legged poet; Thor, the inexhaustible (but befuddled) inventor; Peter, the rhetorician of the absurd; Clumsy Carp, the happy blunderer; and Curls, the suavely sarcastic sophist; not to mention an existentialist anteater and a couple of peace-loving dinosaurs. (Despite this abundance of talents, however, B.C.'s world doesn't seem to be in any better shape than ours.) Johnny Hart later added to his *dramatis per-*

sonae the barely human Grog, a hirsute, macrocephalic freak, and Hart's idea of the "missing link."

By renovating the conventions of the humor strip, *B.C.* became the graphic prototype of the modern sophisticated comics. To express the passing of time, the relativity of space, Hart makes use of all the signs and symbols of the earlier cartoonists but places them

"B.C." Johnny Hart. © Field Newspaper Syndicate.

in a shifting context where, by their presence, they add an element of uncertainty. (*Krazy Kat* had earlier used such devices, but the effect was mainly circumstantial; in *B.C.* the changing moon and the moving rocks are at the heart of the matter and the objects of the cave-men's fascinated incomprehension.)

Hart's drawing is accordingly functional, linear, and elemental. Even the characters are drawn in conformity with geometrical patterns, which freeze in a same perspective living creatures and inanimate objects. The prehistoric setting is not just a source of gags but a dimension of the action. By going back to the dawn of time, Johnny Hart shows the permanence of human nature (this would seem to be in contradistinction to the widely held—but unsubstantiated—notion that *B.C.* is an "existential" strip).

In spite of the seriousness of its intent, *B.C.* is studded with rib-splitting slapstick, hilarious dialogue, and a delightful sense of the absurd, which make it a masterpiece of light comedy and an irrepressible parody all rolled into one starburst of a comic strip.

B.C. has been reprinted in paperback form by G. P. Putnam and by Fawcett and was made into an animated cartoon for ABC-TV.

M.H.

BEA, JOSÉ-MARIA (1942-   ) Spanish cartoonist and illustrator, born in Barcelona in 1942. José-Maria Bea attended the School of Art of Barcelona, studying design, sculpture, and drawing for six years. These studies strongly influenced his future career as a cartoonist and gave him the opportunity of meeting and exchanging artistic ideas with the noted painter Francese Artigau. In the first stage of his development Bea worked for the comic syndicate Selecciones Illustradas and produced a great many romance comic stories designed for the English market.

In 1962 Bea moved to Paris and enrolled in the Academie Julian, a well-known art school, and started experimenting with color, alternating between painting and book illustration. He later went back to Spain and opened his own art studio in Barcelona. There, under the influence of Esteban Maroto, he resumed his cartooning career. In 1971, in collaboration with Luis Vigil for the texts, he created the horror strip *Sir Leo* for the comic magazine *Dracula*. The feature attracted the attention of American publisher James Warren, who put the artist under contract. Beginning in 1973 Bea collaborated for the Warren magazines, notably *Creepy*, *Eerie*, and *Vampirella*.

L.G.

Bea wrote and drew his acclaimed series of science-fiction tales, *Historias de la Taberna Galactica* ("Stories from the Galactic Tavern"), for the Spanish magazine *1984*; started in 1979, the series ended in 1981 with the closing of the tavern on account of financial difficulties. Among his later works, mention should be made of *En un lugar de la mente* ("In a Place of the Mind," 1981-82), *La Muralla* ("The Wall," 1983) and *Siete Vidas* ("Seven Lives," 1984), the last two in the form of animal strips, with the cat Gatony as the protagonist. Bea is also the author of several how-to books on cartooning, and since the late 1980s he has adapted a number of his stories for television.

J.C.

BÉCASSINE (France) In 1905 Maurice Languereau, publisher of the children's weekly *La Semaine de Suzette*, imagined the adventures of a naive young peasant girl as a simple filler story for his magazine. Drawn by cartoonist Jean-Pierre Pinchon, the story met with immediate success and a sequel was eventually concocted, followed in short order by an entire series named *Bécassine* (from the French word *bécasse* meaning a scatterbrain).

Annaik Labornez ("Bécassine"), a native of Brittany, was a maid in the affluent household of the Marquise de Grand-Air, in the little town of Clocher-les-Bécasses. Loyal and well-meaning, she would commit the worst blunders out of a kind heart and an easily abused credulity. Later on, however, she became somewhat wiser, and even made a contribution to the victory of the Allies in World War I. After Pinchon's death in 1953, the series passed into the hands of Jean Trubert (with scripts contributed by various authors), who tried, without success, to jazz up the character of the little Breton girl.

Bécassine never was (and is still not) a genuine comic strip. The written text (quite good) takes up a disproportionate amount of the total allotted space. The drawings themselves are not interconnected but instead serve as illustrations to the narrative, which can be read separately. In fact *Bécassine*, in tone and in structure, is a picture-story more in the tradition of the 19th-century *Bilderbogen* and *histoires illlustrées* than in the form of the modern comic strip. Unlike its contemporary *Les Pieds-Nickelés* (1908), *Bécassine* never developed into a major feature.

In spite of these drawbacks, *Bécassine* enjoyed tremendous popular success before and immediately after World War I. It was reprinted in over 30 hardbound volumes from 1913 onwards, adapted to radio, and celebrated in song and records; and in 1939 Pierre Caron directed a movie version, with Paulette Dubost in the title role. While no original *Bécassine* story has been produced in the last two decades, the little maid continues to live in endless reprints of her old adventures more than 90 years after her debut.

M.H.

BECK, CHARLES CLARENCE (1910-1989) American comic book artist, born June 8, 1910, in Zumbrota, Minnesota. After studies at the Chicago Academy of Fine Arts and the University of Minnesota, C. C. Beck broke in as a humor illustrator for Fawcett's pulp magazines in 1933. In 1939, Fawcett comic book editor Bill Parker created the *Captain Marvel* strip and assigned Beck to design the character. Using American motion picture actor Fred MacMurray as a model, he created the character and drew the first 13-page adventure.

In 1941, the strip became the best-selling feature on the American market, and Beck was promoted to chief artist. That same year he formed his own comic book studio in New York City; most of the work was for *Captain Marvel*, but his studio later drew for Fawcett's *Spy Smasher* and *Ibis, The Invincible* strips. As the *Captain Marvel*–related features continued to expand in the mid-1940s, Beck also became de facto editor and applied his rigid personal standards to scripts as well as artwork. His shop, which was managed by fellow artist Pete Costanza, later took on advertising work and Beck created *Captain Tootsie*, a single-page advertising comic strip for the Tootsie Roll candy company.

Beck opened a second studio in Englewood, New Jersey, in 1944, but when Fawcett folded their comic book line in 1954—partly due to lagging sales and partly due to National Comics' celebrated copyright infringement lawsuit against *Captain Marvel*—he closed his shops and moved to Florida. He eventually formed his own studio of art and design and even sold a text story to *Astonishing Science Fiction* magazine.

Beck returned to the comic book industry briefly in 1966 when Milson Publications, a combine of old *Captain Marvel* artists, writers, and editors, convinced him to draw *Fatman, The Human Flying Saucer.* It lasted only three issues before the company went bankrupt. He made a second and equally short return in 1972 when National Periodical Publications—the company that had originally helped drive *Captain Marvel* into obscurity—revived the character in their *Shazam!* book. Beck was hired to draw the character he made famous, but left after nine issues in a bitter dispute over the feature's editorial direction. His last years were spent writing opinionated articles on the subject of comics and contributing an irregularly published column, *Crusty Curmudgeon,* for comics fanzines. He died at his Florida home on November 22, 1989.

Beck's artistic style remains one of the cleanest ever used by a comic book artist. The stories he drew were told simply and humorously, and he disliked portraying violence. "Let the readers imagine the violence," he said, and it was not uncommon for him to draw only the scenes before and after a punch rather than the punch itself.

As chief artist on *Captain Marvel,* Beck was meticulous in his control of the strip's other illustrators. Everyone was made to conform to his clear, crisp, fast-moving style, and the artists who draw the feature today still utilize and emulate C. C. Beck's classic simplicity.

J.B.

BECK, FRANK HEM (1894-1962) Frank Beck, one of the most skilled and amusing of the strip cartoonists who built their fame and fortune on funny drawings of boys and dogs (and made his particular hit with the dog strip *Bo*), blinked into the light of day in Tacoma, Washington, on March 17, 1894. Brought up in a rural, middle-class family, Beck underwent routine childhood schooling in the Northwest, then went to Chicago to study cartooning at the Art Institute there. He found a job on the art staff of the *New York Tribune,* where he drew a general panel series with individual titles, commenting on the current scene. Beck later drove an ambulance on the western front in World War I, and then returned to draw such popular daily series as *Hem and Amy, Down the Road, All in a Lifetime,* and *Gas Buggies,* all based on men's and boys' relationships with cars, women, and dogs; most were syndicated by Beck himself. In the late 1920s, Beck bought an English bloodhound and became so enchanted with the dog's antics that he developed the daily and Sunday strip that is today most associated with his name: *Bo. Bo,* however, was anything but a thoroughbred of any breed; he was a tumbling, stumbling composite of every big, long-legged dog that ever lived, with a lolling tongue and a black patch of fur over one eye.

Like many cartoonists, Beck went to the West Coast to live after his success with *Bo.* He died in San Diego on March 21, 1962, at the age of 68. *Bo,* distributed by McNaught Syndicate, did not survive its creator.

B.B.

Franziska Becker wishing a happy New Year to readers of a comics fanzine—in typical character and style.

BECKER, FRANZISKA (1949-   ) Franziska Becker was born on July 10, 1949, in Mannheim, Germany. She studied to become an art teacher, but her career took another turn when, in 1977, she started to work for *emma,* the premiere feminist magazine in Germany, founded by Alice Schwarzer. She has since become the quintessential female cartoonist in Germany.

Becker, whose favorite artist and influence is Wilhelm Busch (her favorite Busch character is "pious Helen"), has drawn spot cartoons and comic strip pages for *emma,* and she has become popular among feminists as well as the general public. She emphasizes the female view of life, but she does it with so much versatility that men are also able to see the humor in her stories. Her comics deal with feminist issues, women's views on men, fitness, and pop culture; they include indispensable tips for a multitude of situations.

Collections of her work were first published in 1980 with *Mein Feministischer Alltag* ("My Everyday Feminism"), and continue to appear. In 1992, her comic album *Feminax und Walkürax* was published as a feminist answer to the new *Asterix* album *Asterix and Maestria.*

In addition to the more feminist cartoons she produces as house artist for *emma,* Becker also creates cartoons for weekly magazines, including *stern.* Freelancing offers her a means to explore the humorous antics of both genders. Today, because of her intrinsic humor and her simple but effective style, Becker, along with Claire Brétecher, is considered one of the most important female artists in Europe.

W.F.

BEEP BEEP THE ROAD RUNNER (U.S.) The characters of the Road Runner and Wile E. Coyote were created for Warner Brothers animated cartoons by director Charles M. ("Chuck") Jones with the help of story man Michael Maltese. The duo first appeared in the film *Fast and Furry-ous* in 1948, which was followed by a successful series under Jones' direction until 1964, when Warner Brothers closed the cartoon department and subcontracted the work to DePatie-Freleng. In July 1958, Western Publishing Company named the Road Runner "Beep Beep" and added him and the Coyote to its line of Dell comics starring the Warner Brothers characters. *Beep Beep* first appeared in a special issue of the Dell Color Comics series, number 918. Two more tryout issues followed before the first issue of *Beep Beep the Road Runner* was issued in 1959.

The comic books followed the same basic format as the animated cartoons: The Road Runner raced about the desert, avoiding the schemes and elaborate inventions of Wile E. Coyote. The Coyote had a maniacal obsession with catching and eating the Road Runner and this, coupled with his vast overestimation of his own brainpower, inevitably caused his machinations to backfire. In the cartoons, the Road Runner never spoke, his dialogue being limited to "Beep beep!" (The Coyote spoke in only one film—a 1951 Bugs Bunny short called *Operation: Rabbit*.) For the purposes of the comic book, both were given the powers of speech and it was designated that all road runners speak in rhymed dialogue. The Road Runner was clearly a male in the comic books, there having been some question previously. (Some publicity material on the cartoons gave the Road Runner's name as Mimi.) The comic book Road Runner was given three identical, unnamed sons who followed him about and, on occasion, a female road runner named Matilda who was featured as Beep Beep's wife.

Dell's comic book version proved very popular, and after 14 issues, Western Publishing Company continued it under the Gold Key company logo, starting the numbering over. A wide selection of writers handled the scripting over the years, including Michael Maltese, Jerry Belson, Lloyd Turner, Vic Lockman, Don Christensen, Jack Cosgriff, Cecil Beard, and Mark Evanier. Most of the artwork was handled by Pete Alvarado, Jack Manning, or Phil DeLara.

Beep Beep the Road Runner and Wile E. Coyote were the subjects of hundreds of merchandising items, including games, children's books, dolls, puzzles, jewelry, and even an automobile, "The Road Runner," produced by the Chrysler Motor Company. Both characters appeared in Gold Key comics of other Warner Brothers characters, including the revived *Looney Tunes* comic (1975), *Golden Comics Digest*, *March of Comics* and a cover-featured "guest stars" spot in some issues of *Daffy Duck* (1972-1973).

M.E.

BEETLE BAILEY (U.S.) Created by Mort Walker and bought by King Features in 1950, *Beetle Bailey* was the last comic introduced by that firm for several years; it was also the last comic personally approved by William Randolph Hearst. Debuting on September 3, 1950,

"Beetle Bailey," Mort Walker. © King Features Syndicate.

Beetle soon became one of the most popular of comic strips. It is still among the five most popular strips.

The cast of the army strip, based at Camp Swampy, is one of the largest in the comics. For more than 45 years of turbulent history, the camp has remained untouched by any disturbance, domestic or foreign. By resisting temptations to localize or inject issues into the strip, Walker's aloof world has fared better than George Baker's *Sad Sack* and Bill Mauldin's *Willie and Joe*.

Beetle Bailey, whose eyes (like those of his magazine-cartoon prototype, Spider) have never been seen from under hats and helmets, is Mort Walker's Everyman. He resists authority, seeks easy ways out, and was, like Walker, a reluctant draftee.

Sergeant Orville Snorkel, the authority figure, is Beetle's eternal antagonist. He relishes food as much as ordering his men, is very shy around the girls, has only one real friend (his dog, Otto, one of the funniest dogs in the comics) and, in spite of the constant battle with Beetle, maintains a covert affection for the hapless private. Every year Beetle brings Sarge home on leave.

Other characters include Gen. Halftrack, the elderly symbol of inept authority; Chaplain Staneglass, utterly ineffectual but lovable; Beetle's chum Killer Diller, the self-appointed ladies' man; chubby Plato, the intellectual; and Zero, a village idiot who is always trying and absolutely never succeeding at doing good. Lt. Sonny Fuzz, a punky upstart, was in fact inspired by Walker's own regrets about his swelled head when he attained that rank; Lt. Flap is an Afro-coiffed black officer who seems to run his own army; and Miss Buxley, Gen. Halftrack's secretary, is a bosomy blonde who takes over the gags for weeks at a stretch.

The gags in this stylized, slick strip rely almost exclusively on the interplay of personalities; virtually no outside characters or locales are introduced.

Beetle Bailey appears in approximately 1,300 papers around the world and has inspired dozens of games, toys, puzzles, and patches. A dozen paperback books have appeared, as well as a series of animated cartoons, which were artistic and commercial failures.

R.M.

Beetle Bailey has continued virtually unchanged through the Vietnam War, the Cold War, and the Gulf War, without its soldiers ever leaving Camp Swampy. It is a tribute to Walker's talent and sense of timing that the strip's popularity has never flagged in all this time.

M.H.

BEKER, ŽARKO (1936-   ) The talented cartoonist Žarko Beker lives in Zagreb, Croatia, where he was born on December 2, 1936. Besides soccer, he liked drawing very much, and was happy to have the famous academic artist Željko Hegedušić for his art teacher. Unfortunately, Beker's father read an unhappy biography of van Gogh and decided not to allow his son to be an artist. Therefore Beker turned to architecture, but he never graduated.

His first comic strip, produced under Disney's influence, was published in 1951 by *Pionir* magazine. After that, while pursuing his schooling, he continued to illustrate some magazines until 1956, when he involved himself in the cartoon film field. For three years he worked as an animator on seven films and, in 1968, became a regular collaborator to *Plavi Vjesnik* magazine in Zagreb. Then he began a long series of comic strips; *Pavel Biri, Bint el Hadra, Zaviša, Mak Makić, Operacija palac, Suparnici, Špiljko, Demonja,* and *Magirus* were only a few of them. But most popular of all was *Zaviša*, written by Zvonimir Furtinger, which only lasted for four episodes. Beker collaborated with Furtinger on all of his comics except for two, which were based on his own scripts. One of them was *Špiljko*, a parody of prehistoric life, and another was *Magirus*, about a super-hero. With superheroes appearing all over the world, even Yugoslavia had to have its own,

but *Magirus* lasted for only one episode. Unlike Superman, who could fly, Magirus lived and worked in the sea.

Beker developed his graphic style based on that of Frank Bellamy, but in *Magirus* and in the last episode of *Zaviša*, he copied directly from Alberto Breccia's Western strip *Roy Renk*. Nobody knows why Beker imitated, because he is really a very talented cartoonist and commercial artist.

After he stopped working on comics, Beker became art director of Vjesnik's Marketing Agency in Zagreb.

E.R.

BELINDA BLUE EYES (G.B.) Brave, big-hearted *Belinda Blue Eyes*, who would lose her slightly embarrassing "surname" with the war, came into the *Daily Mirror* on September 30, 1935. She was a cross between Shirley Temple and *Little Orphan Annie*, with the mop of curls of the former and the big, blank eyeballs of the latter. She also had Annie's philosophical bent, which kept her cheerful through many a misery, as she wandered waiflike through the world. "I reckon there's nothin' like good honest work to make you forget ya troubles, Mrs. Frizzle!" she smiled bravely as she sweated over the hot fat in the chip shop. She had a dog (like Annie), a Scottish terrier that faded away in 1944, and an equivalent to Daddy Warbucks, Daddy Pilgrim, forever turning up in time to end an episode, then departing in time to start another. In a close survey of 10 months of the strip made during 1943 by Margot Bennett, Belinda offered 19 pieces of advice, performed 28 courageous actions, and said "Gee!" 139 times and "Gulp!" 11 times.

Belinda's boyfriend—and staunch supporter—was Desmond Dare, one of the Bomb Alley Kids dating from 1944. But among readers her favorite supporting players were the bad girls, teenage Spitfire Kitty, Mrs. Frizzle's sporty daughter, and especially saucy Suky Schoolgirl, rebel of Magdala House. And when Daddy Pilgrim was not around, which was often, who better to go to for comfort and cuddles than bosomy Mrs. Bounty?

Originally drawn by the pseudonymous "Gloria," the strip was taken over by Steve Dowling, then by Tony Royle from 1943 to the end on October 17, 1959. Reprints include: *Belinda and the Bomb Alley Boys, Belinda in Shooting Star,* and a monthly comic book published in Australia.

D.G.

BELL, STEVE (1951-   ) This left-handed lad from Walthamstow, where he was born on February 26, 1951, is one of the few "adult" cartoonists to come up from the ranks of children's comics—and in a very short time he established himself as one of the up-and-coming artists. He began to draw for three I.P.C. weeklies, *Whoopee, Cheeky,* and *Jackpot* in 1978, and by 1979 was drawing the satirical anti-Tory strip cartoon, *Maggie's Farm* (Maggie, of course, being Prime Minister Margaret Thatcher) for *Private Eye,* the radical comic fortnightly. Two years after that he started his own cruel daily strip, *If . . .,* for the *Guardian* newspaper, where it has run ever since.

Educated at Slough Grammar School, Bell studied art at the Teeside College of Art, graduated in Fine Art from Leeds University in 1974, and began a career as an art teacher in Birmingham in 1977. He started strip cartooning in that same year as a freelancer, turning

Žarko Beker, "Magirus." © Žarko Beker.

Steve Bell, an affectionate tribute to Leo Baxendale's "Little Plum." © Steve Bell.

full-time in no time. After a year on the comics, he began to appear in the political press, including the *New Statesman* and *New Society*. His first comic strip was the left-wing series *Good God Almighty* in the Socialist weekly *The Leveller* (1978). Always busy, he took up animation and joined Bob Godfrey in making adult cartoon films for Channel Four Television and the BBC. He was voted Humorous Strip Cartoonist of the Year 1984 by the Cartoonist's Club of Great Britain.

Among his books are: *Maggie's Farm* (1981), *Further Down on Maggie's Farm* (1982), *If* (annual series from 1983), *Waiting for the Old Uptown* (1986), *Maggie's Farm: The Last Roundup* (1987), and *Funny Old World* (1991).

D.G.

BELL, WALTER (1893-1979) Walter Bell was one of those cartoonists whose work for children's comics was both prolific and unoriginal. Able to impersonate almost any of his contemporaries, his talents were used by editors at the Amalgamated Press to fill in for other artists' regular characters during the artists' holidays or

illnesses. However, as a freelancer working from an art studio, and later running a studio himself, he was able to create several successful heroes of his own.

Walter Bell was born in Newcastle upon Tyne, England, on January 23, 1893, and died in 1979. He was still cartooning in his eighties: in 1976 he worked on the revival of *Ally Sloper*, Britain's first strip cartoon hero and the cartoon Bell cut his teeth on back in 1920.

Fresh from a distinguished army career in World War I (where he was an officer in the cavalry and won the Military Medal), Bell bought a copy of the cartoonists' bible, *The Writers and Artists Year Book*, and armed with his portfolio of work samples, began to call on every agency in the book. He met with Ralph Hodgson at Byron Studios on Fleet Street, which was then the world's center for newspaper publishers. Hodgson had once drawn *Airy Alf and Bouncing Billy* under the pen name "Yorick." This strip, originated by the genius of British comics, Tom Browne, had served as the model for Walter Bell's style, and so Bell and Hodgson became lifelong friends and collaborators.

Bell's first published cartoon appeared in the *Daily Chronicle*, substituting for W. F. Thomas, the *Ally Sloper* artist who, at the time, was drawing a daily thumbnail cartoon for the newspaper. While working in the studio, Bell was given the opportunity to draw some Tom Browne creations, titled *Weary Willie and Tired Tim*, for Amalgamated Press. His substitute front page for their weekly vehicle, *Illustrated Chips*, impressed the art editor, Langton Townley. He offered Bell the chance to take over *Casey Court*, the back-page panel of pranks that inspired a young Charlie Chaplin. Bell drew the cartoon weekly for 10 years.

Now well established in the comics world, Bell soon had a roster of characters to draw each week: *Mat the Middy* for *Merry Moments*; *Lottie Looksharp* for *The Golden Penny*; *The Sporty Boyees* for *The Monster Comic*; and *Sonny Shine the Page Boy* for *The Jolly Jester*. These were all independent comics, but by 1922 Bell was working exclusively for the Amalgamated Press chain. He drew *Geordie Brown* in *Funny Wonder*, and many characters for the Nursery Group, which was aimed at younger readers, including *Children of the Forest*, an early picture serial, for *Bubbles*; *Fun and Frolic in Fairyland* for *Playbox*; *Bobbie and his Teddy Bears* in *Sunbeam*; *Redskin Chums* in *Bo-Peep*; and *Snow White and Her Friends* in *Happy Days*.

In 1930 the rival firm of George Newnes and C. Arthur Pearson invented the idea of a seasonal comic and launched *The Seaside Comic*, published that summer. Bell illustrated the entire 12-page color tabloid. It was a great success with children on vacation, and Newnes-Pearson followed it a few months later with *Christmas Comic*, then *Holiday Comic*, *Spring Comic*, *Summer Comic*, and other annual titles, all illustrated by Bell. Amalgamated Press expressed its displeasure with Bell's defection to Newnes-Pearson by reducing the amount of work offered to him. Undeterred, Bell found further work outside Amalgamated's near-monopoly as national, and later local, newspapers began to publish comic supplements of their own. Bell's parade of characters now included *Molly the Messenger*, in the *Daily Mail Comic* and *Jolly Jenkins* in the *Daily Express Comic*.

Bell moved from the comics to the boys' weekly story department at Amalgamated, where he drew *Mike, Spike and Greta* for *The Pilot*, *Mustard and Pepper* for *The Ranger*, and *The Professor and the Pop* for *Detective Weekly*. His full-blown return to A.P. Comics came with the sudden death of George W. Wakefield, who had just begun drawing the weekly adventures of Bud Abbott and Lou Costello for *Film Fun*. Bell completed the first unfinished page and from that took over the series. He later worked for many of the one-shot comic books, most of which were published by P.M. (Phillipp Marx) Productions, with such titles as *Starry Spangles* and *Jolly Jack-in-the-Box*, and his final series, *Flipper the Skipper*, which appeared in 1954 in the A.P. weekly, *Jack and Jill*. In his retirement, Bell drew single cartoons for his local newspaper, the *Barnet Press*, until his death in 1979 at the age of 86.

D.G.

BELLAMY, FRANK (1917-1976) Frank Bellamy, British cartoonist, was born in Kettering, Northhamptonshire, in 1917. On leaving school in 1933, he became junior assistant in a local art studio. During his six-year stay there, he painted and designed display boards and cutouts for films showing at the Regal Cinema, Kettering. He was conscripted into the army in 1939, where he spent six months painting every known aircraft for an Aircraft Recognition Room. After the war he returned to the art studio, where he remained until 1948, when he went to London to look for work. Taken on by the first studio he showed his samples to (Norfolk Studio), he was soon designing advertisements for the *Daily Telegraph*. This led to freelance work through the International Artists agency, love story illustrations for *Home Notes* magazine and story illustrations for *Boy's Own Paper*, *Lilliput*, *Men Only*, etc.

Bellamy's first strip was *Commando Gibbs*, an advertisement for Gibbs Toothpaste; it was published in *Eagle*, a portent of things to come. *Mickey Mouse Weekly* gave him the chance to take over the adventure strip *Monty Carstairs*, created by R. MacGillivray, and his serial *Secret in the Sands* began on July 25, 1953. This led to his first full-color strip, a version of *The Living Desert*, to which he was required to add the signature "Walt Disney!" Now fully freelance, he drew for *Swift*, a weekly comic for younger readers: *Swiss Family Robinson* (1954), *King Arthur* (1955), *Robin Hood* (1955), all scripted by Clifford Makins, who later edited *Eagle*. Bellamy's first work on *Eagle* was a serial strip biography of *Winston Churchill* (1956), in which he pioneered his unique use of splash panels and contrasting color techniques, together with deep research, working from photographs, for example. The complete serial was reprinted in book form by Hulton Press, and Sir Winston was presented with a leatherbound copy. Then came *The Shepherd King* (1958), a Bible strip; *Marco Polo* (1959); and the ultimate *Eagle* accolade, *Dan Dare* (1960). After redesigning the Space Fleet uniforms, spaceships, etc., he abandoned the strip after a year for *Frazer of Africa* (1960), *Montgomery of Alamein* (1962), and the acme of his comic achievement, *Heros the Spartan* (1962-1966). This two-page center spread, painted in full color, took Bellamy five to six days a week to complete. It was scripted by Tom Tully. In 1967 Bellamy changed publishers to draw the strip version of the television series *Thunderbirds* for *TV Century 21*. His last comic page was published September 11, 1969, in the third issue of the combined comic, *T.V. 21 and Joe 90*.

He began to change directions toward newspapers in 1967 with an Edgar Allan Poe story as a strip for *Sunday Extra*, the comic section of *Sunday Citizen*. Later came illustrations in comics technique for *Sunday Times Magazine* and *Radio Times* (1970), the first time strips had appeared in such adult publications. This drew the interest of the *Daily Mirror*, and from December 7, 1971, Bellamy took over the daily fantasy strip *Garth*. A reprint of his strips, entitled *Daily Mirror Book of Garth*, was published in September 1974. He died on July 5, 1976.

Bellamy was considered by many to be the top British comics artist (Best Foreign Artist Award, American Academy of Comic Book Arts, 1972). His work was in the tradition of his early idols, Hal Foster and Burne Hogarth, and the line originated by Frank Hampson.

D.G.

BERG, DAVID (1920-   ) American comic book artist and writer, born June 12, 1920, in Brooklyn, New York. After studies at the Pratt Institute, the Art Students League, and Cooper Union—all in New York—Dave Berg broke into the comic book business as the writer and artist of Quality's *Death Patrol* strip; his first material on the adventure series appeared in the

Dave Berg, "Summer Resorts." © *Mad magazine.*

November 1941 issue of *Military Comics*. Besides his early Quality work (which also included work on *Uncle Sam*), Berg worked for many comic book producers during 1941 and 1942. For Ace Publications, he wrote and drew the Captain Courageous adventure character; at Fawcett, he worked briefly on *Captain Marvel*, *Sir Butch* and several others; at Fiction House he drew and wrote *Pvt. Pippin*; and at Western, he wrote and drew the *Jinx* feature.

Most of his comic book work during the 1940s and 1950s was done for the Timely/Marvel/Atlas group edited by Stan Lee. Between 1941 and 1958, Berg produced a wide range of stories for whatever type of books were then in vogue, whether horror or humor features. His most notable work came as a writer/artist/editor on Marvel's *Combat Kelly* war feature, which Berg handled sporadically between 1945 and 1957. During the 1950s, he also contributed to the Archie group (1951-1955), EC (1952), St. John (1953), and Ziff-Davis (1952).

But it was not until Dave Berg moved to *Mad* magazine in 1956 that his work was recognized. Under the direction of Al Feldstein, Berg started "The Lighter Side" series that eventually expanded from its two-page premiere to a five-page mainstay in the *Mad* lineup. The feature's premise was simple enough: Berg selected a common topic (like "love," "television," or "automobiles") and drew a series of gags about the ironies of American society in that context. Using a clean, straightforward, and realistic approach to drawing, Berg commented that he often sketched at cocktail parties and always carried a pad with him to capture the foibles of American life. Rather than being roughly satirical, however, "The Lighter Side" was more often slanted toward humorous observations and good-natured ribbing.

Over the years, Berg began utilizing set characters in his issue-by-issue vignettes. One of his favorites was his boss, publisher William M. Gaines, whom he drew as the rotund, bearded neo-hippie that he was. More often, however, Berg injected himself into the strip, meticulously rendering himself with ever-present pipe,

glasses, silver-grey hair, and sport jackets with patches at the elbow.

Berg's "The Lighter Side" feature became one of the most popular series in *Mad*, and the writer/artist has published seven paperbacks under the Mad imprint. They are under the general title of "Mad's Dave Berg Looks At . . ." and do essentially the same observatory work as his magazine series. He also had two paperbacks ostensibly about "God," entitled *My Friend God* and *Roger Kaputnik and God*. In 1996 he marked his 40th anniversary of working for *Mad*.

His wife, Vivian Lipman Berg, was a writer/artist/editor in comic books during the 1940s.

J.B.

BERGDAHL, GUSTAV VICTOR (1878-1939) Gustav Victor Bergdahl, Swedish illustrator, painter, and graphic artist, was born December 12, 1878, in Osteråker. He died in Stockholm on January 20, 1939. As a youth, Bergdahl worked as a seaman but, after an accident in 1899, gave up the sea to devote himself to a career in art. At first his main source of income was from editorial cartooning and newspaper illustration. Then, in 1915, Bergdahl conquered a new medium—animated cartoons. Bergdahl, a Swedish pioneer of animated cartoons, also transformed one of his cartoon characters, *Kapten Grogg* ("Captain Whiskey"), into a comic strip version between the World Wars.

Well known for his work in daily newspapers and humor weeklies, Bergdahl was so impressed by Winsor McCay's animated cartoons that he wanted to try his hand at it, too. With no one to teach him the art of animated cartooning, Bergdahl attempted to devise his own method. He tried selling motion picture producers on his ideas, without much luck. Finally, in 1915, he was able to go ahead on production of his first animated cartoon, *Trolldrycken* ("The Magic Brew"), which premiered in November 1915. The public and the critics liked the feature, so Bergdahl continued producing animated cartoons centering on circuses. Finally, he returned to his first love, the sea, with *Kapten Groggs underbara resa* ("Captain Whiskey's

Wonderful Voyage"). The adventures of Kapten Grogg were continued in a number of episodes that were also popular outside Sweden because they were well made and, most importantly, funny. Bergdahl continued producing animated cartoons until his death in 1939.

The success of Kapten Grogg's adventures led to their publication in book form in 1923 under the title *Kapten Grogg och Kalle* ("Captain Whiskey and Kalle"). In 1937 *Kapten Grogg* was included in the first comics magazine published in Sweden, *Musse Pigg-Tidningen* ("Mickey Mouse Newspaper"). Eight issues appeared in 1937, 15 in 1938. It is only thanks to Sweden's comic fandom that Bergdahl's pioneering work in animated cartoons and comic strips has been rediscovered.

W.F.

"Bernard Prince," Greg and Hermann. © Editions du Lombard.

BERNARD PRINCE (Belgium) *Bernard Prince* was created for the Belgian weekly magazine *Tintin* by Hermann (Hermann Huppen) as artist, and Greg (Michel Régnier) as writer, on February 17, 1966.

Bernard Prince is a former Interpol agent turned adventurer and soldier of fortune. Aboard his yacht *The Cormorant* and in company of his loyal crew—the hirsute and hard-drinking Barney Jordan and the teenaged Djinn—he has traveled to the wilds of Amazonia, the deserts of Central Asia and the "jungles" of Manhattan.

An adventure strip in the classic tradition, *Bernard Prince* has introduced its readers to some colorful villains: the sinister Kurt Bronzen, international agitator and criminal mastermind; the bloodthirsty captain of a band of assassins, General Satan; the mad dictator Mendoza; and other smaller fry that Prince and his companions would usually round up after a festival of gunfights, chases, and assorted mayhem. Hermann's drawings are bold and powerful, filled with restless energy, and excellently complementing the whirlwind proceedings of the strip.

Bernard Prince has been reprinted in book form by Editions du Lombard, and one of the early adventures

has been published in the American magazine *Wonderworld*.

After Hermann left the series in 1977, it was turned over to Dany (Daniel Henrotin), who managed to carry it to the end of the decade. It was revived in 1992, with Greg still writing the continuities and Edouard Aidans providing the artwork.

M.H.

BERNDT, WALTER (1899-1979) American cartoonist, born November 22, 1899, in Brooklyn, New York. At age 16 Walter Berndt, a high school dropout, took a job in the *New York Journal* art department as an office boy for the likes of famed cartoonists Herriman, Gross, McCay, Segar, and Sterrett. After closely studying their techniques and giving them an occasional hand when they had trouble meeting a deadline, Berndt had, within five years, risen to full-fledged cartoonist status. As early as 1915 he was doing sports cartoons and occasional fillers, and in 1916 he took over the gag panel *And then the Fun Began* from the overworked Milt Gross.

In 1920 Berndt left the *Journal* to create his own comic strip; entitled *That's Different*, it lasted only a little over one year. He then went to the *New York World* to create a feature based on his reminiscences, *Billy the Office Boy*. Fired for insubordination after a couple of weeks, he took the strip to Captain Patterson, who changed its name to *Smitty* and distributed it through the Chicago Tribune-New York News Syndicate in 1922. From then on Berndt's time was devoted to *Smitty* (and its companion strip *Herby*, which came along in 1930), which he drew and wrote until his retirement in 1973. He died in 1979.

Walter Berndt was not an outstanding cartoonist, but his work exhibits an infectious charm and an obvious love for the medium. As the artist stated: "Drawing was really never work for me," and his enthusiasm and dedication can be seen shining through his life-work of over 50 years.

M.H.

BERRILL, JACK (1923-1996) Jack Berrill was an American cartoonist born in Brooklyn, New York, in 1923. Following service in the air force during World War II, Berrill went to work for Eastern Color Printing Company on their comic book line, including *Famous Funnies*. After many of their titles were discontinued in the mid-1950s, Berrill became an assistant on Martin Branner's *Winnie Winkle*. The job proved to be a stepping stone to better things when he sold a comic strip of his own creation, *Gil Thorp*, to *Winnie Winkle's* distributor, the Chicago Tribune-New York News Syndicate; the first release was dated September 8, 1958.

Gil Thorp was a clean-cut, earnest sports coach at fictional Milford High. In addition to his professional duties, he had to cope with problems ranging from rock-and-rolling and hot-rodding in the early years of the strip to teen pregnancy, drug abuse, and the AIDS epidemic in later episodes. Gil also had a series of mild romances with a string of nubile maidens, but those never amounted to much or contributed anything to the overall action of the strip.

Berrill drew *Gil Thorp* in a pleasant, unobtrusive style, and his plots were leisurely played out over weeks, or even months, in routine soap-opera fashion. He turned out the feature daily and Sunday for almost four decades, making it into one of the longest-running sports strips of all time until illness forced him to leave the drawing board late in 1994. Berrill died of cancer at his home in Brookfield, Connecticut, on March 14, 1996.

M.H.

BESS, GORDON (1929-1989) American cartoonist, born in 1929 in Richfield, Utah. Gordon Bess followed his parents from mining camp to mining camp throughout the West. After high school (where he had already displayed a talent for cartooning and caricature) he joined the Marine Corps, with which he spent 10 years, including one year in Korea. During his service with the Marines, Bess produced illustrations for the Corps Training Aid Section, and in 1954 he became staff cartoonist for *Leatherneck*, the Corps magazine.

In 1957 Gordon Bess left the service, married, and got a job as art director for a greeting card company in Cincinnati, with which he remained for over 10 years. At the same time he contributed cartoons to various magazines around the country. In 1967 he created *Redeye* for King Features Syndicate, a rollicking humor strip about a screwball tribe of comic-opera Indians. The success of the strip allowed him to return to the West, in this case to Boise, Idaho, where Bess devoted his spare time to hunting, fishing, and skiing. He died of cancer at his Idaho home in December 1989.

Gordon Bess belongs to the post-*Pogo* and *Peanuts* school of humor cartoonists. Unassuming, and even modest about his accomplishments, he nonetheless succeeded in maintaining the high tradition of American comic art.

M.H.

BESSY (Belgium, Germany) *Bessy*, created by Flemish writer/artist Willy Vandersteen in 1951 for publication in *La Libre Belgique* (Free Belgium), then picked up by *Belang van Limburg* and *Gazet van Antwerpen* before being published in album form, is today largely produced in comic book format for German audiences.

After having created a number of funnies, Vandersteen felt it was about time to enter into the field of realistic comic strips and did so with *Bessy*, a comic strip starring a collie dog much in the *Lassie* vein with the added interest of a Wild West setting. The success of the strip, especially in Germany, proves that Vandersteen did not miscalculate reader interest. Spreading out with an ever-increasing number of newspaper strips and comic books also led to the founding of the Studio Vandersteen in 1951 where gagmen, scriptwriters, and artists helped to create a line of diversified strips. Thus, the earliest *Bessy* strips were signed Wirel, a contraction of the names of artists Willy Vandersteen and Karel Verschuere. Later on, the artwork on *Bessy* was left completely to Verschuere, with other artists like Frank Sels filling in when the workload grew heavier.

In 1962 the stories of *Bessy* were exported to Germany, where they appeared as one of the features in *Felix*. Some of the stories were also published in giveaway customers' magazines. It was publication in *Felix*, however, that made *Bessy* a success in Germany. Broadcasts of the perennial *Lassie* on German television may have boosted reader enthusiasm, which finally resulted in a 32-page *Bessy* comic book that started publication in May 1965. It was published monthly for the first five issues only, then was stepped up to biweekly and, with number 58, turned weekly.

"*Bessy*," Willy Vandersteen. © Bulls Pressedienst.

Bastei Verlag, the publishers of the *Bessy* comic book in Germany, put the character in digest-sized comics as well. The feature was also dramatized for records. After spreading out into various forms of publication, the regular weekly comic book ended after 992 issues in 1985. The weekly format, by that time, had already downgraded the artwork, giving it a hurried, industrialized look. Sometimes the painted covers by German illustrator Klaus Dill were the only redeeming factor of the books.

Reprints of classic *Bessy* comics were issued by various publishers starting in 1989. Bastei Verlag, which shut down its comic production almost entirely in 1995, has picked up the feature once again for a new reprint series.

W.F.

BETTY (U.S.) *Betty* was the *New York Herald*'s entry into the girl-strip sweepstakes. Spurred on by the success of Hearst's *Polly and Her Pals*, in 1914 the *Herald*'s editors came up with their own idea about a working girl whom they named Betty. They turned the drawing of the Sunday page over to a young staff artist named Russell Westover. Westover (who was already doing the daily *Fat Chance*) does not seem to have taken on the added burden with much relish. When the *Herald* merged with the *Tribune* in 1918, he left the paper.

Betty was taken over by the noted illustrator Charles Voight, with whom it is most often associated. Voight remade the feature into a model of the new, crisp style of illustrated strip. Except for Betty's grotesque suitor Lester de Pester, all the characters were drawn straight, the girls being especially depicted with loving care. However much admired and imitated (the strip gave rise to a number of rivals, *Connie* and *Jane Arden* being the most notable), the feature was rather dull. It was more like a succession of well-turned-out vignettes

"Betty," Charles Voight. © New York Tribune.

"Betty Boop," Max Fleischer. © King Features Syndicate.

than a full-blooded comic strip. The readers must have felt the same way, for *Betty* never reached any heights of popularity, and finally folded in June 1943.

M.H.

BETTY BOOP (U.S.) Betty Boop, the earliest representation of the "French doll" figure in animated films, made her first appearance in the 1931 Max Fleischer cartoon short "Betty Co-Ed." It was a fair success and Fleischer decided to initiate a series of Betty Boop cartoons. Betty's falsely angelic face was modeled after that of the famous singer Helen Kane (who sued the Fleischer studios to no avail) and her figure patterned after that of Mae West (who had sense enough not to sue). Betty's success continued to grow, and a catchy title tune added to her popularity.

In 1935 King Features decided to distribute *Betty Boop* as a Sunday feature: drawn by Bud Counihan, it was given only second-class status and in New York ran in the *Mirror* (a sure-fire indication that the strip occupied a very low position in the Hearst pecking order). The feature was not without merit, nonetheless, although King toned down its more blatant sex suggestions (on the screen Betty was nothing if not a flirt, throwing kisses and hearts at the audience, and demurely batting her long eyelashes).

In the strip Betty worked in the movies, and there were some good satirical takeoffs on Hollywood. Around 1937, however, the spotlight shifted to Betty's overwhelming Aunt Tillie and her midget lover Hunky Dory. The charm of the screen original never really worked in the strip version, and when attacks from the bluenoses began to mount against the Betty Boop animated cartoons, King—always one to play it safe—quietly dropped the feature (1938). The animated films went on for a while longer, until Max Fleischer too decided to throw in the towel with one last cartoon defiantly titled "Yip, Yip, Yippy" (1939).

Three decades later, Betty Boop's underground fame grew, with revivals of her cartoons playing to packed houses in Europe and the United States; and a collection of *Betty Boop* comic strips was published in paperback form by Avon in 1975.

Betty's enduring popularity prompted King Features to resurrect the character in the comic pages. Under the title *Betty Boop and Felix*, the animated screen vamp costarred with the little black feline in a newspaper strip that made its debut in November 1984 and was turned out by four of Mort Walker's sons. The new feature failed to catch fire, however, and Felix made his exit in 1987. The strip, now rechristened *Betty Boop and Friends*, lasted only through January 1988.

M.H.

BEVÈRE, MAURICE DE (1923-   ) Belgian cartoonist, born December 1, 1923, in Courtrai. At 20 Maurice de Bevère was already working as an artist in an animation studio specializing in short features and screen commercials. In 1945, with the studio floundering, de Bevère joined the Belgian magazine *Le Moustique,* for which he contributed over 300 cover illustrations. In 1946, under the pen name "Morris," he created *Lucky Luke*, a humorous Western strip that started appearing as a regular feature in the comic weekly *Spirou* the following year.

In 1948, in order to perfect his knowledge of the American West, de Bevère left for the United States. During his six-year stay (in the course of which he continued to draw *Lucky Luke* for *Spirou*) he met American cartoonists such as Harvey Kurtzman and Jack Davis. In New York he met René Goscinny, with whom he was to start a long collaboration.

De Bevère returned to Belgium in 1954, with Goscinny as his scriptwriter on *Lucky Luke*. In 1968 he left *Spirou* for the French weekly *Pilote* (of which Goscinny was then editor), a decision that proved unfortunate. In 1971 de Bevère, in collaboration with Goscinny and Pierre Tchernia, produced a feature-length animated cartoon of *Lucky Luke* for Belvision. After Goscinny's death in 1977, he continued to turn out the strip with the help of a number of writers and assistants. In 1987 he started *Ran-Tan-Plan*, a *Lucky Luke* spin-off, and in 1990 he established his own publishing company, Lucky Productions.

Maurice de Bevère has received a number of European awards and distinctions for his work on *Lucky*

Luke. His graphic style, flowing and clean, parodic without being caricatural, has been widely imitated by scores of aspiring cartoonists in Europe and elsewhere. In 1993 a vast retrospective of his work was mounted by the Comic Strip Museum in Angouleme, France.

M.H.

BIB AND BUB (Australia) Created by author-cartoonist May Gibbs for the *Sydney Sun News* in 1925, the strip was adapted from her own book, *Gumnut Babies*, which was first published in 1916. The strip appeared as a weekly and adopted the European comic strip format of no speech balloons and placing the text below each panel. For many years, the doggerel verse text was hand-lettered by Gibbs, but in time this gave way to typesetting.

Bib and Bub has a unique place in the history of Australian comic strips, as it was the most successful of any strip (local or imported) aimed at very juvenile readers. Despite its unprecedented long run and undoubted popularity, the strip was not an honest translation of the delightful, fairytale world of Gibbs' books. In her books, Gibbs was able to express her many-sided originality with her loving treatment of the bush creatures and to contribute her messages of kindliness.

At her bidding, the gumnut babies, wattle blossom elves and creatures of the bush, came tripping forward to assist Bib and Bub play out their fantasy adventures. The kookaburra, wattle sprite, beetle, Christmas-bell baby, and butterfly gambolled in an atmosphere of gum leaves, golden sunshine, and gossamer. Like all good children's fantasies, the stories followed a simple plot that contained elements of danger or apprehension.

As a comic strip, *Bib and Bub* did not contain the unique quality of the books. Each strip was complete in itself, and the restrictions imposed by panel limitations did not allow Gibbs to develop characters and plots and weave the same patterns of fantasy as she had done in her books. May Gibbs tried to counter this by giving the comic strip a separate identity. Bib and Bub took up residence in Gumnut Town, where they lived with Mr. & Mrs. Wuzzy Bear. More often than not, Bib and Bub were relegated to the roles of spear-carriers as they observed the antics of Bill Bandicoot, Dad and Mum Platypus, Mrs. Roo, Lizzie Lizard, and other birds, animals, and reptiles that inhabited the town. While this formula proved successful, the downgrading of the contribution of Bib and Bub, the transfer of the locale to a pseudo-village, and the almost total elimination of danger robbed the strip of the opportunity of duplicating the charm and appeal of Gibbs' books. The comic strip also introduced anomalies in the form of elephants, giraffes, monkeys, llamas, and other animals not indigenous to the Australian bush— but their presence helped, rather than hindered, the strip.

While many strips were reprinted in their latter years, *Bib and Bub* was the longest-running strip by one artist to appear in Australia. The strip survived mergers with the *Guardian* (1929), the *Sunday Sun* (1931), and the *Sunday Herald* (1953), and the last strip appeared in the *Sunday Sun-Herald* in September 1967.

J.R.

BIBI FRICOTIN (France) Louis Forton created *Bibi Fricotin* in October 1924 for the French comic weekly *Le*

"Bibi Fricotin," Louis Forton. © SPE.

Petit Illustré. Partly autobiographical, *Bibi Fricotin* chronicles the bittersweet adventures of a lonely young boy who learns how to survive in a cruel world the hard way. Bibi is an orphan and at first something of a juvenile delinquent. But Forton later changed him into a world-wise youngster, smart-alecky and resourceful, with a quick wit and a golden heart, the very epitome of the Parisian *gavroche*. His most famous adventure involves a round-the-world odyssey in which he manages to come out ahead of friend and foe alike.

Following Forton's death in 1934, *Bibi Fricotin* passed into the hands of Callaud. After a wartime interruption from 1940 to 1948, the strip was revived by Pierre Lacroix, who drew it in a style reminiscent of Forton's until 1988, when the series came to an end. The hero's character had changed by then, however: Bibi had become less rebellious, more conventional—a typical good boy, closer to Hergé's Tintin than to Forton's original conception of the character.

Less original than Forton's more famous series *Les Pieds-Nickelés, Bibi Fricotin* nonetheless occupies a respected position among European strips. It has been reprinted in book form and was made into a movie in 1950.

M.H.

BIG BEN BOLT (U.S.) *Big Ben Bolt* was created for King Features Syndicate in 1949 by Elliot Caplin, no doubt in response to the success of the premier boxing strip, *Joe Palooka.* Caplin sought the services of illustrator John Cullen Murphy, who had done fine boxing sketches for *Collier's* magazine. The samples were accepted (*Big Ben Bolt* was the second-to-last strip bought by William Randolph Hearst himself) and was first released to newspapers in February of 1950.

The strip concerns Bolt, heavyweight champion of the world (although the title has been won from him several times) and his adventures, most of them out of

THIS IS CALLED A TYPEWRITER. IT'S A USEFUL BUT STUBBORN LITTLE GIMMICK—INSISTS YOU THINK OF THE RIGHT WORDS BEFORE IT'LL PRINT 'EM.

"Big Ben Bolt," John Cullen Murphy. © King Features Syndicate.

the boxing world. He lives with his kindly aunt and uncle on Beacon Street in Boston. The other continuing character is Bolt's manager, Spider Haines; the rest of the cast (including a string of non-steady girlfriends) changes with each episode of mystery, murder, romance, and adventure revolving around the rough but kind fighter.

Murphy's art was tense, cinematic, and highly illustrative, surviving the crippling onslaught of newsprint shortages and strip reductions. The strip was voted "Best Story Strip" by the NCS for 1971.

R.M.

After 1971 Murphy spent less and less time on *Ben Bolt* to devote himself to *Prince Valiant*. In 1975 the Sundays were discontinued, while a succession of artists worked on the daily strip, including Al Williamson, Angelo Torres, and Gray Morrow. Neal Adams brought the feature to an end, with the hero shot down by an assassin in April 1978.

M.H.

BIG BOY (U.S.) So popular was the medium of comic books in the 1940s and 1950s that a multitude of these publications were printed to be given away free in the furtherance of a variety of political, religious, or educational causes. A majority of these giveaways, however, served to publicize commercial enterprises, and in this field none was as active as the Big Boy family-restaurant chain.

To advertise their double-decker hamburger, the Big Boy (a precursor of the Big Mac), the restaurant chain brought out their corporate mascot, a burly 10-year-old in checked overalls, and featured him as the hero of a monthly comic book that started its run in 1956. *Adventures of Big Boy* (later *Adventures of the Big Boy*) was the brainchild of Manfred Bernhard, who approached Stan Lee of Timely Publications with the offer to write the first year's worth of stories, which were then illustrated by such artists as Bill Everett and Dan De Carlo. Compared to the superhero fare Timely (the predecessor of today's Marvel Comics) was turning out at the time, Big Boy's adventures were rather tame. Big Boy, his girlfriend Dolly, and his dog Nugget would go exploring a cave in the surrounding countryside in search of treasure, or Big Boy would straighten out the school bully, even foil a robbery attempt. Each five-to-

seven-page story ended with a moral homily, often mouthed by Big Boy's Grandpa.

After the first year, Bernhard took charge of the production, employing a variety of artists and writers, often well-known names, sometimes using rank amateurs or pulling former artists out of retirement. Given away free at each of the chain's restaurants, the *Big Boy* comic book, usually 16 pages thick and consisting of puzzles and games in addition to the stories, was meant to entertain the children. It enjoyed an astounding run of 40 years. Its farewell with issue number 466 in August 1996 (it was replaced by a series of activity books) not only signaled the end of a era but also confirmed the sad fact that comic books were no longer a surefire attraction, not even for children. The activity books came out in 1997, and they contain comic stories done by Craig Yoe.

M.H.

BILAL, ENKI (1951-   ) A French cartoonist, illustrator, and filmmaker born in Belgrade, Yugoslavia, on October 7, 1951, Enki Bilal moved to France with his parents when he was 10 years old. After studying at the Paris School of Fine Arts, he started his career in 1972 with several short stories that were published in the weekly comics magazine *Pilote*. Beginning in 1975 with *La Croisière des Oubliés* ("The Cruise of the Forgotten"), he illustrated the cycle "Today's Legends," which had been initiated by scriptwriter Pierre Christin. This uncertain attempt at a longer story was followed by increasingly more skillful artwork in each succeeding narrative: *Le Vaisseau de Pierre* ("The Ship of Stone," 1976); *La Ville qui n'Existait Pas* ("The Town That Didn't Exist," 1977), which American publishers called "a docufantasy about a small town saved from disaster and pushed into utopia"; and the 1979 *Les Phalanges de l'Ordre Noir* ("The Ranks of the Black Order"), the authors' first openly political tale. Bilal's most impressive achievement of the decade, however, had come in 1978 with *Exterminateur 17*. With a script by *Métal Hurlant* editor Jean-Pierre Dionnet, this innovative graphic novel successfully mixed elements of science fiction and theological musings in almost equal measure.

In 1980 Bilal released his first solo comic, *La Foire aux Immortels* (released as "Gods in Chaos" in America), a disturbing story set in a dystopian Paris of the near future. It was well received by the public and critics alike, but was eclipsed several years later by *Partie de Chasse* ("The Hunting Party"), with a script written by Christin. The authors' second foray into political allegory, this "historical fantasy," as Bilal termed it, related the chilling schemes of Soviet bloc oligarchs hunting for wild game and for one another. Bilal followed this with two solo sequels to *La Foire, La Femme-Piège* ("The Woman Trap," 1986) and *Froid Equateur* ("Cold Equator," 1992). From the 1980s on, the artist devoted an increasing amount of his time to other media, notably cinema, designing the sets of Alain Resnais's 1982 film *Life Is a Novel*, and even directing his own feature film, *Bunker Palace Hotel*, in 1989. He directed a second movie, *Tykko Moon*, which came out in 1997.

Bilal has been the recipient of many honors and awards, not only in his adopted country, but in many other parts of the world. In the United States, *Publishers Weekly* called him "one of the great comics artists working today"; and in 1997 the San Francisco Cartoon Art Museum organized a 25-year retrospective of his work.

M.H.

BILBOLBUL (Italy) Bilbolbul, created by Attilio Mussino, was the first Italian character to appear in the pages of the *Corriere dei Piccoli*, the weekly supplement of the daily newspaper *Corriere della Sera*. This took place in the very first issue (December 27, 1908) of the supplement. Bilbolbul was also the character most popular with the young readers and he accordingly appeared with a greater frequency than any other of the *Corriere's* creations (this was a time when a number of features would rotate instead of a few of them appearing weekly).

True to tradition and stereotype, Bilbolbul was a half-naked, mean little black savage who, at the end of each episode, would meet his well-deserved punishment. In the illustrations (accompanied by verse captions in the tradition of the *Corriere dei Piccoli*) there was a mixture of paradoxical and metaphoric happenings finely drawn by Mussino's clever brush strokes. The poor child underwent punishments so realistic that they became frightful, while Mussino built his metaphors to the point where they turned into paradoxes. Bilbolbul actually became "green with rage," his eyes really "burned with fire," his tongue would truly "hang out," and so on.

Bilbolbul's transformations no doubt fascinated the children, but they also frightened them. In a conservative country such as Italy was at the beginning of the century, such a novelty could not be tolerated for long. In spite of *Bilbolbul*'s success, Mussino was advised by his editors in 1912 to turn his talents to more sedate creations—one of which was to be an imitation of *Little Nemo*—but those were all short-lived. (Besides the moral reasons for *Bilbolbul*'s cancellation, there was also a political one: the recent annexation by Italy of Cyrenaica and Tripoli made the environment of the strip look out of place.)

Bilbolbul made a few fleeting appearances after World War I, still in the pages of the *Corriere dei Piccoli*, but only in recent years has its status as a pioneering comic strip been recognized in Italy and abroad.

G.B.

BILLY BIS (Italy) The word *playstory* usually means a series of interrelated adventures with several protagonists. The concept was thought up by scriptwriter Antonio Mancuso for Universo's two comic weeklies, *L'Intrepido* and *Il Monello*. These stories mix a touch of romance with a heavy dose of crime and suspense, and always end up in a clinch.

One of these stories, *Billy Bis*, was conceived by Mancuso in 1966 and drawn by Loredano Ugolini. Billy Bis is an eccentric U.N. secret agent who sports long hair and casual attire. He usually drives an Isotta Fraschini, and his adventures take place in a typically American environment, from the beaches of Florida to the skyscrapers of Manhattan. In the background lurk America's social problems: racial strife, the consumer revolt, political infighting, the clash between old ideals and pressing social needs.

Billy Bis is officially engaged to the beautiful Dorothy Matson, but he is not always faithful to her; contrary to tradition in this kind of story, Dorothy does not just sit up waiting for him, but has her own adventures in which she is the heroine.

The feature has been warmly received by its readers because it presents all types of crime stories and offers gripping suspense, with a few glimpses at social life and frequent romantic interludes, spiced with a bit of sex and violence.

The success of *Billy Bis* as a magazine feature prompted the publishers to issue a monthly comic book called *Billy Bis Super*; at first a reprint of old stories, the comic book later contained only original material drawn by Ugolini, with the frequent help of Ferdinando Corbella. It ended in the 1980s.

G.B.

"Billy Bunter," Frank Minnitt. © Knockout Comic.

BILLY BUNTER (G.B.) This strip is the classic example of survival by transference from the printed word to the picture story. William George Bunter, Billy to his pals, the "Famous Five" of the Remove Form of Greyfriars School, was created by Frank Richards (real name: Charles Hamilton), prolific author of school stories, in the first issue of *The Magnet Library*, dated February 15, 1908. Billy, known as "the Owl of the Remove," was by no means the first "Fat Boy" in British school stories, but he is certainly the most famous and, thanks to comics, the longest-lived. His talents (greed, petty larceny, lying, and cheating) have remained unchanged for almost 70 years.

The first *Magnet* illustrator to depict Bunter was Hutton Mitchell, and the last was C. H. Chapman, and it was Chapman who first tried his hand at a Bunter strip, a half-page, six-panel item in *Magnet*. This was a trial balloon for a full two-page picture story by Chapman, which ran from the first issue of *The Knock-Out Comic* (March 4, 1939). This weekly duly absorbed *Magnet* from May 25, 1940. Chapman did not stay long as illustrator, however; perhaps his style proved too detailed for slicker comic strip work. *Billy Bunter* was soon taken over by Frank Minnitt, not tremendously talented as an anatomist but the possessor of an old, rounded style suited to his subject. Minnitt continued the Frank Richards characters of teacher Mr. Quelch and gatekeeper Gosling, but added a supporting stooge of his own, the diminutive, studious Jones Minor (1942). The strip remained at two pages for some years, but expanded to 24 panels in the space of the original 12. In 1950 the strip was printed in two colors (red/black) instead of one, and soon another idea was tried: a serial strip, *Nobody Wants Billy Bunter*.

After the death of Minnitt, other artists were tried, including Reg Parlett, Arthur Martin, and Les Barton. The best was A. T. Pease, under whose slapstick style *Billy* expanded to fill a five-page weekly strip, including the full-color cover and the actual title of the comic: *Billy Bunter's Knockout* (June 10, 1961). When his comic was discontinued, Bunter lived on, transferring to *Valiant* (February 23, 1963), where he outlived artist Pease. Both he and the strip, however, did end in the late 1970s.

D.G.

BILLY PACK (Japan) *Billy Pack* was created by Mitsuhiro Kawashima and made its first appearance in the October 1954 issue of the Japanese monthly *Shōnen Gahō*. Billy Pack is a private detective, the son of an American, Professor William Pack, and his Japanese wife Tokiko. Professor Pack was arrested on the charge of spying by Japanese policemen, at the start of the Pacific War. He was shot to death along with his wife, who had tried to protect him.

After the war, Billy was adopted by his paternal uncle in the U.S. but could not dispel the memories of his native Japan and the image of his mother; and after completing a detective-school course he went back to his native country.

Billy Pack started his career as a private eye in Tokyo. Always wearing a striped hunting cap and a double-breasted coat, the tall and handsome Billy and his friendly rival, Chief Investigator Onihara Sōsa Kachō, make up a dynamic pair, responsible for the apprehension of an endless number of malefactors. The detection scenes alternate with episodes of violent action in a constantly inventive story line.

After Kawashima's untimely death at the age of 30 on March 19, 1961, the strip was taken over by his former assistant Riichi Yajima. *Billy Pack* has been adapted to radio, and later, to television. The TV dramas were introduced in the United States by CBS without success. *Billy Pack* made its last appearance in the June 1962 issue of *Shōnen Gahō*.

H.K.

BINDER, JACK (1902-198?) American comic book artist, born in Austria-Hungary on August 11, 1902. Binder immigrated to the United States in 1910. He attended fine art courses at the Chicago Art Institute and later studied under the renowned illustrator of the Edgar Rice Burroughs novels, J. Allen St. John. After stints as a commercial artist, pulp illustrator, and animator, he joined the Harry "A" Chesler comic shop in 1937 as the group's art director. In 1940, he left the Chesler studio and formed his own shop, producing thousands of pages of comic book art for companies like Fawcett, Pines, Street and Smith, New Friday, and Marvel. After three years of high-paced work, most notably on the secondary line of Fawcett characters, Binder closed his shop and became the sales manager for C. C. Beck's studio—the company that produced the bulk of Fawcett comics. He resigned in 1946 to continue his personal art career.

Jack Binder's own talents as a draftsman and storyteller were just average. Although his work was always slick and clean, his material lacked the stylized excite-

ment of a Jack Kirby or the sharp realism of a Lou Fine. And even though his material was well drawn and technically flawless, he never utilized the cinematic techniques that Will Eisner did. His stories were usually composed of standard medium-range shots and static poses that lacked significant drama or impact.

In earlier years, Binder had drawn several minor superhero and adventure strips for MLJ (*Press Guardian, Scott Rand*) and Marvel (*Destroyer, Flexo*), but while he ran his own shop and worked for Beck's, he rarely had much drawing time. His most notable work in that period were two Fawcett features, *Mr. Scarlett* and *Mary Marvel*. Producing the former in *Wow* from 1941 through 1947, Binder drew the red-clad Batman imitation in a clean, refreshing style, and, though the strip lacked a novel gimmick or particularly innovative story line, Binder managed to keep the feature readable. With *Mary Marvel*, however, which he drew from 1943 to 1950, he had the advantage of well-written scripts and the natural Marvel Family appeal. The strip carried Binder's best artwork, and while not as classically simple as C. C. Beck's *Captain Marvel* or as flamboyantly beautiful as Mac Raboy's *Captain Marvel Jr.*, Binder's drawings were finely done and well conceived.

Jack Binder, whose brother Otto was a famous comic book writer, retired from the comic book industry in 1953 and returned to commercial art. He will be remembered more for his organizational skills than his artwork. His shops pioneered the technique of breaking down comic pages into eight areas, each of which could be handled piece-by-piece by a specialist. And during the hectic, high-pressured "Golden Age" of the 1940s, that achievement was a key innovation in the still embryonic comics industry. He reportedly died at the end of the 1980s.

J.B.

BINDER, OTTO O. (1911-1974) American comic book writer and brother of Jack Binder, born August 26, 1911, in Bessemer, Michigan. Between the years 1932 and 1942, Binder spent the bulk of his time writing short stories, books, articles, and pulp novels in collaboration with his brother Earl under the pen name "Eando" Binder. He began his comic book career in 1939 as a writer for the Harry "A" Chesler shop, and later began writing for his brother Jack's shop in 1941; there he came in contact with Fawcett's Marvel Family of comic books.

Binder was a workhorse—and he showed this best as the main scripter for *Captain Marvel Adventures* and other books. Historian/artist James Steranko once estimated that he "wrote a staggering fifty-seven per cent of the entire Marvel saga." And while producing fast-paced, enjoyable stories for the Captain occupied the bulk of his time—he wrote 451 of the possible 618 stories, according to Steranko—he also helped create some of the other Marvel features, including *Mary Marvel, Marvel Family*, and the *Jon Jarl* text feature. In addition, he created many of the superb Marvel Family supporting cast: Tawky Tawny, a phenomenally popular talking tiger; Mr. Mind, the evil worm who almost defeated Captain Marvel many times; and The Sivana Family, arch-enemies of the Marvel Family. And this is not to mention his scripts for other already-established Marvel characters like *Captain Marvel Jr.* and *Hoppy, The Marvel Bunny*.

In a comic book career that spanned 32 years, Binder wrote stories for 18 major comic book publishers and well over 200 features, among them *Blackhawk* (1942, 1943), *Captain America* (1941-1946), *Superman* (1953-1969), *Spy Smasher, Bulletman,* and *Hawkman.* He also created dozens of other characters, including The Young Allies (Timely), Uncle Sam (Quality), and Captain Battle (New Friday). Binder also showed tremendous flexibility, writing all types of stories, from science fiction and horror tales for E.C.'s "New Trend," to humor stories for *Campy Chimp* and Fatman, to straight superhero material for *Dollman, Steel Sterling, Spy Smasher,* and *Captain Midnight,* to spin-offs of established features. "Comics," he once said, "were like a drug," and he did not retire from active comic book writing until 1969.

Binder's career as a writer also had great success outside the comic book industry. After he dropped the pen name "Eando"—"E" for his brother/collaborator Earl, and "O" for Otto—he began writing material under his own name. Binder has dozens of science-fiction novels to his credit, was an editor of *Space World* magazine, and wrote for the National Aeronautics and Space Administration among dozens of other writing projects.

Binder died on October 13, 1974.

J.B.

BINET, CHRISTIAN (1947-   ) French cartoonist, born in Tulle in central France on March 27, 1947. Christian Binet showed an early disposition for cartooning, selling his first drawings to *Humour Magazine* at age 14, before going on to art school in Paris. Prior to and after military service, he embarked on a career as a magazine cartoonist, working for such national publications as *Top, France-Dimanche,* and *Plexus.*

Binet made his first foray into comic strips in 1969 with a number of humorous creations, notably the children's strip *Poupon la Peste* ("Poupon the Pest," 1975), followed by *Kador* in 1977. Kador was a thinking dog, capable of reading Kant's treatises in the original German, whose intellectual brilliance, however, proved no match for Poupon's terrible pranks.

These early cartoons were to lead directly to Binet's most famous comic feature, *Les Bidochon.* The Bidochon couple, Robert and Raymonde, were initially Kador's masters but soon graduated to a series of their own. As obtuse as their pet is bright, they find themselves confronted by the myriad frustrations and vexations of a society with which they can barely cope. They are badgered by bureaucrats, harassed by their neighbors, snubbed by their relations, and gypped by their local shopkeepers. So popular did the couple become that their misadventures were brought to the stage in 1990 and made into a movie in 1995.

Throughout the years, Binet has widened his targets to include the Roman Catholic hierarchy (*L'Institution,* 1981) and the political establishment (*M. le Ministre,* 1989), but *Les Bidochon* remains his undisputed masterpiece.

M.H.

BIRO, CHARLES (1911-1972) American comic book writer, artist, and editor, born in New York in 1911. After studies at the Brooklyn Museum School of Art and the Grand Central School of Art, Biro became the writing and artwork supervisor of the Harry "A" Chesler Shop in 1936, a post he held until 1939. That year he moved over to a similar job at MLJ Comics, drew and wrote some stories, and even created the *Steel Sterling* strip.

But not until he joined the Lev Gleason (also known as Comic House) group in 1941 did his real talent become known. If Jack Kirby was the most important artistic force in comics during the 1940s, Biro certainly proved to be the finest editor and writer. While others were providing escapist fantasy in their comic books, Charles Biro decided his books would be different and better. He even dubbed them "Illustories," but the name never caught on. Throughout his 16-year stint as editorial director and chief writer at Lev Gleason, Biro proved to be the most innovative and certainly most advanced writer in the comic book field.

Christian Binet, "Les Bidochon." © *Christian Binet.*

His most miraculous job was possibly on the *Daredevil* feature, Gleason's top seller and a fine superhero concept in its own right; it was created in 1940 by Don Rico and Jack Binder. Biro assumed immediate control over the strip and wrote, drew, and edited for the book throughout the strip's life. In 1942, he introduced the Little Wise Guys, four youngsters who started as Daredevil's sidekicks. His third Little Wise Guys strip became a classic as he killed off Meatball in a gentle and heroic story rarely matched since. The strip took a similarly surprising turn in 1950 when Biro simply wrote Daredevil out of the strip—his own strip in his own book—and allowed the Little Wise Guys to carry the feature.

In 1942, Biro and coeditor Bob Wood created Chuck Chandler in the *Crimebuster* strip. Appearing in *Boy Comics*, Crimebuster was just that, a boy. A hero, yes, but first a boy who had a delightful monkey side-kick named Squeeks. The strip remains arguably the best-handled boy's adventure feature ever to appear in comics.

Biro's third innovation in 1942 was changing the superhero-oriented *Silver Streak* comic into *Crime Does Not Pay*. Usually regarded as the comic book industry's first crime title, it brought on an almost mind-boggling number of imitators, all of them vastly inferior. Throughout its run, *Crime Does Not Pay* was always the best-written, best-illustrated, and best-edited crime title, and it was always the best-selling title, as well. And although its imitators were gory and excessive, and eventually brought on a ruinous round of censorship of comics, the stellar title was the last book to succumb.

Perhaps the best indicator of the obvious popularity of Biro's material was the fact that for several years during the late 1940s and early 1950s, *Boy*, *Daredevil*, and *Crime Does Not Pay* were the three best-selling titles in a comic field of over 400 competitors.

Biro also had other highlights in his comic book career: his marketing of the first adult comic book, *Tops*, a 1949 experiment in full color and standard magazine size; his *Poppo of the Popcorn Theatre*, an outstanding but virtually ignored humor book of the 1950s; and his creation of Hillman's *Airboy*.

The artist/writer/editor left the field for television in 1962. He died on March 4, 1972.

J.B.

BLACK CAT (U.S.) When the superhero craze seized the comic book industry in the early 1940s, it was only natural that the publishers experimented with all types of formats. Men dominated the scene, but women eventually appeared, and the Black Cat was one of the longest-lasting women heroes. Created in August 1941 for Harvey's *Pocket Comics* number one, the Black Cat was really movie actress Linda Turner; she had no superheroic powers, but did have an intricate knowledge of karate.

Text-wise, *Black Cat* was never particularly appealing. Apart from riding her motorcycle, the character was shown fighting and capturing criminals while giving detailed karate lessons on the side. *Black Cat* was primarily a visual feature. Creator Al Gabriele gave the movie actress a tight, skimpy costume and illustrated her adventures until the end of 1941. Art Cazeneuve (1942) and Alex Schomburg (1944) also handled the strip before Joe Kubert took over in 1945 and 1946. Kubert jazzed up the red-haired Black Cat and exaggerated the anatomy. But the strip reached its artistic "height" when Lee Elias handled it between 1946 and 1951. He meticulously drew the Black Cat as a beautiful, sexy creature, someone sure to attract the young and mostly male comic book audience. It was this aspect that kept the strip in print for 11 years.

The strip also gained some notoriety when Dr. Frederic Wertham attacked it in his 1953 *Seduction of the Innocent*. He was particularly disturbed by what he claimed were zealous efforts to emphasize the karate aspects of the strip. He said that the lessons, which were dispensed at every opportunity, could cause children to hurt each other. Twenty years later, Juanita Coulson noted in *The Comic-Book Book* (Arlington House, 1974) that, "In these days of militant Women's Lib groups chanting, 'Rape is not a party—learn karate,' *Black Cat* would seem a bit tame. She never taught the reader how to *really* cream a male assailant."

In all, *Black Cat* appeared in four issues of *Pocket* (through January 1942), in *Speed* 17 through 38 and 44 (April 1942 to January 1947), and in 29 issues of *Black Cat* (June 1946 to June 1951).

J.B.

BLACK CONDOR, THE (U.S.) Some comic book features deserve mention in any history of the comic medium solely on the strength of their artwork. *The Black Condor*, graced with the superb artwork of Lou Fine, was just such a strip.

Writing under the pen name of Kenneth Lewis, Fine introduced the strip in Quality's *Crack Comics* number 1 (May 1940). But throughout the feature's 31-issue run (ending with the October 1943 issue of *Crack*), the story line was mediocre. It told the story of an infant named Richard whose parents were killed by raiders. He was raised by a flock of black condors and eventually simulated their power of flight. Meeting an old, hermetic missionary, who was also later killed by raiders, the grown Richard decided to use his aerial abilities to aid mankind. He adopted the identity of the Black Condor and wore a black costume that incorporated a pair of glider-like wings, which stretched from the wristband to the torso.

Eleven issues into the series, the Black Condor adopted the guise of Senator Tom Wright, a murdered legislator who looked remarkably like him. He also inherited the late senator's fiancée, Wendy, but his impersonation was known only to Wendy's father, Dr. Foster. Fighting an assortment of run-of-the-mill villains and lackluster adversaries was Richard's fate both in his Black Condor role and in his political duties.

But Fine's artwork was never deterred by the inconsequential stories. Although early issues were rather tame as Fine used a straightforward style with 12 panels per page and then 9, as the series progressed, Fine's work developed. He began to use *The Black Condor* as a showcase for his anatomic genius and a variety of shading and stippling techniques.

The work excelled when Fine began drawing expansive flying scenes. The Black Condor in flight often took up a half-page by himself, and the best issues were replete with panel after panel of aerial shots shown close up and in great detail. Besides Fine's amazing photographic accuracy, his artwork had a quality of weightlessness and ease of execution that made the flight scenes workable. The Black Condor was always swooping and diving and maneuvering in uncanny poses never seen before or since in the comic book medium.

When Fine abandoned the strip in 1942, a less talented group of illustrators, including Rudy Palais, Charles Sultan, and Gil Fox, could not match the technical excellence of Fine's work.

J.B.

BLACKHAWK (U.S.) *Blackhawk* was created for the first issue of Quality's *Military Comics* in August 1941, and while no one can claim exclusive credit for the feature's creation, Chuck Cuidera was the strip's prime mover and first artist. *Blackhawk* was different from the standard superhero fare of the early 1940s. While the majority of strips were steeped in fantasy and utilized outlandishly costumed supermen, *Blackhawk* was conceived for the World War II era, complete with grim, mercenary characters. In fact, the only differentiation between the methods used by the *Blackhawk* team and their Fascist enemies was that they were fighting for good and not against it. In its early years, *Blackhawk* was a violent strip with a heavy emphasis on military escapades, soldier-of-fortune ethics, and a vigilante-like method of dealing out justice. Blackhawk was one of the few comic book characters to carry a pistol.

The feature and its characters went through many changes in the early issues of *Military*, but seven men eventually became *Blackhawk* regulars: Hendrickson, a stereotyped anti-Nazi German and weapons expert; Chuck, a young American communications specialist; André, a French ladies' man and Blackhawk's second-in-command; Olaf, a Swedish gymnast; Stanislaus, a physically massive Pole driven from his homeland after the 1939 German invasion; and Blackhawk himself, a grim, expatriate American who was the leader. For comic relief, there was Chop-Chop, a roly-poly ponytailed Chinaman who wielded a meat cleaver and screamed, "Yippee! Me make hamburger." Flying scenes and realistic scripts were the most important factors in the early strip, and the group was usually depicted as ready to jump into their planes and fly into battle at any moment.

"Blackhawk," Reed Crandall. © Comic Magazines, Inc.

Blackhawk's greatest years were from 1941 to 1953. Designed for that time period, the stories didn't require much "willing suspension of disbelief." These were grim, violent tales of war and death. There could never be a Superman—everyone knew that—but there could have been a Blackhawk, an Andre, or a Chuck. And for many years, most notably while artist Reed Crandall and writer Bill Woolfolk were in control, the strip relied heavily on realism. Crandall's fine line and Woolfolk's fast-paced scripts made *Blackhawk* one of the best-known features ever produced. The Blackhawks outlasted most of their "Golden Age" compatriots and, unfortunately, it was their longevity that eventually destroyed them.

At the end of the Korean War, the team had no one left to fight. Created to fight wars that had already been won, they were forced to surpress revolutions in two-bit banana republics and combat the "Red Menace." Their fatalistic, men-of-their-time image began to fade. As the 1950s progressed and Quality sold the feature to National Periodicals, *Blackhawk* became littered with outlandish gimmicks, super-duper aircrafts, demagogic patriotism, and mushy science fiction. The group that had once fought tyrants like Hitler was now fighting mad scientists, crazed super-animals, and common, garden-variety thieves. Changes in the strip came quickly. Chop-Chop, who once rated his own strip, went from a fat, buck-toothed Chinaman to a hip Oriental. The fatalistic, semi-militaristic atmosphere became passé, and the group's oft-moved hideout, Blackhawk Island, began to look more and more like a playground. In the 1960s, innovations like "Lady" Blackhawk, Blackie the mascot, and the "Tom Thumb" Blackhawk robbed the strip of its old glory. Finally, their utilitarian, Gestapo-like blue uniforms were phased out in favor of garish green and red outfits. Writers even advanced the theory that André was secretly afraid of women! As the feature began its final years, the once-proud men were turned into CIA-employed superheroes with another set of uniforms—all in a vain effort to boost sales. When that too failed, new editor Dick Giordano returned the Blackhawks to their former posture and uniforms. But the Blackhawks had lost their following, and the feature was cancelled in 1969.

Blackhawk remains one of the greatest comic strips of all time, and it lasted through 243 issues of its own book as well as 102 issues of *Military* (later *Modern*) *Comics*. At the height of its popularity in 1952, Columbia produced a movie serial with Kirk Alyn as Blackhawk. There was also a short-lived radio drama during the mid-1940s.

J.B.

Ever loath to waste a character, the editors at DC brought Blackhawk back to life again and again. He resurfaced first in 1976, lasting into the next year, then was revived in 1982, 1984, 1988, and 1989-90. His last appearance to date was in *Blackhawk Special* (1992).

M.H.

BLACK HOOD (U.S.) *Black Hood* was created in October 1940 by MLJ editor Harry Shorten and made its first appearance in *Top-Notch* number nine. Quickly becoming one of MLJ's most popular creations, "The Man of Mystery" soon began appearing in *Jackpot* (Spring 1941), and then in his own magazine (starting with issue number nine, Winter 1944).

Shorten concocted a melodramatic motif for the character, and for a long time, Black Hood ran into one misfortune after another. "The Dark Knight" was actually New York patrolman Kip Burland, who had been attacked by a villain called the Skull, who looked like a skeleton. The Skull not only dazed Burland, but made it appear as if he had looted a jewelry store, too. Instantly discharged from the force, Burland set out to capture the Skull; however, it was he who was captured, and his body was riddled with bullets and thrown into a river. But Burland survived because of an old man called The Hermit, who had also been framed by the Skull. The Hermit saved his life and trained him as The Black Hood. After another long series of mishaps, all spread out over several issues of *Top-Notch*, everything was set right and The Black Hood concentrated on catching criminals.

Artistically, *Black Hood* was handled briefly by Charles Biro (1941) and *Archie* artist Bob Montana (1942). But Al Camerata and Irv Novick handled most of the stories. Novick, who drew the strip between 1943 and 1946, was more stylistic; Camerata, an underpublicized artist who drew the strip sporadically throughout its tenure, portrayed more action and adventure.

Black Hood appeared in *Top-Notch* (later called *Top-Notch Laugh*) until April 1944's 44th issue. It also appeared in *Black Hood* until Summer 1946's 19th issue, and made its last showing in *Pep* 60 (March 1947). The character was revived in MLJ's "camp superhero" drive of 1965, but was back in mothballs the following year.

J.B.

BLACK TERROR (U.S.) *Black Terror* was created by writer Richard Hughes and artist D. Gabrielsen in May 1941 and made its first appearance in Better's *Exciting Comics* number nine. The character became Better's (later Nedor and Standard) top superhero, appearing in more than 170 stories.

The Black Terror was really meek druggist Bob Benton, who developed a super potion that gave him extraordinary physical powers. He donned a primarily black costume and domino mask, and a skull and crossbones was emblazoned upon his chest. As the strip continued, Tim Roland, Benton's assistant, and Jean Starr, secretary to the mayor, became the primary supporting characters.

Editorially, the strip was never exceptional, although the stories were always well handled and fast-paced. Before the war, *Black Terror* stories dealt mainly with street crime. As with many of his costumed compatriots, World War II found the character battling the Axis, and the postwar period saw the Black Terror back on the police beat. Cocreator Hughes handled most of the scripts in 1941 and 1942, but he later gave way to Edmond Hamilton, who began scripting in 1941 and lasted through 1945.

Alex Schomburg, an underrated draftsman and illustrator, handled the bulk of the series' stories from 1943 through 1949. As the strip began to fade, however, George Tuska and Mort Meskin also contributed outstanding material to the feature.

The Black Terror outlasted many of the more-heralded superheroes and remained in *Exciting* through September 1949's 69th issue. The character also appeared in 27 issues of his own magazine, from 1942 to June 1949. He also was featured in *America's Best* for the first 31 issues, running from February 1942 through July 1949.

J.B.

BLAKE ET MORTIMER (Belgium) Edgar P. Jacobs created *Blake et Mortimer* for the first issue of the Belgian weekly *Tintin* on September 26, 1946.

Captain Francis Blake (from British Intelligence) and Professor Philip Mortimer join forces in a series of powerful adventures in which mystery, suspense, and even archaeology are cleverly woven into the overall science-fiction theme. In his strip, Jacobs has dealt with some of the most important themes of post-World War II science fiction: survival after a nuclear holocaust ("The Secret of the Swordfish," "The Diabolical Trap"); the horrors of mind-control ("The Yellow Mark"); the strangers among us ("The Enigma of Atlantis"); the dehumanization wrought by a techonology-mad society ("The Diabolical Trap"); and the callous unleashing of unknown cosmic forces ("S.O.S. Meteors"). Very often the enemies of our two heroes are the blind emissaries of a science gone mad (like the demented Professor Septimus) or the willing agents of (totalitarian) darkness best personified by the demoniacal and sinister Colonel Olrik, one of Jacobs' most powerful creations.

In all of Jacobs' stories there can be found the same currents of humanistic concern and passionate commitment to truth as in the works of Ray Bradbury, Arthur C. Clarke, and Richard Matheson.

The graphic excellence of the strip is not as readily apparent as its spellbinding plot and subtle characterization. *Blake et Mortimer* nonetheless constitutes one of the high points in visual storytelling. In epic sweep, in breadth and scope of imagination, in sheer imagery power, *Blake et Mortimer* often equals, and sometimes surpasses, *Buck Rogers, Brick Bradford*, and even *Flash Gordon*.

Eight *Blake et Mortimer* adventures have been published so far (all of them later reprinted in book form). Next to *Tintin* and *Asterix* they are probably the best-sellers among French-language comic strips. Jacobs' series has also been adapted to radio-plays and records.

One last episode, "Professor Sato's Three Formulas," left incomplete at the author's death in 1987, was finished by his former assistant Bob de Moor in 1990. An entirely original Blake and Mortimer adventure, written by Jean Van Hamme and drawn by Ted Benoit, came out in 1996.

M.H.

BLASCO, JESUS (1919-1995) Acknowledged as the best artist of the Spanish comics, Jesus Blasco was born November 3, 1919, in Barcelona. Entirely self-taught, Blasco started his cartooning career in his teens with a series of comic strips for various comic weeklies of the time, such as *Mickey, Boliche* (where he created the first version of *Cuto* in 1935), and *Pocholo*. Later he became a member of the staff of the juvenile magazine *Chicos*; in its pages Blasco revived *Cuto*, and it became his most popular success. Simultaneously he drew *Anita Diminuta* in *Chicos'* sister magazine, *Mis Chicas* (1941).

Other important works in Blasco's early career include: *La Escuadrilla de la Muerte* ("The Death Squadron," 1941), *El País del Oro Negro* ("The Land of Black Gold"), *El Planeta Misterioso, Los Tres Inseparables* ("The Inseparable Three," 1943), a series of war comic books, *Episodios de Guerra* ("Tales of War"), and the humor

"Blondie," Chic Young. © *King Features Syndicate.*

strips *Chispita* (1946), *Kul-Hebra* (1949), *Tontote y Cia* ("Tontote and Cy"), and *Rabituerto*. Mastering further his style with each new creation, Blasco produced *El Condor y el Bebé* ("The Condor and the Baby"), *Una Aventura en la India, Dan Jensen* for *Alcotan* magazine, *Jim el Terrible* ("Jim the Terrible"), *Wild Batson*, which he did along with another Western, *Smiley O'Hara* (1950), and *Dos Hermanos* ("Two Brothers") for *El Coyote*. At the same time he created the adventures of two little girls, *Marcela y Kiki*, for the girl's magazine *Florita*.

The eldest son in an artistic family that includes the illustrators Pili, Alejandro, Adriano, and Augusto, Jesus Blasco formed a partnership with his brothers Alejandro and Adriano for the production of comic features designed for the French, English, Portuguese, Belgian, and Spanish markets. During this international phase Blasco produced, among his more important titles, *Billy the Kid, Wyatt Earp, Buffalo Bill, Blackbow,* and *Shot Basky*, all Westerns, as is his masterwork, *Los Guerrilleros*, published in *Spirou, Chito,* and other magazines since 1968.

The most prolific among Spanish cartoonists, Blasco has also created *Montezuma's Daughter, Miss Tarantula, The Indestructible Man, The Slave of the Screamer, Phantom of the Forest,* and, foremost, *The Steel Claw*, for the English market. In the tradition of English picture stories with captions, he produced the whimsical *Edward and the Jumblies*, and illustrated a lovely series of children's tales, among which his version of *Alice in Wonderland* stands out. Jesus Blasco, a master of the *chiaroscuro*, has been able to endow his pictures with great dynamism and action by using the brush exclusively. Among his later contributions to the comics, mention should be made of *The Return of Captain Trueno* (1986) and *El Chacal de Bir Jerari* ("The Jackal of

Bir Jerari," also 1986). He died at his home in Barcelona on October 21, 1995.

L.G.

BLONDIE (U.S.) *Blondie* was created for King Features Syndicate on September 15, 1930, by Murat (Chic) Young. Blondie Boopadoop was, in the beginning of the strip, a bird-brained flapper pursued by Dagwood Bumstead, a rather ineffectual playboy and the son of a railroad tycoon. On February 17, 1933, Blondie married Dagwood, who was promptly disinherited by his father. Since that time the strip has assumed the look and the character it retains to this day, midway between the humor strip and the family series.

Blondie became a devoted wife and affectionate companion, as well as the actual head of the Bumstead household. While losing none of her charm, she acquired solid virtues of pluck and level-headedness, and often has to rescue Dagwood from the many jams he gets himself into. In 1934 a son, Alexander, joined the family, followed in 1941 by his sister Cookie. There are many colorful characters revolving around the Bumsteads, the most important being their neighbors Herbert and Tootsie Woodley; Mr. Dithers, Dagwood's irascible boss; the harried mailman, Mr. Beasley; not to mention Daisy the family dog and her five pups. This little world is in a state of perpetual agitation, and this provides *Blondie* with most of its gags as well as its hectic, loony atmosphere.

The simplicity of the series and its happy, optimistic outlook have won a remarkable international popularity for *Blondie*. It has been for a long time the most widely circulated comic strip in the world, translated into most languages and with an international audience reaching into the hundreds of millions. It has inspired 28 movies from 1938 to 1951 (Penny Singleton played

"Bloom County," Berke Breathed. © Washington Post Writers Group.

Blondie and Arthur Lake, Dagwood) as well as a TV series and a novel. The strip has also given rise to countless imitations in the United States and abroad. There is also a *Blondie* comic book drawn by Paul Fung, Jr.

After the death of its creator in 1973, the strip was taken over by Chic Young's two former assistants, Jim Raymond (brother of the late Alex Raymond) and Chic's own son Dean. They have managed to keep the strip's original look, and *Blondie* has so far lost none of its appeal. In 1984 Stan Drake took over the drawing, which he carried on until his death in 1997.

M.H.

BLOOM COUNTY (U.S.) While attending the University of Texas, Berke Breathed published from 1978 to 1979 in the school newspaper a comic strip entitled *Academia Waltz* that served as the origin of *Bloom County.* Set in a fictional town deep in the American heartland, it was syndicated by the Washington Post Writers Group and first appeared on December 8, 1980.

Initially, the strip was populated mostly by human characters; Milo Bloom, the irreverent blond-haired 10-year-old boy who worked as a general assignment reporter for the *Bloom Beacon* (sometimes called *Picayune*). His favorite target was Senator Bedfellow, whom he loved to photograph in embarrassing situations and whose statements he would always distort. His best friend, Michael Binkley, a "nincompoop" so lacking in virility that he asks Santa Claus for "machismo," is full of anxieties, feeling nothing in the world has been right since Marie Osmond's divorce. Not even his love for Blondie, a cool girl from Los Angeles, can possibly save him. Oliver Wendell Jones is an African-American boy genius on the cutting edge of science (he discovered that cat sweat stimulates hair growth).

The recurring adults are Cutter John, a paraplegic Vietnam vet, who loves to race around in his wheelchair/starchair "Enterpoop." When not riding with his Star Trek companions, he is heavily engaged with

Bobbi Harlow, a dark-haired beauty and elementary school teacher who loves his reckless *joie de vivre*, if not his hooked nose. She is constantly pestered by a self-centered, clothes-conscious, shallow young lawyer by the name of Steve Dallas. That this unenlightened "elitist boob" (her words) became ashamed of defending murderers and other criminals and is now a feminist and a man in touch with his feelings (he cries during *Bambi*) is not at all surprising in light of the fact that the young Binkley's ultra-conservative gun-loving father had himself metamorphosed into an ultra-liberal Democrat filled with guilt for hating Bill Cosby and his pudding commercials.

To earn a living, Steve becomes manager of the heavy-metal band "Deathtöngue," renamed "Billy and the Boingers" under pressure from sanctimonious censors. The band's members are Bill the Cat (on tongue), Opus the bow-tie adorned penguin (on tuba), and Hodge-Podge the rabbit (on drums). In fact, animals had invaded Bloom County earlier and soon took over the strip. Opus came first, a refugee of the Falklands war, whose mother had been abducted in 1982 by Mary Kay Cosmetics "commandos" ("Even their Uzis are pink."). Just like his human friends, Opus enjoys TV, car rides, Diane Sawyer's good looks; at the newspaper, he works in various positions from classified ad-taker to film critic, not to mention as Bill's vice-presidential candidate in 1988, in a hilarious send-up of presidential politics. Opinionated, but in a gentle way, he pronounces the final moral on human foibles and stupidity.

Bill wanted to be a comic-strip cat, not unlike Garfield, whose merchandising empire he envies and resents. Unfortunately for his dreams of fame and fortune, he drinks too much and takes too many drugs to ever achieve his goal. Even a presidential campaign run does not bring him happiness, despite lots of dirty tricks and illegal contributions. Perhaps his "Ack!" exclamations explain his disgusted view of life. The grumpy woodchuck Portnoy, Hodge-Podge the sharp-tongued rabbit, Rosebud the basselope (part basset hound, part antelope), and Milquetoast, Milo's pet cockroach, round out the menagerie.

Bloom County attacked liposuctions, cable TV, home shopping networks, and other wonders of the universe. In fact, there are few sacred cows in this wickedly funny strip, as it satirizes creationism, the moral majority, and football, and is not afraid to name names; Carl Sagan and his "biiillyuns of years," the British royal couple and their bratty son, William, the no less bratty Sean Penn and Madonna, the publicity-hungry Lee Iaccocca, Jim and Tammy Faye Bakker, members of the press, and politicians ("Bozos," in Opus's opinion).

The humor is pointed but not wounding, and the art clean, simple, and imaginative, favoring profiles. The strip won the Pulitzer Prize for editorial cartooning in 1987 and has been reprinted in a number of best-selling collections. However, wishing to go on to his next project, *Outland*, Breathed stopped the daily *Bloom County* strip on August 5, 1989, and the Sunday page the following day.

P.H.

BLOSSER, MERRILL (1892-1983) American cartoonist, born in Napanee, Indiana. After graduation from high school, Merrill Blosser attended Blue Ridge College in Maryland for one year, and then went on to the Chicago Academy of Fine Arts. Blosser started his professional career in 1912, when he sold his first cartoon to the *Baltimore American*. Thus encouraged, he decided to pursue his avocation, working variously for *Motor-Cycling* magazine in Chicago, and with the Denton Publishing Company in Cleveland, contributing political cartoons to the *Wheeling* (West Virginia) *Register* and sports cartoons to the *Cleveland Plain Dealer*.

In 1915, "tired of drifting" as he himself put it, Merrill Blosser joined NEA Service and, later that same year, started *Freckles and His Friends* in both daily and Sunday form. The strip, which recounts the various exploits of an enterprising youngster and his no-less-adventurous pals, met with great success (at one time it was carried in over 700 newspapers around the country). Blosser drew and wrote *Freckles* for more than 50 years (it was then taken over by Henry Formhals). He later retired to California, where he died in 1983.

Merrill Blosser is the perfect example of the old-style journeyman cartoonist whose entire life was devoted to the drawing and writing of one strip. Blosser's creations may have been humble and his penmanship short of graphic perfection (but with a bite of its own, nevertheless), but he was among the last in a breed faced with extinction, in a time of fast-changing popular tastes and short-sighted syndicate policies.

M.H.

BLOTTA, OSCAR (1918-   ) An Argentine cartoonist born in 1918, Oscar Blotta studied at the National Academy of Fine Arts in Buenos Aires. After working as a freelance cartoonist for a number of publications, he started his comic strip career in the 1940s with two humor features produced for the publisher Dante Quinterno: *El Gnomo Pimentón* ("Hot Pepper the Gnome"), published in the children's magazine *Patoruzito*, and *Ventajita*, which appeared in *Patoruzú*.

The titular heroes of these two strips inspired the first feature-length animated cartoon ever produced in Argentina: *Upa en Apuros*. Blotta collaborated in a decisive

way in the production, while simultaneously doing illustrations for children's books. He retired in the 1980s.

L.G.

BLUE BEETLE (U.S.) *Blue Beetle* was created by Charles Nicholas and made its first appearance in Fox's *Mystery Men* number one for August 1939. One of the earliest superheroes, the character quickly merited his own book (Spring 1940), and *Blue Beetle* became one of the most intriguing strips of all time.

The origin most often cited reveals that rookie policeman Dan Garrett was given his superhuman powers from a vitamin known as "2X." He also wore an almost invisible suit of blue chain mail. Almost all of this changed over the years, however, and the uniform rarely looked like actual mail armor. Inconsistencies aside, the strip became immensely popular, and the character was soon appearing on radio and in an ill-fated newspaper strip. He even picked up a sidekick named Spunky in 1943, but this character did not last long. In fact, the only regularly featured supporting characters were Mike Mannigan, Garrett's police partner, and Joan Mason, the ever-present love interest.

The strip was never outstanding, either editorially or artistically. Illustrations were crude and stories infantile, yet the feature remained popular. Besides creator Nicholas—who drew *Blue Beetle* between 1939 and 1942 and received the syndicated strip byline—Jack Kirby, Don Rico, Alex Blum, and Allan Ulmer contributed to the feature. Overall, during this initial run, *Blue Beetle* appeared in all 37 issues of *Mystery Men* until its discontinuation in February 1942. He also appeared in 60 issues of *Blue Beetle* from Winter 1939 to August 1950. Oddly enough, the issues between numbers 17 and 26 were published by Holyoke and not Fox. He also appeared in *Big Three* and other books.

Charlton purchased the rights to the strip and produced a new series of *Blue Beetle* comics, but the series lasted less than a year—November 1954 to August 1955. Charlton made another attempt in 1964 and 1965, but these 10 issues are among the worst comics ever produced. Notable, however, is the fact that Roy Thomas began his career here.

The strip finally got superior writing and drawing when Charlton revived it again in 1967. Handled primarily by artist Steve Ditko, the feature was gutted of all its previous affiliations. The Blue Beetle was now a duo-toned, gadget-minded hero known in civilian life as Ted Kord. A scientist, Kord was originally suspected by police of killing the Dan Garrett Blue Beetle, but this story line eventually became overworked and was dropped. Ditko's rendition was easily the best *Blue Beetle* ever produced, but poor sales dictated its cancellation after five issues (June 1967 to November 1968). A sixth Ditko *Beetle* tale, produced in 1968, was finally published in the *Charlton Portfolio* in 1974. A new version was published by DC in 1986–88.

J.B.

BLUE BOLT (U.S.) *Blue Bolt* was created in June 1940 by Joe Simon and made its first appearance in *Blue Bolt* volume one, number one, published by Novelty Publications.

The Blue Bolt was really Fred Parrish, a football star struck by lightning during practice. Almost immediately after, he crashed his private plane into a lost valley and was saved only by massive doses of radium administered by a Dr. Bertoff. The doctor also supplied

Parrish with his blue costume, a crash helmet and a lightning gun—all of which Parrish was supposed to take back to civilization. For a long while, however, the character remained in the lost valley and battled a lady known as the Green Sorceress, one of the best-remembered villains of the 1940s.

Artistically, *Blue Bolt* is significant because it was the first collaboration of Joe Simon and Jack Kirby. And although they did not begin their partnership until a year later, Simon and Kirby handled the strip during 1940. After the pair jumped to Timely, George Mandel (1941-1942), Dan Barry (1943), and others began illustrating the character.

Despite his relatively unique lightning bolt motif, Blue Bolt began faltering, and Lois Blake was given a similar costume and powers in volume two, number seven. But by volume three, number four, Blue Bolt abandoned his costume and spent the rest of his career in civilian garb. *Blue Bolt* ended after September 1949's volume 10, number two. The feature lasted exactly 100 issues. The company began a *Blue Bolt* reprint title in 1950, but it ended after a few issues.

J.B.

BLUE SEA AND RED HEART (China) This tale of heroism was adapted from an original story by Liang Hsin into a comic book published in 1965 by the People's Art Publications in Shanghai. The script was by Wan Chia-ch'un and the artwork by Hsü Chin.

Blue Sea and Red Heart recounts in some detail the exploits of Captain Hsiao Ting of the People's Liberation Army during the reconquest of Hainan in 1949. The script reads like an adventure movie in its single-mindedness and high purpose: there is not one dramatic device missing, from the daring raid on enemy headquarters to the obligatory rescue of a comely, if headstrong, damsel in distress. It all ends with Hsiao Ting maneuvering his explosive-laden junk onto the enemy flagship and blowing it up. The last panel (looking suspiciously like a shot from *The Sands of Iwo Jima*) shows Hsiao Ting in a heroic posture, leading his men onto the beaches, while the caption reads: "At dawn, our army has already set foot on the northern shore of Hainan. Hsiao Ting at the head of his troops pushes fearlessly forward. The island of Hainan is liberated at last!"

Childish as the narrative may sound, *Blue Sea* provides a good example of comic book art. Hsü Chin is an accomplished craftsman; his drawings are detailed without being cluttered, his line is simple and effective. Best of all are his compositions: brooding, suspenseful, and functional. On the strength of this one example, Hsü Chin's artistry is far superior to that of any number of American cartoonists currently doing comic book work.

Blue Sea and Red Heart was reprinted (as "Bravery on the High Seas") in *The People's Comic Book* (Doubleday, 1973).

M.H.

BLUEY AND CURLEY (Australia) Created by Alex Gurney for the *Herald and Weekly Times Ltd.* in 1940, the strip appeared briefly in *Picture News* magazine before transferring to the *Sun-News Pictorial* on February 1, 1941, as a daily strip. Soon the strip was appearing in all Australian states and servicemen's newspapers and later was syndicated in New Zealand and Canada.

The strip accurately reflected the Australian soldier's vision of himself as a fighting man without peer but more interested in his beer and gambling; resenting all military authority (and later, all forms of authority); a confidence man with the ability to laugh at himself and a ready disciple of the "You can't win" attitude. More than any other strip, *Bluey and Curley* gave civilians an insight into the hardships of army life and the slang expressions of the period. It also projected the mood of envy directed towards the more highly paid U.S. soldiers. Still, all subjects were handled in a gentle, smile-provoking manner—for, while Gurney was not particularly subtle, he was never cruel. His handling of "fuzzie-wuzzies" or "boongs" and their Pidgin English were classics. The strip perpetuated traditional back-block humor, and the army cook was often the butt of jokes and situations, previously reserved for the shearer's cook.

Bluey had a protruding nose, long jaw, and straight red hair (hence the traditional Australian nickname of Bluey) and, with a cigarette hanging from his bottom lip, was usually a foil for his more exuberant mate. Curley had a baby-face, small up-turned nose, and curly, blonde hair and was the ladies' man of the team, with a girl in every town. Their dialogue was purely Australian, right down to the cursing and swearing, which only lacked the great Australian adjective, 'bloody,' to make it fully authentic. They wore their slouch hats at a jaunty angle, pushed back off their foreheads as an added mark of their disrespect for authority. Yet, despite their rebellious attitude, they were never to be seen drunk or A.W.O.L.—points raised by Gurney when the strip was dropped from an army newspaper as setting a bad example for the service. An immediate protest by the soldiers assured that the strip was reinstated.

Bluey and Curley was a very nationalistic strip that covered all facets of Australian humor. It was at its peak of popularity during the 1940s but tended to lose some of its punch and individuality when it made the transition to civilian life. The common enemies of army life were then missing.

When Gurney died of a heart attack in December 1955, the strip passed on to Norm Rice, who died in a car accident less than 12 months later. The strip was then taken over by Les Dixon, a former *Smith's Weekly* artist and art editor. Dixon gradually altered the art style and added new characters (e.g., a swaggie Jazzer; an old reprobate Trotters), assisting the strip's continued popularity—but it is Alex Gurney's wartime adventures of *Bluey and Curley* that made this strip a household name. The strip finally ended in July 1975.

J.R.

BOBBY THATCHER (U.S.) George Storm's second adventure strip, entirely his own and one of the most popular ever drawn, the daily *Bobby Thatcher* began publication with the McClure Syndicate in a number of papers between March and August, 1927. Since the *Thatcher* episodes carried numbers rather than dates (as did those of many adventure strips to follow), papers could begin the strip months after its original release date and still run the full continuity. Not as exciting at the outset as Storm's earlier, bloodier, and grimmer (but premature) seafaring strip, *Phil Hardy*, *Thatcher* possessed elements that appealed more to the public of the time. An attractive, 15-year-old tow-headed kid (physically similar to Chester Gould's Junior Tracy sev-

"Bobby Thatcher," George Storm. © McClure Syndicate.

eral years later), Thatcher was often on the road in a peaceful, rural American locale immediately recognizable to millions of readers. A public highly partial to *Little Orphan Annie* was more than ready to welcome a well-done male equivalent, and that was what the McClure Syndicate meant to provide.

But *Bobby Thatcher* (which moved to the Bell Syndicate with episode 1013 on June 6, 1930) was more than an *Annie* imitation. Storm's charming narrative imagination, skilled sense of pace, and stunning graphic style followed their own highly individual course in combining to produce an adventure strip that stood second to none but *Annie* and *Wash Tubbs* at the close of the 1920s. At first slow to develop permanent characters, Storm established several close friends for Bobby by 1931, such as Marge Hall, Bobby's longed-for but elusive girlfriend; Lulu Bowers, his "regular" girl; and Ulysses "Tubby" Butler, Peewee Nimmo, and Elmer Bowers, three of his juvenile companions. All these characters are inhabitants of rural Jonesboro, where Bobby, his sister, Hattie, and his Aunt Ida Baxter live for much of the central continuity of the strip. The most powerful character of Storm's *Thatcher*, however, was introduced somewhat later: the tough-hewn, Popeyesque sailor, Hurricane Bill, with whom Bobby is involved in a shipboard struggle against the hulking, brutal Captain Bottlejohn in 1935. This story, featured in the only *Bobby Thatcher* book reprint, was a Whitman Topline paper-covered book of that year.

Storm tired of strip work in 1937, however, hired a full-time ghost (Sheldon Mayer), and abruptly closed down *Thatcher* with a publisher's printed farewell to the readers on various dates in 1938 (depending on the point at which subscribing papers ran out of *Thatcher* continuity). Storm went on to draw other strips of brief duration, largely for comic books, through the 1940s,

but *Thatcher* remains his unique triumph, a major comic strip work of its period, richly deserving of reprinting in full.

B.B.

BOB MORANE (France/Belgium) The Belgian writer Henri Vernes created the character of Bob Morane in a series of best-selling novels published since 1955 by Editions Marabout in Belgium. In 1958 Bob Morane was adapted into the comic strip medium by Dino Attanasio in the pages of the women's magazine *Femmes d'Aujourd'hui*.

Bob Morane is a modern-day adventurer who performs his exploits in all parts of the world. He is clean-living and crew-cut in the best tradition of the 1950s, and he is more than a little on the dull side. The color is supplied by his inseparable companion, the red-haired Scottish giant Bill Ballantine (a chicken farmer in his spare time), whose earthy humor and lively she-nanigans make him the favorite of readers. Among the many enemies that Morane and Ballantine encounter—saboteurs, mad scientists, master spies, and other miscreants—the most implacable is the cruel Mister Ming, also known as "the Yellow Shadow," whose niece, the enigmatic Tania, is the hero's secret love. Science fiction and fantasy agreeably mix with derring-do and suspense in Vernes's well-plotted tales.

In 1960 Attanasio was succeeded by Gerald Forton, who drew the feature in a more up-to-date style; in turn, in 1967 Forton left the drawing of the strip to William Vance, who proved himself as the series' definitive artist. (In addition to his work for *Femmes d'Aujourd'hui*, Vance has also done a few *Bob Morane* episodes for *Pilote*.) In 1979 Vance handed the art chores over to his assistant (and brother-in-law) Francisco Coria; and in 1993 Forton came back to draw *Bob*

Morane for the second time after a quarter-century absence.

Bob Morane has been reprinted in book form by Editions Dargaud in France. In 1970 it also inspired a French TV series with Claude Titre in the title role.

M.H.

BŌKEN DANKICHI (Japan) *Bōken Dankichi* ("The Adventures of Dankichi") was created by Keizo Shimada, a pioneer in the field of children's comic strips, and made its first appearance in the Japanese monthly *Shōnen Kurabu* ("Boys Club") in April 1934.

Dankichi was a little Japanese boy who went fishing one fine day along with his pet mouse Kari-kō; while fishing they fell asleep and drifted to sea. Landing on a South Seas island inhabited by ferocious cannibals, they managed by cunning to defeat the island's chief, and Dankichi ascended to the throne. Under Dankichi's wise leadership, and with the assistance of Kari-kō, the island became a haven of peace and serenity, which did not fail to attract interlopers. Dankichi fought against a crew of pirates intent on seizing the island. His army (consisting of hippopotami used as submarines, vultures serving as dive-bombers, elephants substituting for tanks, and the like) defeated the pirates. Other perils loomed, however, and Dankichi had to fight again until May 1939 when the strip was temporarily discontinued.

Bōken Dankichi reappeared after the war in several monthlies: *Yōnen Book, Shōgaku Ichinensei,* and *Norakuro*. The strip tried to explain the rules of the American military administration and the new ways of Japan to its readers.

"Bōken Dankichi," Keizo Shimada. © Shōnen Kurabu.

In spite of the simplicity of its story lines and the bareness of its drawings, *Bōken Dankichi* enjoyed the highest popularity of any strips in its day, and it is one of the longest-lasting strips in Japan.

H.K.

BONELLI, GIOVANNI LUIGI (1908-   ) Italian writer, editor, and publisher, born December 22, 1908, in Milan. Bonelli's entire output was directed at a juvenile public. He started as a contributor to the *Corriere dei Piccoli* in the late 1920s with a series of poems, which were followed by some articles for the *Giornale Illustrato dei Viaggi*. At the same time he wrote two adventure novels: *Le Tigri dell'Atlantico* ("The Tigers of the Atlantic") and *I Fratelli del Silenzio* ("The Brotherhood of Silence").

In the mid-1930s Bonelli entered the comics field as writer, and later as managing editor of the comic weeklies *Primarosa, Robinson, L'Audace, Rintintin,* and *Jumbo,* published by SAEV in Milan. His stories were illustrated by artists of the first rank, such as Franco Chiletto, Rino Albertarelli, and Walter Molino. When *L'Audace* was taken over by Mondadori, Bonelli stayed on as editor until 1939, when he bought out the magazine and started publishing it himself. He decided immediately to change the format of the publication, from tabloid to comic-book size, foreshadowing the change in illustrated magazines in Italy by some six years.

When the war broke out, Bonelli resumed his writing career, mainly for small publishers, until 1947, when he joined forces with Giovanni De Leo to launch several ventures, including a Western magazine with no illustration and the adaptation of a string of comic books produced in France by Pierre Mouchot.

In 1946 Bonelli wrote a short story, *La Perla Nera* ("The Black Pearl"), and in 1947 *Ipnos*. In 1948 Bonelli initiated a long and successful series of Western strips, starting with the popular *Tex Willer* and *La Pattuglia senza Paura* ("The Fearless Patrol," the adventures of two brothers, Alan and Bob Gray, drawn by Guido Zamperoni and Franco Donatelli). Among his other creations, there are: *Il Vendicatore del Oeste* ("The Western Avenger"); *Yuma Kid* (both 1948); *El Kid* (drawn by Dino Battaglia, most notably); *Davy Crockett* (1956); and *Hondo* (1957). In 1962 Bonelli took over *Un Regazzo nel Oeste* ("A Boy in the West"), which had been originated by Nolitta, and he brought this long saga to an enjoyable end. He retired in the early 1980s, leaving his flourishing publishing house in the hands of his son Sergio.

G.B.

BONER'S ARK (U.S.) Mort Walker, under his real first name Addison, created *Boner's Ark* for King Features Syndicate on March 11, 1968.

Boner is the skipper of an ark that wanders the world's seas aimlessly—never sighting land more than postage-stamp size. On Boner's Ark the animals are not in pairs, although each is accompanied by a singular psychosis or bit of nuttiness that keep an essentially limited basis for gags always fresh and funny.

Boner himself is a gentle, victimized, and sometimes befuddled human. The short skipper briefly sported a blonde mustache in the strip. In 1974 his bushy-haired wife Bubbles was introduced (she was found drifting on a raft). She is flaky, wears tennis shoes, and

"Boner's Ark," Addison (Mort Walker). © King Features Syndicate.

unleashes as much madcap terror on the ark as the wildest of the animals.

The animals include Cubcake, a lovable koala bear; first mate Arnie Aardvark, Boner's blasé sidekick; Priscilla Pig, who stretches a little bikini to its limits and fantasizes about herself as a beauty queen sought after by suitors; Sandy Ostrich, a pal of Priscilla; Dum-Dum, a large, strong, and very stupid gorilla; Duke, the suave penguin in a tuxedo; Spot the dog, a perpetual flunk-out from obedience school; Rex the dinosaur, the hippopotamus, and the giraffe—large-size vehicles for gags about their weight and height problems; and, perhaps the funniest, the trio of the nameless hyena, bear, and mouse, eternal mutineers.

The interplay of the personalities provides ample room for latitude in the strip, which is consistently fresh. Another factor that helps the flow of ideas is Walker's "factory" of gagmen—Ralston Jones, Bob Gustafson, and Jerry Dumas, chiefly—who devote every Monday to conferences on *Boner*. Since 1971 the indefatigable Frank Johnson has pencilled and inked the strip.

The artwork is particularly engaging and individualistic, closer in originality to *Sam's Strip* than Walker's other post-*Beetle Bailey* pastiches, *Hi and Lois* and *Mrs. Fitz's Flats*. The style is sketchy but firm, and simplicity is the hallmark. Panoramas of the ark on the horizon, with an enormous drop of water or two at the crest of a wave, achieve almost a poster effect. The strip, which runs daily and Sunday, has maintained its level of about 145 papers for several years.

R.M.

Frank Johnson, who had been assisting Walker since 1971, finally got to sign *Boner's Ark* in 1982. Despite multiple false sightings, the ark's inmates are as far from land in 1997 as they ever were since the strip's inception.

M.H.

BONVICINI, FRANCO (1941-1995) Italian cartoonist, born March 31, 1941, in Modena, Italy. After attending classes in several universities without getting

any degree, Franco Bonvicini decided upon a career in animated cartoons. He entered the comics field in 1969, creating his first strip, *Sturmtruppen*, about a batallion of inept German storm troopers in World War II, which immediately gained wide acclaim in critical circles as well as from the public. *Sturmtruppen* won a contest organized by the Roman daily *Paese Sera* where it was published, then went on to the short-lived weekly *Off-Side*, and later to the *Gazzetta di Parma*; it now appears in the monthly *Eureka* and in the illustrated weekly *Corriere dei Ragazzi*. A number of *Sturmtruppen* episodes were collected in two hardbound volumes and in two paperbacks. (All are signed with the pen name "Bonvi.")

Along with his *Sturmtruppen*, Bonvi produced several other features for the magazine *Giorni* and the *Gazzetta*

Franco Bonvicini, "Cattivik." © Bonvi.

di Parma, as well as a series of strips drawn for the publications of Edizioni Alpe, the most notable being *Cattivik* ("The Baddie") and *Posapiano* ("Slowpoke"). He also contributed short stories to the monthly magazines *Psycho* and *Horror*.

In 1972 Bonvi created *Nick Carter* (a parody on the fabled detective) in cooperation with Guido de Maria for a TV series called *Gulp! Comics on TV*. The character was an immediate success and the films enjoyed a number of reruns. It was announced that, beginning in 1975, Nick Carter would be the leading character in *Supergulp!* (a spin-off from *Gulp!*). Bonvi and de Maria also produced another series for television, *Saturnino Farandola*, a science-fantasy story based on a novel by Albert Robida. As for Nick Carter, he also appeared in a short series of comic books as well as in the *Corriere dei Regazzi* and in several foreign publications.

In 1973, in collaboration with Mario Gomboli, Bonvi created *Milo Marat* for the French weekly *Pif*. In the meantime *Sturmtruppen* had inspired a stage play, and a movie was also announced. Bonvi succeeded in creating a school around him, made up of some excellent artists, and this strongly contributed to the success (and to the multiplicity) of his comic creations. In the last 20 years of his life he devoted himself more and more to the field of animated cartoons. He died in a car accident on December 9, 1995.

Bonvi was the recipient of a number of awards, including the "Saint-Michel" (Belgium) in 1973, and the "Yellow Kid" (Italy) in 1974.

G.B.

BONZO (G.B.) Bonzo, a happy, laughing, pudgy pup with one black ear, a couple of black spots, and a stump of a tail, was created by George E. Studdy. Bonzo's birthday is unknown, as is his form of origin. He appeared in almost every popular medium during the 1920s and 1930s: picture postcards, cigarette cards, pictures, posters, children's picture and story books, magazine illustrations, stuffed dolls, toys, souvenirs, ashtrays—and all before he appeared in comic strips! He was even the star of the only successful series of animated cartoon films made in Britain during the silent film era. The *Bonzo* cartoons, 26 of them, were produced by his creator in conjunction with animator William A. Ward and scriptwriter Adrian Brunel (1924). A *Bonzo* daily strip appeared briefly around the late 1920s, but seems to have been published abroad rather than in Britain. This is also true of a syndicated Sunday strip page that Studdy drew for King Features in 1930-1931. Bonzo was also featured in color on the cover of *Toby*, a monthly magazine for children, and in an inside strip (1927). The daily strip was reprinted in *Bonzo: The Great Big Midget Book*, published by Dean (1932), the British equivalent of the famous *Big Little Book* series. In addition, Dean published a *Bonzo Annual* each year, with full-color plates by Studdy. After the

"Bonzo," G. E. Studdy. © Studdy.

artist's death, others took over and the annual continued into the 1950s. The early Bonzo material is widely collected today, but the character himself and his artist are almost totally forgotten.

D.G.

BOOB McNUTT (U.S.) *Boob McNutt*, the one considerable and long-lived comic strip Rube Goldberg was to draw, appeared only as a Sunday page during its entire 20-year span. It was Goldberg's second Sunday color feature (the first was a short-lived *Mike and Ike* half-page in the old *New York World* in 1907) and first appeared in the *New York Evening Mail* in May 1915. It did not receive notable national distribution until the growing popularity of Goldberg's daily multititled sports-page gag miscellany (copyrighted by the artist but distributed by the *Mail*) led Hearst's Star Company to contract with the *Mail* for distribution of both the daily panel and the Sunday *Boob* on June 9, 1918. Once the public at large saw *Boob*, primarily in Hearst newspapers, the strip's popularity grew a bit, and when the *Mail* folded in 1924, Goldberg negotiated a new, personal contract with the Star Company, which continued until Goldberg ended *Boob* on September 30, 1934.

Initially, *Boob McNutt* was a weekly gag strip, in which the red-headed, sharp-nosed hero with the tiny green hat and the spotted pants was asked by some trusting person to aid in a minor or major undertaking (from lifting a statue off a roof to piloting a Mars rocket)—and brought about total disaster instead. This

"Boob McNutt," Rube Goldberg. © King Features Syndicate.

Keystone formula was not very different from what was happening in *Happy Hooligan* and a dozen other strips, and though the public liked *Boob* well enough, it was not a wildfire sensation. However, when Boob began to court a flapper named Pearl in early 1922 and managed—usually by dumb luck—to survive the murderous attacks of his rival, Major Gumbo (aided and abetted by Pearl's father, Toby), the public interest in the strip grew. And when the complications that followed on the appearance of a new and richer rival, Shrimp Smith, led to a sudden cross-country trek by Boob, Pearl, Shrimp, and Toby and the creation of genuine week-to-week narrative suspense, more and more readers turned to *Boob* first every Sunday to see what would happen next to this preposterous quartet. Noting this, Goldberg exercised his developing talent for anecdotal narrative during the tense summer of 1924, when attempt after attempt by Boob to marry Pearl went maddeningly awry. Finally, again by dumb luck, the two made it to the altar on September 24, 1924—only to tumble into fresh trouble in a shipwreck on an ocean isle inhabited by such comic-page innovations as ostrich-legged ikmiks and grass-eating biffs-niffs.

Plot was intrinsic to *Boob McNutt* now, and narrative development brought fresh characters into the strip. First was Bertha the Siberian cheesehound (with her engaging dialogue of "ipple gopple zuk," "gifke nok wup," and the like), bought by Boob as a gift for Pearl on January 24, 1925, but who remained Boob's dog for the rest of the strip. (Later, on January 9, 1926, Bertha became the star of *Bertha*, a companion fifth-of-a-page strip for the Sunday *Boob*, which ran until July 11, 1926. A gag strip, it had no narrative connection with the main page.) Next, as the climax of a months-long search in mid-1927 for the long-lost twins of his adopted parents, Boob discovered the missing twins were the old sawed-off Goldberg characters, Mike and Ike, performing as tramp trapeze artists with a circus, on August 14, 1927. Their compulsive explanatory refrain—"I'm Mike." "I'm Ike."—quickly became a schoolyard catch phrase, while their derby-topped, scraggly-bearded moon faces became a nationally recognized double image.

The strip's permanent adventure team was now complete, and Boob, Pearl, Mike, Ike, and Bertha proceeded to follow Goldberg's imagination into the wildest escapades yet. Sea piracy, foreign intrigue, kidnapping—all made the Sunday page an area of animated excitement amid the surrounding placid sea of domestic gag strips like *Elmer, Polly, Tillie,* and others. Then Goldberg recalled the public's enthusiastic response to the earlier desert island ikmiks and biff-sniffs and decided to populate the strip with an almost limitless array of fantastic creatures in 1931 and '32: flying goppledongs, horn-billed zoppuluses, darting ploffs, and bomb-headed bambams—all being rounded up by Boob and his gang on a crippled dirigible from a stormy sea. This was the beginning of the gorgeously inventive era of *Boob* most readers of the time remember best, and it was followed by more fabulous beasts when a nutty scientist, Dr. Zano, enlarged reptiles and insects to a ghastly size and unleashed them onto a flabbergasted world in 1933. Eventually, Boob and a considerable part of the local constabulary licked this zoological challenge on December 31, 1933, after months of intensive strip action—and then, as if Goldberg could think of nothing wilder for Boob to do, the

strip stumbled into a short series of tired narratives and collapsed for good at the end of September 1934.

For all of its heady imaginative content in its last years and skillful narrative pace, *Boob* was badly marred by the careless, slapdash comic style Goldberg affected at every point, and perhaps fatally flawed by the characterless void where the hero should have been. For, far in the wake of the public's eagerly recalled fantastic animals, the lookalike twins Mike and Ike, and Bertha the mutt straggled the *zilch* hero who was literally nothing more than his name indicated: a boob. The flaw was Goldberg's: talented at creating memorable supporting characters in all of his strips, he could never evoke a gripping central protagonist—and yet just such a vital figure, from Popeye and Paw Perkins to Krazy Kat and Dick Tracy, was essential to the creation of a great strip. But *Boob* remains good reading in spite of this, thanks to its narrative pace.

A third-rate gag strip called *Bill* occupied a third of the Sunday page space Goldberg used for *Boob* between July 18, 1926, and September 30, 1934. There is little to be said in favor of this space-filler: its gags are tired, its story tiresome, and its hero even more of a nullity than Boob himself: the narrative of an ambitious young soda jerk with an empty face and a shock of black hair, *Bill* is probably the nadir of Goldberg's strips, including the ill-fated *Doc Wright*.

B.B.

BOOTH, WALTER (1892?-1971) British cartoonist and illustrator, born in Walthamstow, London. He was educated at Samuel Road School before studying art at Walthamstow Art School. He then joined the staff of Carlton Studio (1908), drawing general commercial work until trying his hand at strips for the James Henderson & Son publishing house in Red Lion Square. His extremely clean style, detailed and neat, yet occasionally extruding beyond the frames, seems fully formed from the start (1911) and hardly changes throughout the 60 years of comic work that followed.

His first strip was *Private Ramrod* (1911) in *Comic Life*, echoed by *Ram and Rod* (1914), more soldiers, in *Sparks*. He created his most famous comic character, *Professor Potash*, in 1915 for *The Big Comic*, continuing him in *Lot O' Fun* in 1919. In this same year he deserted the knockabout comic for the nursery comic with *Peggy and Peter in Toyland*, a series for *Sparks*. When that weekly changed its title to *Little Sparks*, which suited its nursery policy, he created *Jumbo* (1920).

The year 1920 was the year that the powerful Amalgamated Press bought out the Henderson comics, and Booth was welcomed to the higher-class fold. He was brought aboard *Puck*, the leading A.P. color comic weekly, and for this paper he created the first dramatic picture serial in British comics, *Rob the Rover*, in 1920. He took over the full-color front page in 1930 with his *Jingles' Jolly Circus*, a return to humor, but continued to exploit the new picture story field. This expanding productivity was made possible by taking on the young Stanley White as assistant. Booth's serials included *Orphans of the Sea* (1930), *Cruise of the Sea Hawk* (1936), and *Captain Moonlight* (1936), all for *Puck*; *The Adventure Seekers* (1926) in *Lot O' Fun*; and *The Pirate's Secret* (1939) in *Happy Days*.

With the discontinuation of *Puck* in 1940, the war years proved to be lean ones for Booth, but he drew some good strips for *Merry Maker* (1946), a small comic started by his old pupil, White. This led to strips for

"Boots and her Buddies," Edgar Martin. © NEA Services.

Scion comics in their *Big* series of one-shot titles, and eventually, despite living in far-off Wales, he managed a full comeback, drawing for the new nursery comic printed in photogravure, *Jack and Jill*. His *There Was an Old Woman Who Lived in a Shoe* (1954) was a large, action-filled picture that covered the center spread. This transferred to *Harold Hare's Own Paper* in 1964, and proved to be his last contribution to comics. He died in February 1971.

D.G.

BOOTS AND HER BUDDIES (U.S.) Cartoonist Edgar Martin created *Boots and Her Buddies* (the name is almost a play on *Polly and Her Pals*) for NEA Service on February 18, 1924.

Boots was a girl strip, and it followed on the heels of such established staples of the genre as *Tillie the Toiler* and *Winnie Winkle*. Boots was a vivacious, eye-pleasing blonde whose charms moved Coulton Waugh to lyrical heights in his study *The Comics*: "Ah, Boots! Sexy Boots! Curvaceous plump one . . . when she stretches out a long rounded leg with those very small feet, we . . . we had better put on our pince-nez again. How can that girl be both thin and plump at once?" Since 1924 Boots pursued her career undisturbed by outside events, going from naive coed to married woman to mod mother without ever losing her cool. Boots' buddies have included her own brother Bill, always handy for a buck or a piece of advice, her kind-hearted lodgers, Professor Stephen Tutt and his prim wife Cora, her fellow students, the disorganized Horace and his fat girlfriend Babe (who later married and got a strip of their own), not to mention her numerous suitors and admirers.

Boots reached the height of its popularity in the 1930s and 1940s when her adventures were followed by millions of readers. As Boots settled into domestic bliss in the later 1940s, the strip became indistinguishable from the host of other married strips cluttering the comics pages, and went steadily downhill. After being

taken over by Les Carroll for a few years, it disappeared in the late 1960s.

M.H.

BORING, WAYNE (1916-1987) American comic book and comic strip artist, born in 1916. He attended the Chicago Art Institute and the Minnesota School of Art. Boring, sometimes working under the name Jack Harmon, became a comic book artist in 1937, working on detective strips like *Slam Bradley* and *Spy* for National. But the overwhelming bulk of material Boring produced during his 30-year association with National was for *Superman*. Along with Paul Cassidy, he was one of the first ghosts to work on the strip, and he was with creators Siegel and Shuster when they opened their first studio in 1938.

And it was Boring's rendition of the "Man of Steel" that eventually became definitive. Whereas Joe Shuster's *Superman* art was crude and plodding, Boring's work was infinitely tighter and more polished. Influenced by Frank Godwin's work on the *Connie* syndicated strip, he remade Superman's squat and chunky figure into a massive, rippling, muscular body. His Superman always sported bulging chest and thigh muscles, never stood or flew in anything but the most classic poses, and always looked the part of the world's mightiest creature. Boring also excelled in expressive faces, every character flawlessly rendered for the best dramatic effect. But many save their highest praise for Boring's city scenes. When editor Mort Weisinger tried to make the *Superman* feature more futuristic, he resorted to gimmicky science fiction plots, but Boring's backgrounds achieved a futuristic look simply by ingenious uses of vertical lines. Unlike Carmine Infantino's prettier, more rounded, and lower cities in *Adam Strange*, Boring created captivating masses of stylized, rectangular skyscrapers.

Boring finally left National and *Superman* for syndicated strip work in 1968, spending four years assisting Hal Foster on *Prince Valiant* and Sam Leff on *Davy Jones*.

"The Born Loser," Art and Chip Sansom. © NEA.

He returned to comic books in 1972, drawing Marvel strips like *Captain Marvel* and *Gullivar of Mars*. He gave up drawing comics in 1991. He was working as a night watchman when he died on February 20, 1987, in Pompano Beach, Florida.

J.B.

BORN LOSER, THE (U.S.) After working for two decades as a bullpen cartoonist drawing several story features for the Newspaper Enterprise Association, Arthur B. Sansom Jr. added a refreshingly new strip to his syndicate in 1964. Dubbed *The Born Loser*, the new humor strip was one of the more sophisticated features to emerge during the 1960s. The beleaguered subject, Brutus P. Thornapple, is a typical, middle-aged Everyman who is beset by fate and family. His towering wife Gladys delivers smug remarks and derogatory support to her husband, while his seven-year-old son Wilberforce usually gets the upper hand in most situations. Neighbor Hurricane Hattie O'Hara is a formidable opponent, particularly for Brutus—a seven-year-old smart aleck specializing in aggravation, while sardonic mother-in-law Ramona Gargle and lethargic pet mutt Kewpie finish off the dysfunctional domestic cast. The discouraging nature of Brutus's existence is mirrored outside the home, in his dealings with discourteous store clerks, persistent beggars, and obnoxious drunks. His boss, Rancid W. Veeblefester, is a towering menace who belittles and berates his employees during putting practice in his executive suite of an office.

Launched by NEA as a daily on May 10, 1965, and on the following June 27 on Sundays, *The Born Loser* contributed significantly to the modern minimal drawing style now common, with only slight movement indicated in the static, generally verbal sequences. Consistently funny, Sansom managed to instill an accommodating slant to his incisive creation, entertaining audiences in 1,300 newspapers in over two dozen countries.

Sansom's son Chip began apprenticing in 1977, gradually rising from gag writer to artist as well. The two have shared a byline since the mid-1980s, even though the strip has been done entirely by Chip Sansom since Art's death on July 4, 1991. Four book collections of *The Born Loser* have appeared since 1975, and the National Cartoonist Society named it Best Humor Strip for 1987 and 1990. A classic, *The Born Loser* is on par with most of the industry's other great

strips, making Brutus P. Thornapple the winningest loser in the comics.

B.J.

BOTTARO, LUCIANO (1931-   ) Italian cartoonist, born November 16, 1931, in Rapallo, Liguria. After dropping out from a technical college, Luciano Bottaro entered the field of comics in 1949 with a few pages he drew for the magazine *Lo Scolaro*. In 1950 he created his first strip, *Aroldo*, a pirate story that started publication two years later. After military service, Bottaro worked for Edizioni Alpe, producing a number of humor strips, among them *Tim, Pepito, Baldo, Marameo*, and *Whisky e Gogo*. At the same time Bianconi published two more of his comic creations: *Pik Pok* and *Papi Papero* ("Daddy Duck").

In 1951 Bottaro started working for the Italian branch of Walt Disney Productions and in short order became one of the more noted and imaginative artists on *Donald Duck*. When Faisani released the comic monthly *Oscar* (1959), Bottaro contributed a number of strips, all endowed with a special graphic lyricism: *Lola, Nasolungo* ("Bignose"), and the Western parody *Maiopi*. *Pinko e Ponko* of the same period were early forerun-

Luciano Bottaro, "Nel Paese dell'Alfabeto." © C. d. P.

ners of Hanna-Barbera's *The Flintstones*, while his tender strip about a little mushroom, *Pon Pon*, was regarded as one of the most imaginative creations in Italian comics. Two of Bottaro's other strips, *Pepito* (1951) and *Redipicche* (1969) are also his most successful. Collaborating with Bottaro on almost all of his strips has been the scriptwriter Carlo Chendi. In 1982 Bottaro realized a new adaptation of *Pinocchio* in comics form. He has also been very active in computer graphics throughout the 1990s.

Bottaro's characters have been widely utilized in merchandising, while a gift shop in San Remo currently uses the name Pon Pon.

G.B.

BOUCQ, FRANÇOIS (1955-   ) French cartoonist, born November 28, 1955, in Lille in northern France. After art school studies, François Boucq started his professional career in 1974 as a political cartoonist for such publications as *Le Point*, *L'Expansion*, and the daily *le Matin*. The following year he contributed his first, tentative comic strips to the humor magazine *Mormoil*; but it was only in 1978, with *Les Cornets d'Humour* ("Humor Scoops") for *Pilote*, that his talents in the field came to be recognized nationally. For a long time he restricted himself to turning out humor strips, particularly for the comic magazine *Fluide Glacial*, in whose pages he created in the early 1980s *Rock Mastard* (a spoof of superheroes) and *Les Leçons du Professeur Bourremou*, about the ramblings of a zany pedagogue.

Boucq took a job at the comics magazine *A Suivre* in 1983, publishing short, humorous stories, but soon turned his attention to more ambitious fare. In a collaboration with the noted American novelist Jerome Chayrin, he realized two highly original graphic novels. The first, *The Magician's Wife* (1985), set in Saratoga Springs in the shady world of jockeys, race touts, and crooked gamblers, was a thriller with fantastic overtones. *Bouche du Diable* ("Billy Budd, KGB") followed in 1989; it again mixed elements of suspense, mystery, and the fantastic, as it records the fateful progress of a Soviet spy from the KGB's training school in the Ukraine to the streets of New York City.

With these and the equally innovative stories that have come out from his brush in the 1990s, the most outstanding being *Face de Lune* ("Moon Face," 1991) with a story line by famous screenwriter Alexandro Jodorowsky, Boucq has joined the front ranks of international comics creators.

M.H.

BOY COMMANDOS (U.S.) Of all the kid groups comic books that World War II produced during the 1940s, Joe Simon and Jack Kirby's *Boy Commandos* was undoubtedly the most popular and distinctive. Created just three months after their *Newsboy Legion* feature, the four-boy, one-adult combine premiered in National's *Detective Comics* number 64 in June 1942. The group was ethnically balanced—like the adult *Blackhawk* group before it—and showcased one kid from each country fighting the Germans.

America was represented by a tough, swaggering Brooklynite who talked like Jimmy Cagney and dressed in a green sweater and garish red derby; from France, Pierre Chavard joined the group to fight the "Boche," and eventually changed his name to Andre; Jan Haasen came from Holland to help defeat the Nazis because they killed his parents; and finally, there was the

English child, Alfy Twidgett, who battled the "Jerries" mostly with his cockney accent. Leading this brigade of children was Captain Rip Carter, the group's mentor and teacher. He trained the boys for one purpose only: to battle and defeat the Axis and make the world safe for democracy.

Throughout the war years, the *Boy Commandos* did fight the enemy everywhere possible, to the apparent vicarious glee of the readers who eventually helped the group into their own book in the winter of 1942. Their popularity was such that besides the score of imitators that were to follow, Harvey Comics introduced the "quartette of fighting queens" called the Girl Commandos. As the war ended, however—and Simon and Kirby moved elsewhere—the strip slowly began to degenerate. Jan and Alfy were dropped, and in their stead came Tex, an uninteresting cowboy character who was of little value either as an action figure or an ethnic figure. The group was also forced to return to America and fight more common crooks, and without the menace of Nazis and Japanese, *Boy Commandos* became just another comic book strip.

In all, *Boy Commandos* was a durable strip and lasted until *Detective* number 150 and *Boy Commandos* number 36 before disbanding in December 1949. In 1973, however, National reprinted two issues of *Boy Commandos* for a seemingly uninterested audience.

J.B.

BOZZ   *see* Velter, Robert

BRAMMETJE BRAM (Netherlands) A creation of Belgian artist Edouard Ryssack (with Piet-Hein Broenland as writer), *Brammetje Bram* is a fast-paced, humorous strip about pirates in the early 19th century. It first appeared in 1970 in the Dutch comic weekly *Sjors*. Its star, of course, is Brammetje Bram, a red-haired boy wearing red pants and a red striped shirt. Brammetje does not get into the story until page eight of the first episode, well after the stage has been set by introducing his antagonist, the terror of the seven seas, the pirate captain Knevel de Killer. While walking along the street, Brammetje comes across a striped cat pursued by a butcher. Together with the cat he escapes the butcher by running aboard a ship, which turns out to be that of the pirate captain, who has agreed to take the king's daughter to her Prince Charming. The pirate, of course, secretly plans to hold the princess for ran-

"Brammetje Bram," Edouard Ryssack. © Eddie Ryssack.

149

som. These plans, however, do not work out after Brammetje Bram and the cat (who had fallen asleep) are discovered as stowaways far out at sea. Brammetje Bram is hired as cabin boy and turns out to be the one person who can ward off the attacks of fleets of other pirates. It is also he who causes a happy ending.

Besides Brammetje and the captain there is a strong cast of supporting characters, all acting in the best of the (animated) cartoon tradition. Besides being a visual delight with its sense for movement and visual gags, *Brammetje Bram* is also well written. In a way, the series also is an allegory of the constant struggle of Good against Evil. Whatever evil the pirate captain may plan is held in check and eventually turned into good by Brammetje, without the slightest semblance of moralizing.

W.F.

BRANDOLI, ANNA (1945-   ) Italian illustrator and cartoonist, born July 27, 1945, in Milan. Anna Brandoli began her career as a cartoonist drawing the medieval story *La strega* ("The Witch"), written by Renato Queirolo and published in the monthly *Alter Alter* in 1977.

In 1979 she illustrated the comics adaptation of L. Frank Baum's *The Wizard of Oz* for the weekly *Corriere dei Piccoli*. During the 1980s, working with scriptwriter Queirolo, she drew the as-yet-unfinished trilogy *Testamenti di Sant'Ambrogio* ("Saint Ambrose's Testaments/ Wills") of which only the first and second episodes, *Rebecca* and *Scene di caccia* ("Hunting Scenes"), appeared in the monthly *Orient Express*. The trilogy follows the gypsy Rebecca through her wanderings in Northern Italy in the year 1492, which, though considered the beginning of modern times, still marked an era of intolerance and prejudices.

Brandoli's next work was *Alias*, another unfinished adventure written by Queirolo and set in 17th-century Netherlands. It was published in 1987 in the monthly *Comic Art*, which also published *Cuba 1942* (1991) and *Il gigante italiano* ("The Italian Giant," 1993), both written by Ottavio De Angelis. Since then Brandoli has given up drawing comics and has devoted herself to book illustration. This is a real loss to the comic book world, since her powerful graphic style, with expressionist overtones based on violent contrasts between black and white, has left a mark on the Italian comics world. Most of Brandoli's stories have been reprinted in book form. Brandoli was awarded a Yellow Kid in Lucca in 1984.

G.C.C.

BRANNER, MARTIN (1888-1970) American cartoonist, born December 28, 1888, in New York City. Martin Michael Branner was educated in the New York public schools. In 1907, with his 15-year-old bride, Edith Fabrini, he started a song-and-dance act and met with some success on the vaudeville circuit. After service during World War I, he sold his first comic strip, *Looie the Lawyer*, to the Bell Syndicate in 1919. A short time later he started a second Sunday feature, *Pete and Pinto*, for the *New York Sun*. The success of *Looie*, meanwhile, had brought Branner's work to the attention of Arthur Crawford, general manager of the New York News-Chicago Tribune Syndicate. In September 1920, *Winnie Winkle, the Breadwinner*, Branner's most enduring creation, made its debut (later to be joined by *Looie* as its bottom strip). Martin Branner retired from the comic strip field in 1962, leaving *Winnie Winkle* in the hands of his assistant Max van Bibber. Branner died on May 19, 1970, after a long illness.

While he was not an outstanding cartoonist by any means, Branner possessed sufficient charm, originality, and freshness to leave a durable imprint on the history of the comics.

M.H.

BRECCIA, ALBERTO (1919-1993) A resident of Argentina for many years, the Uruguayan cartoonist Alberto Breccia was born in Montevideo in 1919. In 1936 he started his collaboration to Buenos Aires publications with a number of comic strips: in this youthful period only *Mu-fa, un Detective Oriental* (1939) stands out. In 1941 Breccia moved to Brazil but came back to Buenos Aires, where he drew *Vito Nervio* from 1947 to 1959. In this period he also produced *El Vengador* ("The Avenger") for the magazine *El Gorrion*, and *Jean de la Martinica* for *Patoruzito*. His latter works include *La Ejecucion* ("The Execution"), written by Hector Oesterheld, the scriptwriter of other Breccia creations such as *Richard Long, Pancho Lopez* (published in the magazine of the same name), and *Sherlock Time*, which he created in 1958 for *Frontera* magazine. With the latter, Brecia initiated his most ambitious and complex cycle, opening fresh vistas and blazing new trails.

During a long European trip starting in 1960, Breccia was contracted by Fleetway Publications of London and he worked on a number of their publications. Back in Argentina in 1962, Breccia resumed his career with *Mort Cinder* the same year. In 1968 he took over the drawing of *El Eternauta* and created his very personal *La Vida del Che* ("The Life of Che [Guevara]") which was subjected to the rigors of the censors. Soon after, he devoted most of his time to a long-cherished project, the pictorialization of H. P. Lovecraft's difficult and controversial stories, *Los Mitos de Cthulhu* ("The Myths of Cthulhu").

In 1984 he started a new, long-running science-fiction series, *Perramus*, which proved to be his valedictory. He died in Buenos Aires on November 10, 1993.

L.G.

BREGER, DAVID (1908-1970) Born in 1908 into a Russian immigrant family in Chicago, the future coiner of the famed term "G. I. Joe" (in a comic panel series of the same name) was called Dave from the moment he entered a Chicago grammar school. Educated fitfully between stints working with his father in the sausage industry in his teens, the young Breger encountered the Chicago gangsters of the 1920s more than once. (On one occasion, he was actually shot at by a protection racket hoodlum, saving himself only by moving a door between himself and the bullet and catching it miraculously on the metal lock.) In the 1930s, he developed his cartooning talent with serious professionalism and began to sell gag panels to the big slicks (*Collier's, Liberty*, etc.). Entering the army as a buck private in the year before America's entry into World War II, Breger created a comic panel series based on his basic-training experiences as a rookie, selling it to King Features Syndicate under the title *Private Breger*.

Shortly after its appearance in 1941, it caught the eyes of the men who were preparing the publication of an official entertainment and historical magazine for the American forces, to be called *Yank*. They wanted Breger's self-caricature series in *Yank*, but since the

Dave Breger, "Private Breger." © King Features Syndicate.

A large, full-faced man who did not look in the least like the bespectacled, shrimpish Private/Mr. Breger, Dave Breger lived most of his postwar life on an estate in South Nyack, New York, where he died (in a nearby hospital) after a long illness on January 16, 1970, at the age of 61. His highly individual strip died with him.

B.B.

BRENDA STARR (U.S.) *Brenda Starr* was born on June 30, 1940, as a Sunday page, from the pen of Dalia (Dale) Messick, despite the misgivings of Captain Joseph Patterson of the Chicago Tribune-New York News Syndicate, which distributed the feature. The captain's fears were ill-founded as it turned out: *Brenda* went on to become a steadily growing success, and a daily strip was added in October 1945.

Dale Messick wanted to make her heroine a woman-bandit, but settled for a girl reporter on the advice of her editor, Mollie Slott. Brenda is always flying to the far corners of the earth on assignments for her newspaper, *The Flash*, and is always impeccably dressed and coiffured, even in the unlikeliest of situations. Her love life is as restless as her career: relentlessly pursuing her lover, the elusive Basil St. John, who suffers from a "secret disease" and sends her black orchids from afar; and being pursued in turn by every male character in the strip. Her problems are not made any easier by her gruff managing editor Livwright, her homely female colleague Hank O'Hair, or her overbearing cousin Abretha Breeze, from Pinhook, Indiana.

Romance dominates the events in *Brenda Starr*, which has remained popular over the years in spite of its outlandish characterization and the ludicrousness of most of its situations. The strip (which eventually was produced by a team of specialized artists under the direction of Miss Messick) seems to appeal mainly to younger female readers who tend to identify with the heroine and relish her stormy and doomed love affairs. A movie serial, *Brenda Starr, Reporter*, was produced by Columbia Pictures in 1945.

new magazine would be entirely filled by the work of enlisted men done for the magazine, the syndicated strip could not be used. Breger agreed to do a separate weekly panel for *Yank*, under a new name. In thinking of this new name, Breger came up with *G. I. Joe* (for Government-Issue Joe), and sold the *Yank* people on it. Within a week of the first *G. I. Joe* panel in the first *Yank*, on June 17, 1942, the term was on everyone's lips in the services, and a week later it was being heard everywhere in the country, as if it had always been in existence. G. I. Joe had a reality beyond that of Breger's character: it had replaced "Yank" as the popular term for an American foot soldier.

A book collection of Breger's *G. I. Joe* panels appeared in 1945, and was a best-seller for months, being read avidly by the same people who treasured their collections of *The Sad Sack* and Mauldin's *Joe and Willie* panels. Breger's King Features panel had its title changed after Breger's discharge at the end of the war to *Mr. Breger*, and a Sunday half-page was added, in comic strip format. *Mr. Breger*, however, was not the universal hit Breger's military life feature had been, for his highly individual wit and acid view of humanity in private life was not to everyone's taste. The strip and panel continued with reasonable success, however, into the 1960s, when the panel was dropped and the Sunday strip continued alone. At this time, Breger wrote what many consider a basic reference work, his *How To Draw and Sell Cartoons* of 1966. (In 1954 he had also written a very funny and revealing exposé on cartoon censorship, *But That's Unprintable!*)

"Brenda Starr," Dale Messick. © Chicago Tribune News Syndicate.

Messick retired from the strip in 1980. The writing was then taken over by Linda Sutter, who turned over the scripting chores to Maria Schmich in 1985. After a 15-year stint drawing *Brenda Starr*, former comic-book artist Ramona Fradon resigned in 1995. The feature is now being illustrated by June Brigman.

M.H.

BRICK BRADFORD (U.S.) *Brick Bradford* was the product of the collaboration between writer William Ritt and artist Clarence Gray. Appearing as a daily strip on August 21, 1933, and as a Sunday page in November 1934, *Brick* was distributed first by Central Press Association and then by King Features Syndicate.

In 1949 Ritt stopped writing the story lines, and Gray became his own scriptwriter. Illness forced him to abandon the daily strip in 1952, but he continued to draw the Sundays until his death in 1957. During Gray's tenure Brick enjoyed his own comic book (done by Paul Norris) in the 1940s and 1950s; and in 1948 Spencer Gordon Bennett and Thomas Carr adapted *Brick Bradford* into a movie serial.

Having taken over the dailies and later the Sundays from Gray, Norris managed to pilot Brick through time and space in his own laborious, plodding way for almost twice as long as his predecessor. Under his guidance *Brick Bradford* lasted until 1987, the dailies ending on April 25, and the last Sunday appearing on May 10.

Brick himself is a hero devoid of neuroses and ambiguities. He represents the tradition of an earlier, more optimistic era. In his actions he is motivated by nothing more than his curiosity and love of adventure, which draw him into the most unlikely situations in alternating tales of exploration, suspense, and science

fiction. It is to the latter genre that *Brick Bradford* belongs most firmly, and while it possesses neither the futuristic vision of *Buck Rogers* nor the epic grandeur of *Flash Gordon, Brick Bradford* displays the undeniable qualities of fantasy, poetry, and imagination that put in on a par with its better-known rivals. Brick Bradford's exploration into the atoms of a copper penny and his adventures in the center of the earth were particularly spectacular.

Aside from the hero himself, few memorable characters emerged out of *Brick Bradford*; Kalla Kopak, Brick's scientist companion, and Bucko O'Brien, his loud-mouthed, ill-tempered sidekick, were the only exceptions.

M.H.

BRIEFER, RICHARD (1915-1982?) American comic book artist and writer, born in 1915. He attended New York's Art Students League and entered the comic book business in 1936 as a member of the S. M. "Jerry" Iger studio. Dick Briefer's earliest work appeared in Helne's *Wow* in 1936, one of the first comic books to carry original material. Over the next several years at the Iger studio, Briefer produced material for Fiction House (1938-1941, *Hunchback of Notre Dame, Flint Baker*, others), Fox (1939-1941, *Rex Dexter of Mars*), Worth (1940), Marvel (1940, *Human Top*), and others.

In 1940, however, Briefer approached the Prize group with a proposal to adapt Mary Shelley's 1818 *Frankenstein* to comics. The artist/writer's version, which premiered in *Prize* number seven for December 1940, had Victor Frankenstein creating his monster during an experiment in 1940 Manhattan. The doctor sees his monster begin a crusade against humanity, and in a repentant mood, vows to care for an orphan named Denny; the boy eventually catches up with Frankenstein and puts him into the care of Dr. Carrol for rehabilitation.

Drawing the strip under the painfully obvious pen name of "Frank N. Stein"—much of Briefer's other work was signed "Richard Norman" or "Remington Brant"—Briefer handled the strip poorly. His work was crude, his layouts loose and lackadaisical, and his execution juvenile. It was, in fact, comedic. But after the monster's rehabilitation, Briefer cashed in on his own style and began playing the strip for laughs with great results. His artwork was ideally suited for this twist: his whimsical Frankenstein interpretation was appealing and his scenes and drawings were pleasantly humorous. He relocated the monster in "Mippyville," and this humorous, often underrated version of Frankenstein became a financial success, and a *Frankenstein* title was added to his *Prize* appearances. After six years of good fortune, however, the *Frankenstein* series ended with February 1949's 17th issue, and Briefer returned to serious drawing.

After some horror work for Atlas, Briefer then moved to the romance line in a two-year stint with Hillman on *Rosie Romance*. But Prize recalled him in March 1952 to revive *Frankenstein*. Unfortunately, however, it was the serious version and the artist/writer was obviously bored with the whole concept. His stories were poor and hackneyed, his artwork sloppy. This revival mercifully died in November 1954.

Briefer left the comic industry shortly thereafter to concentrate on advertising artwork, and then in 1962

"Brick Bradford," William Ritt and Clarence Gray. © King Features Syndicate.

turned his attention to portrait painting. He reportedly died in the spring of 1982.

J.B.

BRIGGS, AUSTIN (1908-1973) American cartoonist and illustrator, born September 8, 1908, in Humboldt, Minnesota. After studies at the Detroit City College and the Wicker Art School, Briggs moved to New York City in the early 1930s; there he worked for an advertising agency and freelanced for various magazines while attending classes at the Art Students' League. He started his comic strip career as Alex Raymond's assistant in 1936, then took over the *Secret Agent X-9* strip from 1938 to 1940. On May 27 of the same year he created (uncredited) the *Flash Gordon* daily, and in 1944, following Raymond's enlistment, started drawing the Sunday pages (also including *Jungle Jim*) as well. He also worked briefly on the *Spy Smasher* comic book in 1941.

Chiefly known as an illustrator, Austin Briggs also left his mark as a comic strip artist. As Alex Raymond's successor on both *X-9* and *Flash Gordon*, he showed talent, style, and imagination, proving himself Raymond's most worthy rival.

In 1948 Briggs left the comic strip field to devote himself fully to magazine illustration. A cofounder of the Famous Artists School and a member of the Society of Illustrators' Hall of Fame, Briggs was also the recipient of countless awards. On October 10, 1973, Austin Briggs died of leukemia in Paris, where he had retired.

M.H.

BRIGGS, CLARE (1875-1930) American artist, born in Reedsburg, Wisconsin, on August 5, 1875. When Briggs was nine, his family moved to Dixon, Illinois, where the youngster drew his first sketches, and later

Clare Briggs, "Danny Dreamer."

to Lincoln, Nebraska, where he attended Nebraska University. His first published cartoons appeared during this time in *The Western Penman*.

At age 21, Briggs went to work for the *St. Louis Democrat* as a $10-a-week sketch artist, depicting news events in the days before widespread photographic reproduction. Two years later, in 1898, he switched to the *St. Louis Chronicle* as an editorial cartoonist. He played the Spanish-American War for all it was worth, but when the war ended so did his subject material and Briggs was out of a job.

He then traveled to New York City and failed in various jobs peripheral to the art world: sign-painting, show cards, catalog illustration, etc. He returned to Lincoln in 1900 and married Ruth Owen. Another "invasion" of New York was more successful: Briggs became a sketch artist for the *New York Journal*. A perceptive editor told Briggs he was meant to be a cartoonist, and William Randolph Hearst assigned the penman to his Chicago properties, the *American* and *Examiner*.

Here Briggs shone and became a celebrity (no mean feat in a city dominated by John McCutcheon). For the *American* he pioneered daily strips with the short-lived *A. Piker Clerk*. In 1907 Briggs was lured away by McCutcheon's Chicago *Tribune*, and his humorous panel cartoons earned him a national reputation.

In 1914 he returned to New York at the invitation of the *Tribune*; here he stayed until his death.

Briggs succeeded in producing the synthesis of various newspaper cartoon genres emerging in the early years of the century. His panel creations spanned sports, suburban life, nostalgia, and the kibitzer-vignettes creates by Tad. His series ran to dozens of titles: *When a Feller Needs a Friend, The Days of Real Sport, Movie of a Man, Golf, Someone's Always Taking the Joy Out of Life, There's at Least One in Every Office, Ain't it a Grand and Glorious Feelin '*!

Briggs' humor seldom failed; he was, simply, a genius at recognizing and chronicling human emotion—a boy and his dog at the swimming hole, frustrations on the golf course, or marital squabbling. Perhaps his greatest series is one least remembered—significantly, because it dealt with things in life also seldom noticed: *Real Folks at Home*. Here Briggs glorified the commonplace, visited the homes of ordinary people—streetcleaners, bakers, cab drivers—and imagined the small talk. No funny endings, no glamour—just a brilliant insight into the soul of the common people and a contrast to the flashiness and celebrity addiction of the rest of the newspaper.

Briggs produced several strips besides *A. Piker Clerk* in his Chicago days—Sunday features—and his *Mr. and Mrs.* color page for the Herald-Tribune Syndicate was a funny, realistic picture of the never-ending bickering between Vi and Joe Green.

Briggs' style was breezy and informal, a solid familiarity with anatomy hiding handsomely behind economy of line, abbreviated strokes, little detail or background, and masterful blocking and spotting of blacks.

He died in New York on January 3, 1930, after a long illness; pneumonia followed lung problems and he was bothered by troubles with the optic nerve (drawing was difficult during his last year). He divorced his wife in 1929; she and a common-law wife made headlines as they fought over the estate.

Briggs' kid cartoons were put on the screen in 1919, and *Mr. and Mrs.* became a radio serial in 1929. The latter feature was continued, very badly, by a succession of artists, into the 1960s.

R.M.

BRIGGS, RAYMOND (1934-   ) British cartoonist Raymond Briggs was born on January 18, 1934, in Wimbledon, London, the son of a milkman. He attended the Rutlish School, Merton, and studied at Wimbledon School of Art and at The Slade for two years. His career began in 1957 when his illustrations appeared in magazines and children's books. In 1966 he won the Kate Greenaway Medal for his illustrations in *The Mother Goose Treasury*. Convinced that he could write better stories than the ones he was illustrating, he wrote and drew *Father Christmas*, his first full-color book, in 1973, for which he won his second Kate Greenaway Medal. He based his refreshingly down-to-earth, no-nonsense *Father Christmas* on his father and modeled Santa's house on his parents' home. The sequel, *Father Christmas Goes on Holiday*, was published in 1975.

Having humanized the sugar-coated cliché of Father Christmas, Briggs took on his next project, exploring the hilariously disgusting world of slimy monsters in *Fungus the Bogeyman* in 1977, upsetting some parents but delighting children. The next year, after this detailed and complex book, he switched to a much simpler, completely silent strip book, *The Snowman*. This tells the story of a boy's snowman who comes to life, capturing the beauty of winter landscapes and the comfort of home in evocative drawings done in colored pencil. The book has become a classic and was adapted into an animated film.

In 1980 Briggs introduced Jim and Hilda Bloggs, trusting elderly English pensioners battling the forces of law and society in *Gentleman Jim*. Two years later they returned in his masterpiece, *When the Wind Blows*. Briggs felt passionately about the government's inadequate and misleading contingency planning in the event of a nuclear attack. The early scenes of the Bloggs' simple life are told in small, cheerful panels, interrupted by huge two-page illustrations of the escalating war. These climax in two white pages, when the bomb is dropped. Briggs then shows the couple following the advice of the government, which utterly fails in dealing with the true horror of the situation. The Bloggs hope for the best, but radiation sickness rapidly erodes their health and leads to their deeply moving deaths. The book was discussed in the House of Commons and adapted into a play and an animated feature film in 1987.

Briggs' anger at the lives lost and damaged in the Falklands War inspired *The Tin-Pot Foreign General and the Old Iron Woman*, published in 1984. A political picture book, it contrasts savage political caricatures with haunting pencil drawings of the dead and injured. In recent years, Briggs has created several successful children's illustrated books, starting with *Unlucky Wally Twenty Years On*, which was published in 1989, but so far he has not returned to the complete comic strip format.

P.G.

BRIGMAN, JUNE (1960-   ) Born in Atlanta, Georgia, in 1960, comic strip artist June Brigman grew up reading *Brenda Starr* in the *Atlanta Journal*. Her other favorite strip was *The Phantom*. Brigman studied art at the University of Georgia and Georgia State University.

She freelanced at many different art jobs, including a summer stint working as a quick portrait artist at a Georgia amusement park. In 1982 she sent samples of her work to Marvel Comics in New York City, where she was offered a job. At Marvel she teamed up with writer-editor Louise Simonson to create the *Power Pack* series. *Power Pack* was a group of children, two boys and two girls, ages 6 to 12, who had been given super powers by a friendly alien.

Brigman went on to draw a wide range of comic books, including *She Hawk* for Marvel, *Supergirl* and *Teen Titans* for DC Comics, and a four-book miniseries of *Star Wars* for Dark Horse Comics. Brigman's last comic book work was drawing *Barbie* for Marvel Comics. She also drew illustrations for the children's book *Choose Your Own Adventure* and the comic strip *Where in the World Is Carmen Sandiego?* for National Geographic Society's children's magazine.

After hearing from a friend that Ramona Fradon, the cartoonist who was drawing *Brenda Starr*, was retiring, Brigman contacted Tribune Media Services, submitted samples of her work, and was hired. On November 6, 1995, Brigman became the third female cartoonist to draw *Brenda Starr*. The comic strip about the star reporter for *The Flash* newspaper was created in 1940 by Dalia (Dale) Messick for the Chicago Tribune-New York News Syndicate. Copying neither Messick's nor Fradon's style, June Brigman has successfully kept the traditional *Brenda Starr* look and mood of the strip, while initiating a very clean line style. The future of *Brenda Starr* looks bright with the professional team of June Brigman and Mary Schmich.

B.C.

BRINGING UP FATHER (U.S.) When George McManus created *Bringing Up Father* for the Hearst organization, he was already a cartoonist of high repute. *Bringing Up Father*, which first appeared in the dailies in 1913, was only one of a number of strip ideas that McManus had played around with. It was sometimes missing for weeks at a time, and only in 1916 did it become definitively established (with the Sunday version following on April 14, 1918).

The most striking feature of *Bringing Up Father* is its theatricality. Inspired by William Gill's 1893 play *The Rising Generation* (which McManus saw as a child), the strip, in the neat unfolding of each of its episodes, resembles a skit or playlet, loaded with witty dialogue, nutty characters, and outlandish happenings. The underlying theme of the strip is quite simple (as in all great creations): Jiggs, a former mason, and his wife Maggie, an ex-washerwoman, have suddenly become wealthy by winning the Irish sweepstakes. But while Maggie, the epitome of ugliness, snobbishness, and egotism, seeks to forget her social origins, Jiggs' only wish is to meet his buddies at Dinty Moore's tavern for a dish of corn beef and cabbage and a friendly game of pinochle. Most of the strip's hilarious events derive from this basic situation.

The luxurious setting of the action, an astounding mixture of rococo architecture, Art Nouveau furnishings, and weird-shaped curios, form the appropriate backdrop for this battle of the sexes, in which the immaculately dressed Jiggs is forever ducking out of the house (while ducking Maggie's rolling pin at the same time). These almost ritual proceedings are refereed by

"Bringing Up Father," George McManus. © *King Features Syndicate.*

Maggie's and Jiggs' stylish daughter Nora, and sometimes upstaged by the outrageous shenanigans of the scores of secondary characters who blissfully wander in and out of the plot.

Bringing Up Father is one of the very few comic strips in which all strata of society are represented in an astounding gallery of portraits ranging all the way from the upper crust to the lower depths: genuine and false princes, captains of industry, social climbers, petty-bourgeois, dim-witted cops, shiftless workingmen, querulous maids, smart-alecky errand-boys, loafers, moochers, small-time grifters, and bums of every type and description, who all take part in the great parade.

After McManus' death in 1954, *Bringing Up Father* was written by Bill Kavanagh and the Sunday page was drawn by Frank Fletcher, while Vernon Greene drew the daily strip until his death in 1965, when he was succeeded by Hal Campagna (signing "Camp"). As of 1996 Frank Johnson was doing both versions of the feature.

Bringing Up Father was the first comic strip to enjoy worldwide fame. It has been reprinted in book form, translated into most languages, adapted six times to the screen, and made into animated cartoons. During the war Jiggs was the official emblem of the Eleventh Bombardment Squadron. In the 1920s a stage play, *Father*, toured the United States and Canada, and McManus himself appeared as Jiggs in some of the productions. Several other plays based on McManus' comic strip were also produced in later years.

M.H.

BRINKERHOFF, ROBERT MOORE (1880-1958)

American cartoonist and illustrator, born May 4, 1880, in Toledo, Ohio. R. M. Brinkerhoff's father, R. A. Brinkerhoff, was a cofounder of the *Toledo Post*, which later merged into the *Toledo News-Bee*. Brinkerhoff *fils* developed an early liking for the arts and started studying music at the Cincinnati Conservatory before going on to the Art Students League in New York City. After a brief stay in Paris, he returned to Toledo and became a political cartoonist on the *Blade* before moving to the *Cleveland Leader* and the *Cincinnati Post*.

In 1913 Brinkerhoff moved to New York, where he joined the staff of the *Evening World* and became a successful painter and illustrator. In 1917, at the urging of fellow cartoonist Will B. Johnston, he created his first (and only) comic strip, *Little Mary Mixup*. The tale of this mischievous little girl, drawn in an airy and graceful style, was slight but Brinkerhoff made it enjoyable as well as believable. Conceived first as a little devil with innocent blue eyes and girlish blonde curls, Little Mary eventually grew up and in World War II even

joined the fight against the Nazis. The strip could have reached greater heights of popularity had Brinkerhoff devoted his full time to it. Certainly he was an artist of outstanding talent, but he never gave poor Little Mary more than casual attention. Brinkerhoff had many other interests: he painted, illustrated stories and books, and wrote several books himself. But his real passion was the sea: he owned several yachts—on which he went several times around the world—and even owned an island—Brinkerhoff-Island—in Maine. After a long and productive life, R. M. Brinkerhoff died in Minneapolis on February 17, 1958.

(Brinkerhoff's son, Robert Jr., an advertising artist, also tried his hand at cartooning: he drew the short-lived *Hagen, Fagin and O'Toole*, a comic strip about a Great Dane, a Siamese cat, and a parrot.)

M.H.

BRISTOW (G.B.)

"In the Chester-Perry Building/Massive Chester-Perry Building/Was an office known as Buying/Buying was their occupation/And their names were Jones and Bristow." That was Frank Dickens writing/drawing (his drawing is so basic and speedy it is almost writing) one of his popular parodies in *Bristow*, the first British newspaper strip to follow the non-art tradition begun by James Thurber. The quoted poem continues with references that set Bristow firmly in his milieu: "All the phoning, all the filing/All the dreary dreadful filing/Nine to five for just a pittance/So they hated Chester-Perry/Hated him with all their being/And they lived for going-home time. . . ."

Actually, the "lovely, glorious going-home time" is not all that lovely and glorious to Bristow, who loves his daily routine and encounters with the incredibly badly drawn pigeon, Mrs. Purdie the Tea Lady, his lunch lovingly prepared by Mr. Gordon Blue, master chef of the Chester-Perry canteen, the Blondini Brothers ("scaffolding to the gentry"), the shouting Mr. Fudge, the letter to Messrs. Gun and Fames and the ensuing fun and games, and the rejection slip for the great Bristow novel from Messrs. Heap and Trotwood.

Created and written by Frank Dickens (born 1932), who was fortunately allowed to return to his own handwrought lettering after a period of unsuitable legibility, *Bristow* grew out of *Oddbod*, his first strip for the *Sunday Times* (1960), and the picture stories in his book, *What the Dickens* (1961). It began in the *London Evening Standard* in 1962 and is syndicated by Dickens himself to many provincial British newspapers, as well as to the *South China Morning Post*, the *Sydney Morning Herald*, the South African *Eastern Echo*, and papers in New Zealand and Brazil. Bristow's name varies, even in England. The *Lancashire Evening Post* acted on complaints from a Mr. Bristow and changed his name to Dickens! There is an original book, *Bristow*, published by Constable in 1966, and several reprints of the strip: *Bristow!* (1970); *Bristow* (1972); *More Bristow* (1973); *Bristow Extra* (1974). Dickens was voted cartoonist of the year four times by the Cartoonists Club of Great Britain, has transferred *Bristow* to the stage, and, shortly, hopes for a film and television series. After 35 years of existence, *Bristow* is still going as strong as ever.

D.G.

BRONC PEELER (U.S.) In 1934 Fred Harman created his first comic strip, *Bronc Peeler*, which he syndicated himself, as both a daily and a weekly feature, to a few newspapers (including the *San Francisco Chronicle*).

Bronc was a young ranch hand who fought cattle rustlers and bank robbers, saved innocent young girls from swarthy seducers, and once even worked as an undercover agent for the F.B.I. When he was not out riding through the Rockies or along the Rio Grande, Bronc could usually be found in the company of his sweetheart—blonde, energetic Babs—or with Coyote Pete, his grizzled, slow-witted sidekick. *Bronc Peeler's* locale was New Mexico, and unlike *Red Ryder*, it took place in modern times: Bronc could be seen riding a car or even flying an airplane.

Fred Harman once made a statement to the effect that his early strip was now completely forgotten, and justly so—but he was wrong on both counts. While the artwork in *Bronc Peeler* was sometimes clumsy, it also displayed vigor and zest; the plots were quite imaginative and well handled visually ("The Lost Valley of the Aztecs" is a good example). As to the first point: by some yet unexplained fluke, *Bronc Peeler* was published in France, where it enjoyed wider circulation (and

"Bronc Peeler," Fred Harman. © Fred Harman.

greater popularity) than in the United States—and in recent years fond reminiscences of the strip have appeared in a number of French (and Belgian) publications.

M.H.

"Broom Hilda," Russ Myers. © Chicago Tribune-New York News Syndicate.

BROOM HILDA (U.S.) *Broom Hilda* was created by Russell Myers in 1970 for the Chicago Tribune-New York News Syndicate.

Situated in an undetermined country and at an indeterminate time (possibly the Middle Ages), the strip tells of the adventures—or misadventures—of a rather ineffectual witch. Despite her repulsive aspect and her greenish complexion Broom Hilda is a rather tame and even endearing creature. Her black magic often misfires on her, her spells, more often than not, do not work, and even her pet buzzard Gaylord seldom heeds her commands. In her rare moments of triumph, however, she is capable of flying through the air, of shuttling back and forth in time, and of unleashing lightning and thunder. She uses her awesome powers (such as they are) to satisfy her whims and peeves more than to spread terror in the hearts of her (generally) unbelieving cohorts.

As a counterpart to Hilda's self-aggrandizement, Myers has created the hirsute, uncouth troll Irwin, whose mindless antics seem to mock the witch's attention-getting shenanigans.

Obviously inspired by *The Wizard of Id, Broom Hilda* is nonetheless one of the best and funniest comic strips to come out of the 1970s. It has continued to entertain readers, daily and Sundays, for more than 25 years now.

M.H.

BROOS, PIET (1910-1964) Piet Broos, Dutch artist and cartoonist, was born on December 16, 1910, and died on July 9, 1964. Broos studied art at the Den Haag Academy of Art in hopes of making it his career. In 1939 he debuted as a comic strip artist with *Professor Pienterbult*, a strip done for *Roomsche Jeugd*, a magazine for young people. From the start, *Broos* tended to com-

Piet Broos, "Tommie's Avonturen." © Piet Broos.

plete tales in order to start another one or more with different characters. At times he revived earlier characters either with new stories or by completely redrawing old ones. Thus, *Professor Pienterbult* reappeared in 1948 in the newspaper *Onze Krant*, and in 1954 the character graced the pages of *Maas en Roerbode*, another newspaper.

In 1940 the Flemish comics magazine *Zonneland* published his *Avonturen van Knobbeltje Knop* ("Adventures of K.K."); in 1941 *Tommie's avonturen* appeared in *Panorama*, a newspaper with a weekly children's supplement titled *Sjors*, which had started on January 2, 1936. (*Sjors* is the Dutch version of Martin Branner's *Winnie Winkle* Sunday page. In 1938 an originally Dutch version of *Sjors*, written by Lou Vierhout and drawn by Frans Piet, replaced the original.)

After World War II Broos's first comic strip was *Professor Snip Snap*. It appeared in *St. Antoniusalmanak* in 1946. That same publication published his *Avontuur van Pinkeltree* (1948) and *Keesje Slim* (1949). In 1946 he also created characters like *Daniël* and *Okkie en Knokkie* for the newspaper *Onze Krant* and *Jan Pierewiet* for *Maas en Roerbode*. *Jan Pierewiet* also appeared in *Credo* from 1962 to 1964.

While *Kuif de onverschrokkene* ("Kuif the Intrepid") was the last strip he did for *Onze Krant* in 1948, Broos continued working for *Maas en Roerbode* with features like *Stroppie* (1948), *Streken van Reintje de Vos* ("Pranks of Reinecke Fox," 1950), *Toon Okkernoot* (1950), *Kwikkie Kwiek* (1952), et al. From 1948 to 1964 he drew *Avonturen van Brom, Ping en Ming*, and other features for *Kinderkompas*, a life insurance company's children's magazine. His *Ali Baba* appeared in *Okki* from 1956 to 1964, and he contributed various strips regularly to *Hartentroef* (1957-1964) while working for a number of other magazines and papers. He was nearly omnipresent, making him one of the best-known Dutch comic artists.

W.F.

BROWN, BERTIE (1887-1974) British cartoonist Albert Thacker ("Bertie") Brown was born in 1887 in Epsom, Surrey. Educated at council schools in Sutton and Brockley, he won an art scholarship to the Slade School of Art, but was unable to take it up because of the poverty of his large family. He started work at Elliott's of Lewisham in the blueprint department while studying the strips of Tom Browne in the halfpenny comics. He visited Browne on his sickbed and was encouraged to try submitting joke cartoons.

His first published work appeared in Henderson's *Scraps*. He submitted specimens to Harmsworth's *Illustrated Chips* and was immediately offered a staff job by editor Langton Townley, which he accepted, remaining with that publisher for 50 years, from 1908 to 1958. During this time he drew perhaps a million frames (for many years he drew five full front pages a week, each with 12 panels). His early work closely followed Tom Browne and G. M. Payne, whose characters he often took over. Later he developed a hasty style that nevertheless retained considerable detail, and his eye for contemporary types and backgrounds makes his comic work an important reflection of the social life of his period. He was also particularly adept at capturing a caricatured likeness, and from his creation of the *Charlie Chaplin* strip for *Funny Wonder* (August 7, 1915), Bertie (originally nicknamed "Buster"), drew many stage, screen, and radio celebrities in comic form. He died in February 1974 at the age of 87.

His first original character was *Homeless Hector* (1908), a dog who hunted bones in *Chips* right to the last issue on September 12, 1953. His strips include: 1911—*John Willie's Jackdaw; Nibby Nugget; Peter Parsnips*; 1912—*Marmaduke Maxim; Coffdrop College*; 1913—*Herr Kutz; Cyril Slapdab*; 1914—*Willy & Wally; Ragged Reggie; Brownie Boys* (long run in *Rainbow*); 1915—*Angel and Her Playmates; Gussy Goosegog; Sally Cinders; Charlie Chaplin*; 1916—*Corny Cachou*; 1917—*Rushing Rupert*; 1918—*Dandy and Dinky*; 1919—*Our Kinema Couple* (long run in *Funny Wonder*); 1920—*Pimple; Moonlight Moggie; Annie Seed*; 1921—*Harry Weldon; Wizzo the Wizard; Piggy and Wiggy*; 1922—*Pa Perkins and Percy* (long run in *Chips*); *Billy and Buster*; 1923—*Abie the A.B.*; 1924—*Jessie Joy*; 1925—*Merry Boys of Dingle School*; 1926—*Smiler and Smudge* (long run in *Butterfly*); 1928—*Skinny and Scotty*; 1930—*Jolly Uncle Joe*; 1931—*Snappy Sammy*, 1933—*Nelson Twigg*, 1934—*Kitty Ken and Koko*, 1935—*Captain Skittle*, 1936—*Will Hay*; 1937—*Kitty & Ken*; 1939—*Ping the Panda*; 1940—*Richard Hassett; Little Teddy Tring*; 1941—*Pinhead and Pete; Troddles and Tonkytonk; Vic Oliver*; 1945—*It's that Man Again; Petula Clark; Jimmy Durante*; 1946—*Charlie Chester*; 1948—*Gracie Fields; Derek Roy*; 1949—*Joy Nichols and Dick Bentley*; 1950—*Sid Field; Reg Dixon; Arthur English*; 1952—*Mustava Bunn*; 1953—*Red Skelton; Beverley Sisters; Diana Decker*; 1954—*Martin & Lewis*; 1956—*Frankie Howerd; Shirley Eaton*; 1957—*Harry Secombe*; 1959—*Jimmy Durante*.

D.G.

BROWNE, DIK (1917-1989) American cartoonist, born August 11, 1917, in New York City. Richard (Dik) Browne started as a newsboy on the *New York Journal* and made the customary climb up the ladder to newspaper cartoonist in a few years. In 1941 he joined *Newsweek* magazine as an illustrator but was drafted the following year.

Upon his return to civilian life, Dik Browne resumed a career as book illustrator and advertising artist with the Johnstone & Cushing agency (where he designed the Chiquita Banana cartoon character for the United Fruit Company and the Campbell Soup Kids, among other things). In 1954 he met cartoonist Mort Walker and together, with Walker writing and Browne drawing, they produced *Hi and Lois*, a gentle, genuinely warm and funny family strip. In 1973 Dik Browne created his own strip, *Hagar the Horrible*, the rollicking saga of a comic-opera Viking band of plunderers.

Dik Browne received a number of awards, including the Reuben and the Silver Lady, and served as president of the National Cartoonists Society from 1963 to 1965.

In the late 1970s he moved to Sarasota, Florida, where he continued to work on *Hagar* and *Hi and Lois* with the help of his two sons, Chris and Chance. He died on June 4, 1989.

M.H.

BROWNE, TOM (1870-1910) British cartoonist, illustrator, poster designer, and painter, born in 1870 in Nottingham of "humble parents." He was educated at St. Mary's National School and became a milliner's errand boy in 1882. Apprenticed without pay to a local lithographic printer until 1891, he eked out his living by freelancing cartoons to London comic papers. His first strip was published in *Scraps* dated April 27, 1880: "He Knew How To Do It," which was a prophetic title. For the eight panels he was paid 30 shillings. The boom in comic papers begun by Alfred Harmsworth's *Comic Cuts* (1890) opened the ideal market for Browne's humorous line, and from the close-hatched style of the time he developed a clean approach with bold blacks, ideal for the cheap printing of the halfpenny comics. His work was so much in demand that, once out of his apprenticeship, he became a full-time comic artist, moving to London and setting up a studio in Wollaton House at Westcombe Park, Blackheath. From here he turned out six or more full comic pages per week, together with story illustrations for boys' papers, joke cartoons, illustrations, and full-page features for *Graphic* and other national magazines, full-color postcards in series, huge posters for the theater (particularly pantomimes), and watercolors. He joined the Langham Sketch Club, then seceded to form the London Sketch Club, and was made an R.I. (Royal Illustrator). An avid bicyclist, he rode from London to Paris and to Gibraltar across the Pyrenees, toured Holland, and visited New York, drawing his adventures for newspapers. He established his own color printing

business in his hometown and joined the Territorial Army. When he died in 1910 at the early age of 39, after an operation for an internal illness, he was buried with military honors at Shooters Hill.

Browne's characters in comics were many, ranging from the immortal *Weary Willie and Tired Tim*, who continued in comics 40 years after his death, to their bicycling blood-brothers, *Airy Alf and Bouncing Billy* (1897). He was also responsible for *Doings at Whackington School* (1897), *Dan Leno* (1898), *Don Quixote de Tintogs* (1898), *Robinson Crusoe Esquire* (1898), *The Rajah* (1898), *Little Willy and Tiny Tim* (1898), *Mr. Stankey Deadstone and Company* (1898). He published several editions of *Tom Browne's Christmas Annual* (1904-5¢) and is the only British comic artist to be treated in a serious study: *Tom Brown R.I.* by A. E. Johnson, in the *Brush Pen and Pencil* series (Black, 1909).

The first true comic strip artist in Britain, he set the style and standard of the British comic paper, and his influence may be traced through to the present day.

D.G.

"Bruce Gentry," Ray Bailey. © Post Syndicate.

BRUCE GENTRY (U.S.) Ray Bailey, a former assistant to Milton Caniff, created *Bruce Gentry* for the Robert Hall Syndicate on March 25, 1945.

Bruce Gentry and a small group of friends have started a small airline in South America. Using surplus fixed-wing airplanes, they ply the Andes, carrying the mails and supplies to remote points of the continent. Powerful competitors are watching, however, and soon Bruce finds himself in the role of flying troubleshooter, always putting out fires before they have time to spread.

In 1947 Bailey told Coulton Waugh he felt that "readers are tired of battles, hence he has none." The times weren't ripe for peace and harmony just yet, however, and soon Bruce got involved in some rough fights against smugglers, pirates, and foreign agents, in an effort to retain the strip's readership. But to no avail—it folded early in 1952.

Bruce Gentry was one of a number of aviation strips that sprung up during the war and soon thereafter; it was among the best and deserves to be ranked alongside *Buz Sawyer*, *Johnny Hazard* and *Steve Canyon*. The art was uniformly excellent, but on the writing side, Ray Bailey could not compete with Crane, Robbins, or Caniff. *Bruce Gentry* lacked that special touch of indi-

Tom Browne, "Robinson Crusoe Esq."

viduality which might have made it into a success. In 1946 the indefatigable Spencer Gordon Bennett and Thomas Carr directed a movie serial of *Bruce Gentry, Daredevil of the Skies.*

M.H.

BRUNO BRAZIL (Belgium) *Bruno Brazil* was created in 1967 by scriptwriter Louis Albert (pseudonym of Michel Régnier) and cartoonist William Vance for the comic weekly *Tintin.*

Bruno Brazil was the leader of a commando group, the "Cayman Commando," assigned to desperate missions, mostly espionage. The recruits for the commando were a motley crew of several men and one woman with unsavory pasts who were whipped into shape by the hard-driving, no-nonsense Bruno Brazil. A cross between *The Dirty Dozen* and *Mission: Impossible,* the strip was filled with exciting characters, weird happenings, and outrageous derring-do. In addition to Brazil, the principal protagonists were the strong-willed "Gaucho" Morales and "Whip," the sexy, lash-wielding heroine. There was a good deal of violence, blood-letting, and mayhem in the commando's encounters with master spies, would-be dictators, and Mafia chieftains; death occurred quite frequently and occasionally struck members of the group.

The stories were carefully plotted and enjoyably written by the veteran Régnier, while Vance's graphic style, vigorous and dynamic, kept the action moving at a neck-breaking pace.

Bruno Brazil has been reprinted in book form by Editions du Lombard in Brussels. The feature ended its run in 1983.

M.H.

BUCK DANNY (Belgium) *Buck Danny,* the poor man's *Terry and the Pirates,* made its first appearance in the pages of the Belgian comics magazine *Spirou* on January 2, 1947, drawn by Victor Hubinon and written by Jean-Michel Charlier. Indeed, with the very first episode evocatively titled "Les Japs Attaquent!" ("The Japs Are Attacking!"), *Buck Danny* sounded like a delayed echo of the war's *Terry.* Buck Danny and his comic sidekick Sonny Tuckson (looking a lot like Caniff's Hot-shot Charlie) were pilots with the U.S. Navy

"Buck Danny," Victor Hubinon. © Editions Dupuis.

and took part in the battles of Midway and the Coral Sea. The battle scenes were straight out of old war movies, as was most of the dialogue. After the Pacific War, Danny and Sonny became flying adventurers on dangerous assignments from Arabia to Borneo. Then came the Korean War and the Cold War, and our two heroes reenlisted in the U.S. Air Force (at times *Buck Danny* could sound more bellicose than even *Steve Canyon* or *Buz Sawyer*).

In recent years the war angle has been considerably played down, and the team (now up to three members with the addition of Tumbler, in the strong, silent type tradition) is getting involved more in counterespionage, one of their enemies being the leggy, alluring master spy known as Lady X.

Buck Danny first suffered an interruption in 1979, following Hubinon's death. It was resumed in 1983, with Francis Bergèse supplying the artwork in a very illustrative, dynamic style. A second interruption occurred in 1989, when Charlier died. But the series was picked up again in 1993 on continuities written by various scribes.

Buck Danny is the oldest European aviation strip in existence. While definitely not on the same level as Caniff's *Terry* or *Steve Canyon* at their best, it never got as bad as Wunder's *Terry* at its worst. The adventures of Buck Danny and his friends have been reprinted in book form by Editions Dupuis.

M.H.

BUCK ROGERS (U.S.) The first American science-fiction strip appeared on January 7, 1929. Adapted by Phil Nowlan from his own novel *Armaggedon 2419 A.D.,* drawn by Dick Calkins, and distributed by John F. Dille Co., it was first called *Buck Rogers in the Year 2429 A.D.,* later *Buck Rogers in the 25th Century,* then simply *Buck Rogers.*

Awakening from a five-century-long sleep, former U.S. Air Force lieutenant Buck Rogers finds himself in a devastated America overrun by Mongol invaders. With the help of young and pretty Wilma Deering (who was to become Buck's constant companion), our 20th-century hero almost single-handedly defeats the Mongols and liberates America. But his labors are far from over as new enemies appear on the horizon: the tiger-men of Mars; the pirates from outer space; and most dangerous of all, Buck's arch-foe Killer Kane, and his seductive accomplice Ardala Valmar. Aided by the scientific genius of Dr. Huer, Buck will triumph over all enemies and overcome all perils.

The *Buck Rogers* daily strip has known a long series of artists and writers of varied merit. After Calkins there was Murphy Anderson (1947-49), then Leon Dworkins (1949-51), Rick Yager (1951-58), again Anderson (1958-59), and finally George Tuska, who drew the strip until its final demise in 1967. On the writing side, creator Nowlan was replaced by Calkins himself (1940-47), and the strip was later written by Bob Barton (1947-51), Rick Yager (1951-58) and a variety of other writers, including noted science-fiction author Fritz Leiber.

The Sunday *Buck Rogers* (which first saw publication on March 30, 1930) had a double particularity: it was never drawn by Calkins, who signed it, and for a long time the titular hero never appeared in it. Instead it was given over to Wilma's kid brother Bud Deering and his girl companion Princess Alura from Mars. Their adventures were quite creditable, very imaginative and

"Buck Rogers," Dick Calkins and Phil Nowlan. © National Newspaper Syndicate.

always enjoyable. In later years Buck Rogers took back the Sunday page from his younger stand-ins, and the page was again filled with Buck's space-opera pyrotechnics until the feature was finally discontinued in 1965 (two years before the daily strip).

The most noteworthy contributors to the Sunday version were Russell Keaton (1930-33), Rick Yager (1933-58), Murphy Anderson (1958-59), and George Tuska (1959-65) for the drawing; and for the writing Phil Nowlan (1930-40) and Rick Yager (1940-58).

For a long time *Buck Rogers* was the most popular science-fiction strip, challenged only by *Flash Gordon*. It had its own comic book version (with Frank Frazetta among the contributing artists) and was adapted into a highly successful radio series. In 1939 veteran serial director Ford Beebe directed a movie version of *Buck Rogers* with Buster Crabbe in the title role. In 1969 (the year of the first moon landing) Chelsea House published a hardcover anthology, *The Collected Works of Buck Rogers in the 25th Century* (with a preface by Ray Bradbury), which was followed by *Buck Rogers 1931-32* (Ed Aprill, 1971) and *Adventures in the 25th Century* (Funnies Publishing Company, 1974).

Following on the heels of the *Buck Rogers* theatrical movie and television series (both starring Gil Gerard), the newspaper strip was revived on September 9, 1979, in a new, more streamlined version drawn by Gray Morrow and written by Jim Lawrence. Cary Bates took over the scripting chores in 1981, and the next year Jack Sparling became the titular artist of the series. Distributed by the amateurish New York Times Syndicate (which was not even able to sell any of its strips to its parent newspaper), the feature was never a conspicuous success, and it petered out in the fall of 1983. (From 1979 to 1983 there was also a parallel *Buck Rogers* comic book carried under the Gold Key banner.)

M.H.

BUCK RYAN (G.B.) Buck Ryan, amateur sleuth, receives a cryptic cable from New York: Silas Craig, millionaire, wants him to meet his ward, Sonia Dell, at

Southampton. With youthful assistant Slipper by his side, Buck motors down to the docks. The heiress steps down the gangplank: "What a peach!" Then a pistol pokes into his spine: "Move and I'll plug you!" In four whirlwind panels, readers of the *Daily Mirror* were swept into a world of murder, mystery, and mayhem that lasted for 25 years. From March 22, 1937, to July 31, 1962, Jack Monk's seldom signed, never bylined strip hardly changed: guns, girls, Yankee chat, and action. Only Slipper, the kid assistant cast in the traditional Sexton Blake-Tinker mold, disappeared. He was replaced by Zola Andersen, blonde and beautiful, who

"Buck Ryan," Jack Monk. © Daily Mirror Newspapers Ltd.

could lick any man (or woman)—a crooked lady who reformed for Ryan.

Ryan was created as a stopgap replacement for *Terror Keep*, a serial strip adapted from Edgar Wallace's *Mr. Reeder* novel, when an American syndicate claimed all rights to Wallace. Harry Guy Bartholomew, editor, asked for a character in the style of America's successful *Dick Tracy*. "Buck," close to Dick and inspired by cowboy star Buck Jones, was one of the names on a list circulated by artist Monk and writer Don Freeman among the *Mirror* staff. The most popular combination came out as Buck Ryan—but soon after the strip was published, letters came in from readers asking if there was any connection between the character and the old established London chain of shops, Buck and Ryan! The name stayed.

Many popular characters emerged from the strip. Zola became the pinup girl of a minesweeper, an anti-aircraft battery, a Wellington bomber, and the submarine *Tally-ho*, all in pinups drawn by Monk. The most popular question from readers was: "When will Buck and Zola marry?" Bartholomew answered for Monk: "Never, never!" Outbidding even Zola in the popularity polls was Twilight, the glamorous girl crook, a brunette with a peekaboo bang. This obscured half of her face, the side scarred by acid. The tease was kept going until she finally had a skin graft operation, and her full beauty was revealed. Under a new writer, James Edgar, Twilight reformed her evil ways and replaced Zola as Ryan's helpmate. Monk's second-favorite character was Ma-the-Cache, an old biddy who smoked a pipe and lived on a barge on the River Thames. On the side of the law was Inspector Page of Scotland Yard.

Monk, famous for his authenticity of detail, went to Canada in November 1945-January 1946, on a sketching "holiday" that attracted much Canadian attention and resulted in an excellent series with authentic settings.

Reprints of *Buck Ryan* include: *The Case of the Broken Thistle*, a *Mirror* paperback comic of a 1945 adventure; a number of pocket-size paperbacks in the *Super Detective Library* series; and a monthly comic book published in Australia.

D.G.

BUFALO BILL (Italy) William Frederick Cody (nicknamed "Buffalo Bill" for having killed over 4,300 buffaloes in the course of 18 months) was a hunter, explorer, Indian scout, and show-biz entrepreneur.

Very early in his life, writers got hold of his legend and completely altered the historical character of Colonel Cody. The first was E.Z.C. Judson, who wrote a string of dime novels devoted to the mythical Buffalo Bill for Street and Smith in the 1870s. Their sales were extraordinary and worldwide, and they spawned a multitude of Buffalo Bill stories in every conceivable medium. The comics were not long in following suit, and the fabled sharpshooter was soon the hero of strips from Japan to Argentina (in the U.S. his fame was never so great; let us mention, however, *Young Buffalo Bill*, later retitled *Broncho Bill*, by Harry O'Neill). Among the many Italian versions, the most popular remains the one written by Luigi Grecchi and illustrated by Carlo Cossio. This series differs from the others not only by the missing "f" in the title, but also for its long life.

Conceived in 1950, *Bufalo Bill* made its appearance in 1951 in the weekly *L'Intrepido* when the publication changed from tabloid to comic book format, and it remained there until the mid-1960s. "Silver Cody is killed by Juarez Alvarando, the cowboy boss, who mistook him for a cattle rustler. William, his son, leaves his home and his mother to track down the killer...." Thus begins *Bufalo Bill* in a vein not unlike other Western sagas such as *Il Piccolo Sceriffo*, *Kansas Kid*, and *Capitan Miki*. These adventures were made more entertaining, thanks to the secondary characters introduced into the strip, like Old Toby and Susy, the nice young girl. Carlo Cossio's artwork, usually hurried and superficial, is much more detailed here and fits well with Grecchi's tangled plots. The stories were obvious and larded with rhetorics, but they impressed the readers with their air of authenticity and sophistication.

Other *Buffalo Bill* strips (all spelled with two "f's") have appeared in the Italian market, from an earlier version written by Amilcare Medici and drawn by Lina Buffolente (1945) to a more recent one produced by Armando Bonato (1965). In 1975 an erotic Buffalo Bill made his appearance in a saga called *Zora*, written by Renzo Barbieri and drawn by Balzano and Micheloni.

G.B.

BUFFALO BILL (Germany) *Buffalo Bill* is one of a number of Western comics that, to a degree, are a staple product of the German comics market. The character of Buffalo Bill, known in Germany since the times of the original William F. Cody and made famous through pulps and his Wild West show, was kept alive in postwar Germany by reprints of the Fred Meagher syndicated strip in a *Tom Mix* comic book that appeared from 1953 to 1954 and in a *Buffalo Bill* comic book reprinting of French and/or Italian strips.

Buffalo Bill took a well-earned rest until July 29, 1968, the day the first issue of *Lasso-Sonderheft* ("Lasso Special") was published. The 68-page comic books, which at the time starred Arturo del Castillo's *Randall*, featured *Buffalo Bill*, *Reno Kid*, *Lederstrumpf* ("Leatherstocking"), et al. The initial adventures of *Buffalo Bill* were reprints of a series originating in the Willy Vandersteen stable, written by Rik Dierckx and drawn by Karl Verschuere in a style influenced by Vandersteen and Alberto Giolitti. The Vandersteen material ran only to several books, so the German publishers asked Hansrudi Wäscher to work on the strip.

Reno Kid, one of the features in *Lasso-Sonderheft*, took over the regular 32-page *Lasso* comic book with issue number 82 (September 23, 1968). In order to publish *Lasso* weekly, the specials ended with number 17, and *Buffalo Bill* invaded the regular *Lasso* comic book with number 116 (January 12, 1970), continuing in all of the even-numbered issues, up to number 376 in 1974. *Reno Kid* appeared every other week in the issues with uneven numbers. Still alternating from week to week, *Lasso*, starring *Reno Kid* and *Buffalo Bill*, received individual numbering with issue 377. In 1970 both series were produced by the Giolitti studio in Rome from scripts written by Dirk Hess, with Hansrudi Wäscher doing some of the *Buffalo Bill* stories. In 1971 *Buffalo Bill* was turned over to Studiortega of Barcelona, Spain, with artists like Sola, Andres, and Rojo, and, of course, to Wäscher. Studio Giolitti continued doing *Reno Kid*, which has also been exported to other European countries. While most of the stories of either series make good use of the Western formula, some of the artwork is substandard. If not for Wäscher and some foreign artists of considerable talent, *Buffalo Bill* might not have endured so long.

W.F.

BUFFOLENTE, LINA (1924-   ) One of the few women cartoonists in Italy, Lina Buffolente was born October 27, 1924, in Vicenza. She moved to Milan with her family, where she attended the Brera Academy, but her studies were interrupted by the war. She began her career with a series of adventure comic books without a permanent cast of characters for Edital in Milan (1941), while at the same time assisting Professor Giuseppe Capadonia, one of the most prolific Italian comic strip artists of the prewar period.

In 1942 Buffolente began work with Edizioni Alpe, realizing in collaboration with Leone Cimpellin *Petto de Pollo* ("Chicken Breast"), a humorous comic book. A collaboration ensued, which was to last for the whole period of the war and beyond, during which time Lina Buffolente signed the sagas of *Piccolo Re* ("Little King," no relation to Otto Soglow's character), *Frisco Jim, Colorado Kid, Hello Jim,* and *Calamity Jane.* In 1948 she drew the comic books *Tom Bill* and *Tom Mix* for Casa Editrice Arc, and *Furio Mascherato* ("Masked Fury"), a superhero comic book, for Edizioni Audace. In the same year she drew a series of adaptations of the classics (*Les Misérables, The Mysteries of Paris,* etc.) for the publisher Ventura, for whom she also created the character of Nadia in his bilingual magazine *Per Voi/For You.* Also in 1948, Lina Buffolente began a very fruitful collaboration with Casa Editrice Universo.

In addition to many episodes in the "Albo dell'Intrepido," la Buffolente took over the long-running western saga *Liberty Kid,* created by the painters Toldo and Albanese in *L'Intrepido,* and *Fiordistella* ("Starflower"), a soap opera started by Cesarina Putato in the pages of *Il Monello* (1961). In addition to her work for Casa Editrice Universo, she did occasional works for other publishers: *Mosqueton, Rouletabille* (a detective strip based on Gaston Leroux's famous character), and *Nick Reporter,* published in France by Editions Aventures et Voyages; a revised version of *Sciuscia* for Edizioni Sepim; a few episodes of *Reno Kid* for a German publisher; and the adventures of *Zembla, Ivan il Veggente* ("Ivan the Seer"), and *Gun Gallon* for Editions Lug in Lyons, France.

At the present, Lina Buffolente's time is almost completely absorbed by the production *of Il Piccolo Ranger* ("The Little Ranger"), yet another Western, created by Andrew Lavezzolo and now written by Decio Canzio. In the early 1990s she also drew several episodes of *Il Commandante Mark* and *River Queen.*

G.B.

BUGS BUNNY (U.S.) The *Bugs Bunny* comic books and strip were based on the character in animated cartoons produced by Leon Schlesinger. The creation of the wise-cracking rabbit was done in stages, with contributions by many studio employees. The genesis was in a *Porky Pig* film, "Porky's Hare Hunt," directed by Ben "Bugs" Hardaway and Cal Dalton, based on a story by Bob Clampett. The hare, which was quite unlike the final Bugs, proved popular and warranted another film. "Hare-um Scare-um" was done by the same directors, featuring a remodeled version of the rabbit. Another version appeared in "Presto Change-o," directed by Chuck Jones. In 1939, when it was apparent that the rabbit was becoming a star, two

"*Bugs Bunny.*" © Warner Bros.

more films were assigned: "Elmer's Candid Camera," directed by Jones; and "A Wild Hare," directed by Fred "Tex" Avery. It was in "A Wild Hare" that the character most closely resembled the definitive version and used his famous catch phrase, "What's up, doc?" Upon completion of the film, suggestions were solicited from around the studio for a name for the bunny. "Bugs," inspired by Hardaway's nickname, was chosen.

A long series of *Bugs Bunny* cartoons and comic books followed. The cartoons were released (and later produced) by Warner Brothers until 1969. The bulk was directed by Avery, Clampett, Jones, Fritz Freleng, Robert McKimson, and Frank Tashlin, featuring voices by Mel Blanc. The cartoons have been perennial television favorites and Bugs has been the subject of hundreds of toys, records, books, and other merchandise.

Bugs Bunny's affiliation with Western Publishing started in 1941 when he joined the other Warner characters in the first issue of *Looney Tunes and Merrie Melodies.* The comic ceased publication in 1962 and resumed again in 1975.

The *Bugs Bunny* comic book began as part of the Dell *Four-Color* series and appeared in 27 intermittent issues, many by Chase Craig, before beginning regular publication in 1953 with issue number 28. The feature also appeared in dozens of specials, including issues of *Golden Comics Digest, March of Comics,* and *Super Comics,* in addition to Bugs' guest-starring in other Warner comics, especially *Porky Pig* and *Yosemite Sam.* Among the writers involved in *Bugs Bunny* stories were: Lloyd Turner, Don Christensen, Sid Marcus, Carl Fallberg, Tom Packer, Cecil Beard, and Mark Evanier. Artists have included Wyn Smith, Tom McKimson, Phil DeLara, Ralph Heimdahl, and John Carey. The series was discontinued in 1983 but was revived 10 years later.

The *Bugs Bunny* newspaper strip began in 1942, starting as a Sunday page only. The first few were by Chase Craig, and the strip, syndicated by NEA, was produced by Western Publishing under the supervision of Carl Buettner and, later, Al Stoffel. A great many writers and artists worked on the strip, most notably Fallberg, Stoffel, McKimson, Roger Armstrong, Jack Taylor, and Heimdahl. In 1948, a daily version of the strip was begun, written at first by Taylor and drawn continuously by Heimdahl. Eventually, Heimdahl also assumed the Sunday page and Stoffel handled the writing of both on a regular basis. The newspaper feature was closed down in 1993.

M.E.

BULANADI, DANNY (1946-   ) Danny Bulanadi was born in Tondo, Manila, Philippines, on February 9, 1946. He started working for comic books at the age of 18, after he graduated from high school. His first art job was for *Romansa Komiks*, and for many years he worked as an assistant to Tony Zuñiga. He did pencilling and inking on various Zuñiga assignments, but his first big break was with Craf Publications, where he illustrated short stories for *Theme Song*.

He then collaborated with Mars Ravelo and did graphic-novels for *Bulaklak*. In 1973 he drew for a government-sponsored publication. He did the visual sequences on the feature *The Many Fascinating Islands* and illustrated a historical account of *Jose Rizal*, the national hero of the Philippines.

On June 21, 1974, he teamed up with Ric Poblete to do *Gloria Sagrada*, a fantasy novel that appeared in Top Star. It ran for 32 chapters. Later he joined Pablo Gomez, who wrote *Katakumba*, which was published on August 2, 1974. The story became a success and was made into a movie.

One of Bulanadi's most popular works is *Ako Si Abraham* ("I am Abraham"). It was written by Carlo J. Caparas and appeared in *Philipino Komiks* starting on September 3, 1974. This long, visual-novel was also made into a motion picture.

While doing individual assignments, Bulanadi has also maintained his position as Zuñiga's assistant. He worked on many of the American series that Zuñiga handled, such as *Jonah Hex, Black Orchid, Phantom Stranger, Dr. 13*, and other strips for National Periodicals. He also worked on the Marvel characters Ka-Zar and Conan.

Just before he left the Philippines, Bulanadi had the opportunity to work with Nestor Redondo, learning from one of the most influential artists in the comic book medium. He has recently arrived in the United States. He plans to pursue his career as a freelancer and to continue his work as a comic book artist.

O.J.

BULLETJE EN BONESTAAK (Netherlands) *Bulletje en Bonestaak* ("Fatty and Beanstalk"), which first appeared in the newspaper *Het Volk* ("The People") in 1921, is one of the earliest Dutch efforts in the field of comic strips. Written by Adrianus Michael de Jong

"Bulletje en Bonestaak," G. A. Van Raemdonck. © Het Volk.

(1888-1943) and drawn by George van Raemdonck (1888-1966), from the start *Bulletje en Bonestaak* had a different approach to the comics medium than the earlier *Yoebje en Achmed* by Henk Backer. Although both are humorous, *Bulletje en Bonestaak* is drawn in the more realistic, down-to-earth style that makes the difference between a fairy-tale strip and a kid strip. As their names suggest, Bulletje is the little fat boy and Bonestaak the big thin boy. They are inseparable while journeying around the world, going from one adventure to the next. *Bulletje en Bonestaak* even provided one of the earliest crossovers of comic strip characters when, during one of their journeys, the two visit London and meet Jopie Slim and Dikkie Bigmans, whose adventures were reprinted in the Dutch newspaper *De Telegraaf* as early as 1920.

In 1924 *De wereldreis van Bulletje en Bonestaak* ("Fatty and Beanstalk's Journey Round the World") was the first in a long series of book editions of the comic strip. These books are still reprinted, despite the end of the series in *Het Volk* in 1934. Earlier reprintings deleted scenes in which invalids of World War I appeared, but a 1968 edition included these scenes once again.

Bulletje en Bonestaak, like so many early European comic strips, separated pictures and narrative, but because it was included in a newspaper, it did not have to be printed on a strip of paper. Nevertheless, one such series did exist in early Dutch comics history. These stories were printed on strips of paper two meters long and rolled up for safekeeping in a round box. This strip, by artist W. Heskes and with verse by C. J. Kievit, pictured stories centered on two characters called *Flip en Flop* ("Flip and Flop").

W.F.

BÜLOW, BERNHARD-VIKTOR VON (1923-   ) Loriot, whose real name is Bernhard-Viktor von Bülow, is a German cartoonist and writer/artist, born November 12, 1923, in the city of Brandenburg, 60 kilometers west of Berlin, Germany, the son of an army officer turned police officer. The Bülow family always had a penchant and secret admiration for acting, which in a way influenced young Bernhard-Viktor, who grew up and went to school and high school in his hometown and in Berlin. He left high school with a makeshift graduation to join the army, fighting in World War II as an officer.

When the war ended, von Bülow worked two years doing odd jobs like woodcutting. Then he returned to school for a regular high school graduation before taking up his studies at the Academy of Art in Hamburg, Germany. Having finished his studies, he started working as a graphic artist, his first cartoons getting published in the short-lived magazine *Die Strasse* ("The Road") in 1950. He moved on to the weekly *Stern* in the early 1950s, where he debuted with *Auf den Hund gekommen* ("Gone to the Dogs"), a series of cartoons reversing and parodying the relationship between humans and dogs. These cartoons also were the first to be reprinted in book form by the Swiss publishing house Diogenes. This series of cartoons sent von Bülow well on his way toward having his pen name, Loriot, become a household word.

Never using speech balloons, Loriot entered the realm of the comic strip with the furiously funny *Wahre Geschichten erlogen von Loriot* ("True Stories Made Up by Loriot") and with *Reinhold das Nashorn* ("Reinhold the Rhinoceros"), which originally was scheduled to appear for six consecutive weeks in the mid-1950s but actually ran 15 years in the pages of *Stern*. For legal reasons, the comic strip was signed Pirol (which is the German equivalent to the French "Loriot," the name of a blackbird species). Reinhold das Nashorn and his son Paul were as enjoyable as Loriot's other work. Each episode of four pictures was complemented by verse within the pictures.

In 1966, Loriot got his own TV show, *Cartoon*, which ran until 1972, attesting, among other things, to Loriot's considerable acting talent. A dog used in a 1971 cartoon in *Stern* became his best-known animated cartoon character, the lovable Wum in 1972.

The antics of Wum and his friend, the naive and stubborn elephant Wendelin, who were occasionally visited by a little UFO complete with a green-skinned pilot, were the highlight of a long-running quiz program aimed at collecting funds for charity. The five-minute cartoons usually were made so the characters seemed to be engaged in dialogue with the shows' (real live) host. The cartoons were produced by Loriot, who was also the voice of all the characters. The comedic aspects of the stoic Loriot persona as depicted in cartoons and television shows led to a number of very successful German motion pictures written by and starring Loriot.

W.F.

"Bulletman," Ken Battefield. © Fawcett Publications.

BULLETMAN (U.S.) Early in their publishing history, Fawcett experimented with formats. One of their books, *Nickle Comics*, was a five-cent biweekly, about half the size of a normal color comic. Although the book didn't last long, *Bulletman* premiered in May 17, 1940s first issue and later became a Fawcett staple. Created by artist Jon Small with an origin similar to that of The Batman, Bulletman was really policeman Jim Barr. An orphan dedicated to wiping out crime because of his parents' murder, Barr studied chemistry and became a ballistics expert. He developed a secret serum that gave him tremendous physical and mental powers. He then perfected a bullet-shaped "gravity regulating helmet," which provided the power of flight.

When *Nickle* folded after eight issues in August 1940, *Bulletman* began a regular series in October 1940's *Master* number seven. In the 30th issue, Susan Kent became his partner, Bulletgirl. Together they fought all kinds of crime, perpetrated by crooks, spies, madmen, murderers, and crazed lunatics. Although none of the strips were as good as Fawcett's Marvel Family, *Bulletman* developed several outstanding villains. The Black Rodent, Dr. Mood, the Black Spider, and Dr. Riddle were all constant enemies of the duo, who soon came to be called "The Flying Detectives." Most of the scripts were written by Otto Binder, Fawcett's workhorse, in a snappy, fast-paced style that left no room for humor.

Bulletman had a long series of artists, starting with the crude, almost primitive material of creator Jon Small. Jack Binder eventually handled the bulk of stories between 1941 and 1946 in a straightforward, no-nonsense manner. However, artists like Jack Kirby and Joe Simon (1941), C. C. Beck (1940), and Winsor McCay Jr., son of *Little Nemo* creator Winsor McCay, all did outstanding work. Mac Raboy, who later illustrated Fawcett's *Captain Marvel Jr.*, also drew some of the finest *Bulletman* adventures during 1941 and 1942.

Over the years, the feature has appeared in *Master*, *Whiz*, *America's Best*, and other normal-sized comics. But it was also placed in a wide range of Fawcett's experimental books, including the book-sized *Bulletman Dime Action*, a pocket-sized *Bulletman Miniature*, and even *Gift, Xmas*, and *Holiday*, the company's oversized Christmas specials. There were also 16 issues of *Bulletman* comics, beginning in 1941 and ending in fall 1946. The feature was finally discontinued in September 1949 after its story in *Master* number 106.

J.B.

BUNGLE FAMILY, THE (U.S.) The finest, most inventive, and socially critical of the family strips, Harry Tuthill's *The Bungle Family* first emerged under its original title, *Home, Sweet Home*, as part of a miscellany of staggered daily strips also by Tuthill in the *New York Evening Mail* late in 1918. Before the end of 1919, however, only *Home, Sweet Home* remained as a nationally syndicated daily. Anecdotal for the whole of its five-year life, the strip featured a quarreling married couple initially named George and Mabel, but by the end of 1919 renamed George and Jo (for Josephine). Living in a city flat with their in-laws, George and Jo suffered endless tribulations with their landlord and neighbors.

When the *Evening Mail* was sold in January 1924, Tuthill took George and Jo to the McNaught Syndicate, gave his strip a new name and his team a last name at the same time, and added a grown daughter to the

"The Bungle Family," Harry Tuthill. © McNaught Syndicate.

menage. Peggy Bungle served as the focus for the continuing story structure now utilized in the new *Bungle Family* strip, and her on-again, off-again affairs with the con man and adventurer Hartford Oakdale led George Bungle, a small-time opportunist and harried householder, into a series of scrapes and escapades that ultimately took him to Africa, outer space, and forward in time. With the addition of a gripping narrative (and a hilarious Sunday page in 1925), the public took sharper notice of the strip, and within a few years it became one of the most widely read and printed features of the time.

Aside from George, Jo, Peggy, and Oakdale, the cast of characters was evanescent but ultimately came to include world rulers, gnomes, invisible animals, a superstrong slob beloved by women, magicians, hypnotists—and an endless, horrendous array of scurvy, aggressive, brutal neighbors; outraged and stone-hearted landlords; and cold-faced, nightstick-prodding policemen.

Tuthill himself decided to close down the strip for reasons never fully disclosed, and he ended it with the daily episode of August 1, 1942, after Peggy had married Oakdale and the current story had been wound up. Then, unexpectedly, he revived the strip on May 17, 1943, apparently for the Bungles to do their part in the national war effort. With the close of World War II, however, Tuthill again folded *The Bungle Family* on June 2, 1945. This time the closing was permanent, Tuthill politely refusing the endless requests of readers for revival of the strip.

Only one book publication of *The Bungle Family* is known: a collection of the early anecdotal episodes under the *Home, Sweet Home* title, by M.S. Co. in 1925. The strip was reprinted in early issues of *Famous Funnies* as well, but not prominently or for long.

B.B.

BUNKER, MAX *see* Secchi, Luciano.

BUNKY (U.S.) A Sunday third-of-a-page strip (later a half-page), Billy De Beck's *Parlor, Bedroom and Sink* began on May 16, 1926, replacing a short-lived Sunday gag strip accompaniment of *Barney Google* named *Bughouse Fables* (which became a daily gag panel series). The new strip opened with the marriage of Bunker and Bibsy Hill to a shower of shoes and rice and the discovery of the disillusioned bride that far from getting a honeymoon in Paris, the young Bunker was taking her to a cheap hotel, where he signs for a "parlor, bedroom, and sink" (the cheapest family accommodations of the time). Bunker (whose nickname is Bunky) has a third-rate office job and barely makes ends meet; his financial problems serve as the comic nexus of the strip for the ensuing few months.

Gradually, however, De Beck introduces a new dimension to the strip: continuity based on comic melodrama. Bunker Hill is arrested for robbing his own wife after she has become a newly hailed movie star, is reduced to stark poverty, etc., all in a close satire on the popular newspaper serial stories of the time. However, De Beck makes this garish nonsense oddly suspenseful. De Beck, it is apparent, is a master of comic narrative.

By May of 1927, Bunker and Bibsy are reconciled, still broke, and in the midst of new troubles acquire a child: Bunker Hill, Jr., first seen in the strip on November 13, 1927. Bunky, the baby, grows rapidly and turns out to be preposterously and hilariously precocious, speaking words of world-weary philosophy while still in baby clothes and lace cap. All at once, it dawns on the reader, as the young Bunky is plunged into a dark netherworld of crooks, prostitutes, and dope pushers, where his steadfast morality shines fierce and true against all odds, that De Beck is doing a full-length satire on Harold Gray's *Little Orphan Annie*. In keeping with this aspect, the young Bunky takes over the strip *in toto* by late 1928, and has his name added to the title: *P, B & S, Starring Bunky* (one of the longest strip titles on record). Meanwhile, on February 5, 1928, the nefarious Fagin the Viper enters the strip, attempting to train Bunky in a life of crime (*a la* the Dickens character). Bunky's resultant and oft-repeated cry of outraged alarm: "Fagin, youse is a viper!" became a hallmark of the strip and of an era. During the remainder of the 1920s, through the 1930s, and well into the following decade, Bunky and Fagin meet and part in an endlessly engaging series of sordid or plush backgrounds, the story remaining as absorbing as ever, even when taken over by De Beck's successor, Fred Lasswell. Outright fantasy is often introduced into *Bunky* (as, to a much lesser extent, it was in *Barney Google*), and it is one of the great works of comic strip imagination. It was, unfortunately (in view of Lasswell's ability to maintain the quality of the strip), folded in 1948 by King Features.

B.B.

BUN LOUR SARN (Thailand) In Thailand, Bun Lour Sarn is a name synonymous with comic books. Founded in 1953 by Bun Lour Utsahajit, the company is the oldest and, by far, the country's largest publisher of comics, with a dozen or more titles in its fold.

Bun Lour Sarn titles are humorous, often containing one gag after another in cartoon or story format. Some books are published in two versions—one the size of

American comic books, and one pocket-sized edition. As many as 13 panels are sometimes stacked on a page in the pocket versions. The drawings are black and white, and simple in their execution, characterized by bold and dark strokes.

Bun Lour Sarn's best sellers are *Kai Hua Lok* ("Laughter for Sale"), and *Maha Sanuk* ("Super Fun"), with hundreds of thousands in print. The earliest titles, *Baby* and *Nuja* ("Little Baby"), were first published in 1957 and 1958. Other books include *Ai Tua Lek* ("Little One"), *Konulawang* ("Mess Up"), *Yornsorn* ("Reversed Arrow"), *Pean* ("Fanatic"), *Bakropsuit* ("Completely Mad"), *Parade*, and *Mitti Pisawang*. Bun Lour Sarn's policy is to have a new issue of one of its monthly comics on the market every five days.

Although the company has closed some of its divisions, such as feature film production, it has continued to expand its comics production. By the mid-1990s, four to five new humor titles were in the works, with plans to distribute Chinese, Indonesian, and Japanese language versions of *Kai Hua Lok* overseas.

J.A.L.

BUNNY *See* Schultze, Carl Edward

BURGON, SID (1936-   ) Sid Burgon is a good example of a latecomer to cartooning who succeeded as a gag artist, then transferred his talents to comic strips, and remained happily in children's comics for the rest of his career.

Sidney William Burgon was born in Berwick-on-Tweed, England, on October 3, 1936. His father was a gardener, his mother a housemaid with a natural artistic talent. She taught young Sid the elements of sketching. In 1950 he left school to become a mechanic in a local garage, a job he had for 13 years. He would occasionally display his sketches at work, and his coworkers persuaded him to pursue his talent. He took classes at the London Art School and Percy V. Bradshaw's Press Art College.

Burgon's first success, after years of sending pencil cartoons to various newspaper editors, came when *The Weekly News*, a national newspaper published in Scotland, published one of his cartoons. Burgon signed his drawing "Swab," a name created from his initials, plus his wife Annie's "A." This success led to more of his work being published, and he made the unusual decision to submit only finished artwork to newspapers. Fortunately, this was not much more difficult than only submitting sketches—so simple was his style.

In 1963 he stopped working as a mechanic and began freelancing as a cartoonist. His drawings appeared in many publications, including the *Daily Mirror*, the *Sunday Express*, and *Weekend* magazine, all of which ran plenty of gag cartoons at the time. His mechanic experience paid off as well: he became a staff cartoonist at *Motor World* magazine and supplied a regular motoring cartoon to the *Daily Telegraph* newspaper.

In 1970, at the urging of cartoonist friend Colin Whittock, Burgon sent a strip to the editor of the new comic *Whizzer & Chips*. His work was accepted and his substitution for "Hot Rod," a dragon drawn by the comics' art editor, Alf Saporito, was published. In 1971 he created *Joker* for another new comic, *Knockout*, which was a revival of an old title, but not of the comic itself. Scripted by Roy Davis, *Joker* was designed to be a rival to D.C. Thomson's *Dennis the Menace*, and was

a great success, continuing elsewhere after *Knockout* folded. Burgon's later characters took on the "comic horror" style popular at the time: *The Haunted Wood* in *Knockout*, *The Invisible Monster*, a two-page series for *Monster Fun* (1973), and *The Little Monsters*, a large panel series in the style of Fred Robinson's *Gremlins*. Later still came *The Toffs and the Toughs* (*Whizzer*), which had been created by Reg Parlett; *Milly O'Nare and the Penny Less* (*Jackpot*, 1979); and their male clones, *Ivor Lott and Tony Broke* (*Buster*). Other series Burgon worked on included *Biddy's Beastly Bloomers*, *Shiver & Shake*, *Lolly Pop* (*Whoopee*), and *Bookworm* (1984) for the same comic. In 1982 Burgon won the Society of Strip Illustration Best Comic Artist Award for his long-running series *Joker*.

D.G.

BURGOS, CARL (1920?-1984) American comic book artist and writer, born in New York City; although both Steranko's *History of Comics* and the *Who's Who of American Comic Books* pinpoint Burgos' birthdate as 1917, the artist/writer claims he was born April 18, 1920. After one year at the National Academy of Design, Burgos eventually joined the Harry "A" Chesler shop in 1938 before moving to Lloyd Jacquet's Funnies, Inc. studio. He remained there until drafted for service in World War II in 1942. When he returned, Burgos entered City College and spent most of the next 25 years in advertising art.

But his early work included the creation of one of comic books' most important strips, *The Human Torch*. Burgos had spent most of 1938 and 1939 producing material for the Centaur group, writing and drawing features like *Iron Skull* and *Stoney Dawson*. When he moved to the Jacquet shop, however, he and Bill Everett began working on Timely's *Marvel Comics* number one (November 1939), and while Everett created the aquatic *Sub-Mariner* strip, Burgos created the flaming android known as the Human Torch. Despite his merely adequate scripting and even poorer artwork, Burgos' fiery character caught on and was appearing in his own book by autumn 1940. Burgos' own art style—which was straight-forward and uninspiring, notable only because he refused to "swipe" from other artists—never appreciably improved. He left the strip and comics in 1942.

Burgos made only three brief reappearances in color comics: in the mid-1950s he drew several horror stories for Atlas; in 1964 and 1965, he handled some *Giant-Man* and *Human Torch* stories for Marvel; and in 1966, he created Country-Wide's short-lived version of *Captain Marvel*. Later that year, he assumed the editorship of Country-Wide's line of black and white "horror" titles, poor imitations of Warren's *Creepy* and *Eerie* books. He died in April 1984.

J.B.

BUSCEMA, JOHN (1927-   ) American comic book artist, born in New York City on December 11, 1927. After studies at the High School of Music and Art and Pratt Institute, Buscema broke into the comic business in 1948 with the Marvel/Timely/Atlas group. From that time until 1950, he worked on a wide variety of strips, mostly in the love, crime, and Western genres.

In 1950, he went to work for the Orbit group, where he continued to work on the same type of features he had done for Marvel. He left the firm in 1955, and, after a very brief stint at Charlton, began concentrating on work for Western (Gold Key), which he had been contributing to since 1953. Buscema again worked on a wide range of comic book story types, but he began concentrating on Western's movie adaptations and the *Roy Rogers* book. Although his work was not outstanding or particularly unique, it was clean and realistic, and this made him a perfect choice for the movie books, which always tried to closely parallel their motion picture counterparts.

Between 1958 and 1966, Buscema worked mainly for the ACG group, mostly on forgettable features and in the lucrative advertising art field. He returned to Marvel in 1966, however, about the time editor Stan Lee began a major expansion. Buscema has remained at Marvel ever since, and his uncluttered style became a Marvel mainstay. Along with John Romita and Jack Kirby, Buscema set the Marvel house style, mainly emphasizing straightforward storytelling and bigger-than-life, majestic heroes with staggering drawbacks. Over the years, he has drawn nearly every Marvel superhero and fantasy character, including the much-footballed *Hulk* (1966-1967), *Sub Mariner* (1968-1970), *Captain Marvel* (1969), *Thor* (1970), *Warlock* (1972), *Ka-zar* (1971-1972), *Fantastic Four* (1971-1973), *Black Widow* (1970), and many others. He also had a long, highly successful run on the *Avengers* strip, which he drew more or less regularly between 1967 and 1973.

Despite his herculean effort, Buscema did manage to make two particular strips totally his own. Both of them, strangely enough, had been previously handled by highly stylized artists, and most observers thought Buscema was the sacrificial lamb. When he began drawing the *Silver Surfer* in 1968, he succeeded Jack Kirby, who, along with writer Stan Lee, had elevated the strip to a level where it had a rabid cult following. Nevertheless, he handled the feature until 1970, and his pleasing, steady style and plausible storytelling methods brought him much acclaim. Similarly, when artist Barry Smith—a young Briton with a fascinating and ornate, if not perfect, style—abandoned *Conan* at the height of its cult popularity in 1973, Buscema was expected to generate little excitement. But even though he was saddled with what seemed to be a different inker for every story, he drew *Conan* in a pristine but exciting style that began accumulating a cult following all its own.

J.B.

From the 1960s to the 1990s Buscema has proven to be the ideal Marvel artist, working on every major title put out by the company, from *Savage Sword of Conan* to *Tarzan*, from *Wolverine* to *Punisher*, and returning to *The Avengers* in the 1980s. So valued is his talent that he was chosen as the main illustrator on the *How to Draw Comics the Marvel Way* manual.

M.H.

BUSCH, WILHELM (1832-1908) German poet, artist, and cartoonist, born April 15, 1832, in Wiedensahl (near Hannover, Germany), the first of his merchant parents' seven children. At the age of nine, Busch was sent to his uncle, the pastor of Ebergötzen, who was to educate him so he could enter secondary school. In 1845 they moved to the parish of Lüthorst. At the age of 16 Busch was accepted by the Polytechnic School of Hannover. He stayed in Hannover for about four years, and there made the acquaintance of a painter who suggested that he study at the Academy of Düsseldorf.

From there he went to Antwerp, Belgium, and got to know the paintings of Rubens, Brouwer, Teniers, and Frans Hals, which influenced his own paintings, most of which were not displayed until after his death (and are now valued at about $10 million).

After Antwerp it was back to Wiedensahl, then to Lüthorst, and finally on to the Academy of Munich, Germany. Here, he became a member of the "Künstlerverein" (artists' club), which led to the first publication of his caricatures in the weekly *Fliegenden Blätter* ("Flying Leaves," or "Looseleaves") in 1859. He continued working for them and for the *Münchener Bilderbogen* until 1871, even after he returned to his native Wiedensahl. Busch's first picture story, not unlike "pantomime" comic strips of today, was published in the *Fliegenden Blätter* in 1860. It was titled "Die Maus oder die gestorte Nachtruhe. Eine europäische Zeitgeschichte" ("The Mouse, or Sleep Disturbed. A European Story of the Times"). Busch's picture stories, predecessors of the modern comic strip, were later collected in the books *Schnaken und Schnurren* ("Wit and Drollery") and *Kunterbunt* ("Pell-Mell").

The best-known creation of Wilhelm Busch appeared in 1865. It is, of course, *Max und Moritz*, on which the *Katzenjammer Kids* were based. Actually, the publisher who had printed Busch's earlier picture books *Bilderpossen* ("Pictorial Farces"), *Der Eispeter* ("Icy Peter"), *Katze und Maus* ("Cat and Mouse"), among others, rejected *Max und Moritz*. Nevertheless, the book was published and, because of its grim moral, was harshly criticized by pedagogues. It is not surprising, then, that comics met with similar criticism while their predecessor had long since become a children's classic.

In the 1870s Busch became fed up with having to grind out picture stories week after week for humor

Wilhelm Busch.

magazines and turned to writing and illustrating books, living a hermit's life in Wiedensahl. In 1898 Busch moved to Mechtshausen, where he continued writing prose and verse, illustrating, and painting until his death on January 9, 1908. Busch's narrative figuration still holds up well. His wit, precise line drawing, and humorous verse live on. They have also been of some influence in the development of what is called the comic strip. Maybe art critic Arsene Alexandre sums it up best in his obituary in the Paris *Figaro*: "Wilhelm Busch was one of the most surprising inventors of comic syntheses who ever lived. . . . Many makers of 'simplified' drawings have borrowed from him. Unfortunately they have not borrowed his depth of observation."

W.F.

BUSHMILLER, ERNEST (1905-1982) Ernest Paul Bushmiller was born in 1905 in the Bronx, New York, and went to work at 14 as copy boy on the old New York *World* as soon as he was out of grammar school. At the time, many of the great strip artists drew every day at their desks at the paper (working at home and sending your strips to the syndicate by mail was almost unheard of), and the young Ernie hobnobbed with many of his idols, such as Rudolph Dirks, H. T. Webster, Milt Gross, and others. He spent two of his teen years studying after work at the National Academy of Drawing, and then got his first break as a cub artist in the "comic room"—the strip artist's domain.

A few years later, he sold his first comic strip to United Features: *Fritzi Ritz*, a working-girl feature with more zest than most. *Phil Fumble* was added to the *Fritzi* Sunday page and replaced in 1940 by *Nancy*. Later the instantly popular *Nancy*, a simple gag strip about a young girl (Fritzi's niece), replaced *Fritzi* first as a daily and then as Bushmiller's sole Sunday feature. It is as the creator of *Nancy* that he is widely known today, and *Fritzi* (to say nothing of *Phil Fumble*) is largely forgotten, although both were funnier and better drawn than most of *Nancy*.

The excellent visual comedy of *Fritzi Ritz* led Harold Lloyd to invite Bushmiller to Hollywood in the 1920s, where the Bronx cartoonist spent nearly a year inventing gags and narrative for Lloyd films, managing to

draw *Fritzi* at the same time. He died in Stamford, Connecticut, on August 15, 1982.

B.B.

BUSTER BROWN (U.S.) R. F. Outcault's second great strip, *Buster Brown*, first appeared in the color Sunday section of the *New York Herald* on May 4, 1902, where it replaced Outcault's minor *L'il Mose* page. In sharp contrast to the slum grubbiness of the artist's earlier Yellow Kid, Buster Brown was the markedly well-dressed 10-year-old scion of a well-to-do suburban family, literate enough to write weekly, tongue-in-cheek "Resolutions," which reflected temporary contriteness at having been punished for another of the recurrent pranks he played with savage ingenuity on family and friends. Always accompanied by a toothily grinning evil muse of a bulldog named Tige, Buster—who appeared only in the Sunday pages for the duration of his nefarious career, aside from a few scattered, irregular daily appearances in the early 1910s—plagued the family maids, the deliverymen, policemen, his juvenile peers, and parents with explosives, paint, infuriated cats, wrecked cars, sunken boats, and a multitude of other devices that Outcault seemed able to inexhaustibly invent.

The strip soared to instant, nationwide popularity, provoking William Randolph Hearst to hire Outcault for the second time—the first was when he was drawing *The Yellow Kid* for the *New York World*—and once more put him and his character to work on Hearst's *New York American* Sunday page, where Buster first appeared on January 14, 1906 (after making his last Outcault bow in the *Herald* on December 31, 1905). The dismayed *Herald* reprinted a couple of old, 1902 *Buster* pages, then hired a miscellany of artists to keep its version of the strip going. In a court battle, it was decided that Outcault could keep the characters but not the strip name, while the *Herald* could use both the characters and the name. The public wasn't fooled, of course, but the *Herald* stubbornly kept its ersatz *Buster* running, finally as a half-page, until late into 1910.

Outcault's own *Buster*, appearing weekly under a different descriptive title every Sunday in the Hearst papers, ran merrily on through World War I, with Buster doing his devastating part, and finally retired from comic page action (after Outcault had felt forced

"Buster Brown," R. F. Outcault.

by waning inspiration to repeat more than one earlier sequence in slightly differing context) on August 15, 1920, when the work of other hands on the strip was already evident. But Buster's fame, like that of his dog, Tige, and vigorous feminine aide-de-vamp, Mary-Jane, was far from exhausted, and these characters continued a career already established in newspaper and magazine advertising pages, promoting clothing of all kinds (as a result of the public's early fascination with Buster's outfits), notably the still-popular Buster Brown shoes. Outcault drew or supervised much of the earlier advertising; later work was done by other artists.

A number of books reprinting or based on the *Buster Brown* strip appeared during the first two decades of the century: *Buster Brown's Pranks, Buster Brown and Mary-Jane, Buster Brown's Resolutions, Tige—His Story,* etc., to be echoed many years later by a giveaway *Buster Brown Comics* from the shoe company in the 1940s. There were also minor stage and vaudeville adaptions of the strip, radio ads, and some early short films based on the characters. Curiously, there were fewer Buster Brown toys of all kinds than there had been Yellow Kid artifacts, but the strip itself was much more widely popular and longer lasting. It has been recently reprinted in an inexpensive edition by Dover (*Buster Brown*), and will probably, deservedly, see more extensive textual revival in the future.

B.B.

BUTSCHKOW, PETER (1944-   ) Peter Butschkow was born on August 29, 1944, in Cottbus, Germany, but two months later his family moved to what would later become West Berlin. There he went to elementary school and then studied at a private art school for four semesters, followed by a yearlong apprenticeship as a typesetter. This was followed by nine semesters at the State School for Graphics. While preparing for his career, he was also a drummer in a rock band for nearly eight years.

Butschkow had decided to pursue a career as a graphic designer, and was employed at a Berlin advertising agency before leaving for a 10-year stint as a freelance graphic designer. He had started drawing gag cartoons for the satirical magazine *pardon*, and left Berlin—and advertising—in 1979, intending to continue working with only gag cartoons, comics, and illustrations. It took him almost five years to make a success of this transition.

In 1983 he moved to Hamburg and shortly after had his first collection of cartoons published. Since then, more than two dozen books of his cartoons have been published. Butschkow's work has appeared in numerous magazines and newspapers, as well as on television. His most popular work, however, is published regularly in the weekly magazines *stern* and *Hör zu*. For the latter, Butschkow has created a comic strip titled *Siegfried*. This strip, which began in 1985 and has been running ever since, depicts the very funny antics of a dragon named Siegfried living in a Neanderthal Stone Age world. While making the best of an occasional atrocious pun, the gags about dragons and Stone Age characters have kept readers in stitches ever since inclusion of the strip in the magazine. Unlike Reinhold Escher, Butschkow is not under exclusive contract to *Hör zu*. Therefore, he creates his ever-popular funnies not only for other magazines and newspapers but also for competing television programs.

W.F.

BUTZE OLIVER, GERMAN (1912-   ) Mexican cartoonist and illustrator German Butze was born February 11, 1912, in Mexico City. He studied painting and drawing at the San Carlos Academy in Mexico and later worked under the noted portrait painter Ignacio Rosas.

Butze started his career as an advertising artist, creating many ad characters that were to become famous. In the mid-1930s he turned to comic strip work with such features as *Memo Migaja* and *Pinito Pinole*. His most famous comic creation, *Los Supersabios* ("The Supersavants"), followed in 1936 in the pages of the magazine *Novedades*. The feature was so successful that it soon appeared in daily strip form as well as a weekly page. Later it also appeared in *Mujeres y Deportes* and was carried in the newly created periodicals *Chamaco Grande* and *Chamaco Chico*. Butze also did a strip for the magazine *Pepin* called *Pepe el Inquieto* ("Pepe the Worrier").

For a period, Butze devoted his time exclusively to *Los Supersabios*, which was published in the form of a twice-monthly comic book for a long time by Publicaciones Herrerias before being converted to a weekly format. Serious cardiovascular problems forced him to cease working in the early 1980s. (His older brother Valdemar was also a cartoonist.)

M.H.

BUZ SAWYER (U.S.) Roy Crane's *Buz Sawyer* was one of a number of armed-services strips kindled into existence by the development of World War II. Its first episode, published at the height of war on November 2, 1943, by King Features (followed by the Sunday half-page on November 23) and depicting the launching of the aircraft carrier *Tippecanoe*, from which Naval Lieutenant (J. G.) Buz Sawyer and his gunner, Roscoe Sweeney, were to fly sorties against the Japanese enemy, reflected the openings of other new military strips between 1941 and 1945. The difference between nearly all of those and *Buz Sawyer* is that Crane's strip lasted.

The reason is simple. *Sawyer* was planned over a long period of time by Crane as a means by which the cartoonist could gain control of his own creative work, enabling him to leave his contracted employment with NEA. If the conditions of war hadn't served as a launching pad for the new strip, Crane would have used something else. But essentially it was Crane's

"Buz Sawyer," Roy Crane. © King Features Syndicate.

superb graphic, narrative, and character-creating abilities that built *Sawyer* into a major, and now classic, comic strip.

Buz Sawyer was a clean-cut American boy, just out of flight school, with an apple-pie family in a small American town and a girl named Christy Jameson waiting for him. His gunner, Roscoe Sweeney, a comic-relief character, was older than Buz, and without any home. But the real characters in the strip at the outset were the war, Sawyer's aircraft carrier and crew as a unit, and the fighter planes that filled panel after panel with exciting, authentic air action (for Crane had researched his material thoroughly, even making tours with navy authorization to check details and foreign scenes). Nevertheless, Crane wrote continuously gripping adventure narratives involving his two heroes and their war activity, stories so imaginative that today they seem wholly undated by their war content. (The Sunday material, on the other hand, put more direct emphasis on G. I. humor, via Sweeney and his kooky pals, and consequently does not hold up so well.) The end of the war, of course, reopened the world to adventure, and Crane was prompt to plunge Buz into the kind of goofy, slam-bang, exotic escapades he liked best to write and draw, while he literally farmed Sweeney into exclusive appearance in the Sunday half-page gag sequences (where for the next three decades Sweeney and his sister, Lucille, plagued occasionally by cousinly horrors called Swatleys, tended their farm).

After Buz's discharge in October 1946, the postwar *Sawyer* daily strip got seriously under way. Chili Harrison, a wartime flyer buddy of Buz's (who was a somewhat more realistic equivalent of Mort Walker's Killer—he calls Sawyer "Buzzo," for example), gets Buz involved in a New York skyscraper intrigue, which is at once grisly and comic: Buz's fiancée, Tot Winter, is shoved off a balcony dozens of floors above the street by a woman gang leader's pet tiger, and Tot's death is blamed on Buz by the law. From that point, events simply get wilder and woolier, involving high peril in all parts of the world, man-eating plants, mad Russian exiles on glaciers, and Malay pirates, among others. Buz confronts a fabulous assortment of unique villains: the Tiger of Hong Kong; the phony American named Jerome Pomphrey, who is apparently concealing Hitler himself in an African hideout; Don Jaime of Mexico; and, Harry Sparrow and Gool. Buz himself had a number of tentative occupations, most relating to private investigation and government work, and finally married his wartime girl, Christy.

But *Buz Sawyer* continued, with Crane actively interested in the story line and art, although personal health made it increasingly difficult for him to work directly on the strip, and Ed Granberry began to do the nominal script and Harry Schlensker the bulk of the drawing. Growing taboos against violence in strips since the 1950s cut down much of the range and impact of *Sawyer*, while decreased size in syndicated comics reduced the graphic scope possible in individual panels. As a result, the strip, although still striking in art and intelligence of story line, became but a hearty shadow of the *Buz Sawyer* of the first two decades.

B.B.

Crane's death in 1977 did not signal any marked changes in either style or content. While the Sunday page had been discontinued in 1974, the daily strip continued in the hands of Schlensker and Granberry.

John Celardo guided *Buz Sawyer* in its twilight years from 1983 until the strip's demise in October 1989.

M.H.

Guido Buzzelli, "La Rivolta dei Racchi." © Buzzelli.

BUZZELLI, GUIDO (1927-1992) Italian cartoonist and illustrator, born July 27, 1927, in Rome. The son of a painter, Guido Buzzelli always showed more predilection for the comics than for painting; and at the age of 18 he joined the staff of the illustrated weekly *Argentovivo*. In the period immediately following the war, he produced a few covers for comic books. After drawing the adventure strip *Zorro* for the publisher Gabriele Gioggi of Rome and a multitude of covers for the Italian versions of *Flash Gordon*, *Mandrake*, and *The Phantom*, he started working for the British Daily Mirror Syndicate, later moving to London, where he illustrated the *Angélique* series based on Serge and Anne Golon's popular string of novels.

In 1965 Buzzelli returned to Italy and decided to follow in his father's footsteps, producing a number of paintings that were later exhibited. But he missed comic artwork and in 1969 drew a comic story for the catalogue of the Lucca Comics Convention, *La Rivolta dei Racchi* ("The Revolt of the Racchi"), a wildly surrealistic strip that won him critical acclaim. He was then dubbed "a master of the comics," a title that he confirmed with a series of highly innovative comic strips: *The Labyrinths, Zilzelub,* and *Annalise and the Devil* (these stories were first published in the French monthly *Charlie* and later introduced in Italy in the pages of *Linus* and *Alterlinus*). For a short while Buzzelli authored a series of pornographic parodies (based on comic characters, not unlike the "Tijuana bibes") for the satiric monthly *Menelik*. In the last 15 years of his life he divided his work almost equally between French and Italian publishers. He died in Rome on January 25, 1992.

Buzzelli was awarded the Yellow Kid in 1973 as best comic author, and his works have been exhibited at the Louvre in Paris.

G.B.

BYRNE, JOHN (1950-   ) Born on July 6, 1950, in Walsall, England, but raised in Canada, John Byrne burst onto the comics scene in the late 1960s with his

John Byrne, The Incredible Hulk. © 1998 Marvel Comics.

contributions to *Monster Times* and other fanzines. A graduate of the Alberta College of Art, Byrne made his professional debut in the early 1970s drawing for Charlton Comics on such titles as *Doomsday + 1, Space: 1999,* and *Emergency!*

In 1978 the big time beckoned to Byrne when he began work on a variety of titles for Marvel Comics, including *Iron Fist, Fantastic Four, The Incredible Hulk, Spider-Man, Daredevil,* and *The Avengers.* He is best remembered, however, for his work on the *X-Men* group of titles, for which he created Alpha Flight, which received its own title in 1983. In addition to his pencilling and scripting duties on these and other titles, he also drew close to 200 covers for Marvel.

Attracted by his innovative style and his newfound star status, DC Comics hired him away from Marvel in 1986 to revive its faltering Superman line of comics. This Byrne did, earning even more kudos in the process. During his two-year stint at DC Comics, he also worked with marked success on *Batman* and *Green Lantern.*

Returning to Marvel Comics, he turned his attention to *The West Coast Avengers* and *The She-Hulk,* but the comic-book-buying public's tastes had changed, and Byrne, whose work had been considered "hot" a scant 12 months before, now met with only a lukewarm response, prompting him to leave Marvel Comics for the second time. Since 1993 he has been published by Dark Horse, working on its own titles, *John Byrne's Next Men* and *Critical Error,* and drawing occasional issues of outside comics such as *Aliens* and *Judge Dredd.*

John Byrne's career can be considered a prime example of the fickleness of comic book fans and of the precariousness of the star system in the comics universe. His fall from grace between the mid- and the late 1980s proved as precipitous as his rise had previously been meteoric. Yet his solid craftsmanship and polish endure, and he will be heard from long after some of today's hotshots are gone.

M.H.

BYRNES, EUGENE (1889-1974) American cartoonist, born on Manhattan's West Side in 1889. After graduation from high school, Gene Byrnes embarked on a promising sports career which was unfortunately cut short at the age of 22, when he suffered a broken leg in the course of a wrestling match. During his stay at the hospital, Byrnes spent his time first copying Tad Dorgan's cartoons, then drawing cartoons of his own, which he sent to various newspapers. His first cartoon series, *Things That Never Happen,* was published as a two-column panel in a California newspaper in 1915.

Later that year, Byrnes met Winsor McCay, who got him a job as sports cartoonist on the *New York Tele-*

Gene Byrnes.

gram, for which Byrnes also created his famous humor panel *It's a Great Life If You Don't Weaken* (whose title became the slogan of the American Expeditionary Force in World War I). As a complement to *It's a Great Life*, Byrnes in 1917 began a two-column companion panel, *Reg'lar Fellers*. The new creation was all about a high-spirited gang of kids whose names, "Jimmy Dugan," "Pudd'n Head," "Aggie," soon became household words. Impressed by the success of their new feature, Byrnes' publishers shifted *Reg'lar Fellers* to their more prestigious parent publication, the *New York Herald*, in the form of a full-fledged comic strip (it appeared first as a Sunday page to which a daily version was later added).

Gene Byrnes' influence as a cartoonist was at its peak from the 1920s to the 1940s. His drawing style, detailed, precise, and almost academic, and his lively but gentle humor proved a distinct departure from the slam-bang school of cartooning prevalent during his time.

Byrnes reinforced his preeminent position as a guiding light for cartoonists with the publication of a number of professional textbooks that he wrote and edited himself, starting with *How to Draw Comics and Commercial Art* (New York, 1939) and continuing with *A Complete Guide to Drawing, Illustration, Cartooning and Painting* (New York, 1948), *A Complete Guide to Professional Cartooning* (Drexel Hill, Pa., 1950), and *Commercial Art* (New York, 1952).

Gene Byrnes retired from professional life in the 1960s. On July 26, 1974, he died of a heart ailment.

M.H.